Money, Politics, and the Constitution

Money, Politics, and the Constitution: Beyond *Citizens United*

Monica Youn, editor

Sponsored by The Century Foundation and
the Brennan Center for Justice at NYU School of Law

The Century Foundation Press • New York

About The Century Foundation

The Century Foundation conducts public policy research and analyses of economic, social, and foreign policy issues, including inequality, retirement security, election reform, media studies, homeland security, and international affairs. The foundation produces books, reports, and other publications, and convenes task forces and working groups. With offices in New York City and Washington, D.C., The Century Foundation is nonprofit and nonpartisan and was founded in 1919 by Edward A. Filene.

Board of Trustees

Library of Congress Cataloguing-in-Publication Data

Money, politics, and the Constitution : beyond Citizens United / Monica Youn, editor.
p. cm.
"Sponsored by The Century Foundation and the Brennan Center for Justice at NYU School of Law."
Includes bibliographical references and index.
ISBN 978-0-87078-521-4 (alk. paper)
1. Campaign funds--Law and legislation--United States. 2. Corporate speech--United States. 3. Freedom of speech--United States. 4. Advertising, Political--Law and legislation--United States. I. Youn, Monica. II. Century Foundation. III. Brennan Center for Justice.
KF4920.M67 2011
342.73'078--dc22

2011010347

Manufactured in the United States of America
Cover design and art: Claude Goodwin

About the Brennan Center for Justice

The Brennan Center for Justice at New York University School of Law is a nonpartisan public policy and law institute that focuses on the fundamental issues of democracy and justice. Our work ranges from voting rights to campaign finance reform, from racial justice in criminal law to presidential power in the fight against terrorism. A singular institution—part think tank, part public interest law firm, part advocacy group—the Brennan Center combines scholarship, legislative and legal advocacy, and communications to win meaningful, measurable change in the public sector. Founded in 1995 by the family and clerks of Justice William J. Brennan, Jr., the Center is dedicated to his vision of "common human dignity."

From its beginning, the Brennan Center has played a central legal and intellectual role on the subject of money and politics. It helped draft the Bipartisan Campaign Reform Act of 2002 (BCRA), and successfully defended the law before the U.S. Supreme Court as co-lead counsel in *McConnell v. FEC*. In the wake of *Citizens United*, the Center leads the legal defense of campaign finance laws in federal court. Most recently, it defended Arizona's Clean Elections system in the U.S. Supreme Court in *McComish v. Bennett*. Over the years, its attorneys and experts have testified frequently before Congress and state legislatures, have counseled policy makers nationwide, and have participated in campaign finance litigation in dozens of federal courts. The Brennan Center also serves as constitutional counsel to the Fair Elections Now Act coalition, advocating for public financing laws at the federal level. Recent publications include *A Return to Common Sense* by executive director Michael Waldman and *Small Donor Matching Funds: The NYC Election Experience*.

The Brennan Center would like to acknowledge the Arkay Foundation, Jeffrey Clements, Marilyn and Robert Clements, the Columbia Foundation, the Compton Foundation, The Nathan Cummings Foundation, The Democracy Education Fund, Democracy Alliance Partners, the Ford Foundation, The Joyce Foundation, Open Society Foundations, Rockefeller Brothers Fund, Fran and Charles Rodgers, and Wallace Global Fund for their generous support of our money in politics work. Statements made and the views expressed in this volume are solely the responsibility of the Brennan Center and the authors.

The Brennan Center would also like to thank the NYU's *Review of Law and Social Change*, the *Harvard Law and Policy Review*, the *Georgia State University Law Review*, and the *Harvard Law Review* for their permission to reprint many of the essays published in this volume.

Foreword

In the late 1990s, The Century Foundation and the Brennan Center for Justice at New York University School of Law collaborated to develop two publications focusing on the landmark *Buckley v. Valeo* campaign finance case. At the time, that 1976 decision, which prohibited caps on electoral spending, was viewed as the central obstacle to legislative reforms that could help to reduce the deleterious effects of money on democracy. One of those reports, titled *Buckley Stops Here*, conveyed the recommendations of a group of legal scholars for a strategic campaign to overrule or limit that decision. The follow-up edited volume, titled *If Buckley Fell*, was a collection of essays describing an alternative vision of a First Amendment that tolerates greater regulation of the flow of money into elections, without sacrificing any of the critical First Amendment moorings that are so critical to a free society.

Last year, the Supreme Court reached an even more monumental decision in *Citizens United v. Federal Election Commission*, further inhibiting what Congress can do to regulate campaigns. That unwelcome development prompted the Brennan Center to join forces once again with The Century Foundation to publish a new collection of essays, this time focused on *Citizens United*. Although we are clearly fighting an uphill battle, to say the least, we remain convinced that the influence of money on American democracy denigrates the integrity of the republic. Rather than acquiesce to the ongoing judicial assault against campaign finance laws enacted by elected officials, both the Brennan Center and The Century Foundation remain deeply committed to finding ways to diminish the outsized clout of money in elections and governing.

We thank Michael Waldman, executive director of the Brennan Center, and his colleagues for working with us on this project. Perhaps one day down the road our efforts will lead to a campaign finance decision that we can celebrate together.

RICHARD C. LEONE, *President*
THE CENTURY FOUNDATION

Contents

Preface

The struggle for democracy is at the heart of our history. American politics has long been convulsed by scandal and reform. Results rarely are pretty. The line dividing private economic power and the public realm shifts and slides with the felt necessity of the times.

Then, in *Citizens United v. Federal Election Commission*, the U.S. Supreme Court abruptly erased and redrew that line again. Overturning decades of precedent and dozens of laws, five justices ruled that corporations and unions had a constitutional right to spend unlimited sums in elections. The ruling earned banner headlines, a sharp State of the Union rebuke, and public disapproval hovering near 80 percent in the polls. In the 2010 election, independent spending spiked, much of it secret, with more to come. The decision ranks among the Court's most controversial and consequential.

Yet *Citizens United* was no bolt out of the blue. It was the product of a decades-long legal drive to rethink doctrine and, ultimately, strike down the edifice of campaign law. This jurisprudential movement drew inspiration from the 1971 memo drafted by soon-to-be Justice Lewis Powell that urged corporate leaders to fund scholars and public interest legal groups to promote a "free market" approach in the courts. Former Federal Election Commission chair Bradley Smith bragged to the *New York Times* that *Citizens United* was the fruit of "long-term ideological warfare." This effort was bold, strategic, and willing to rethink basic premises. It has been markedly effective.

Above all, it sought to advance a powerful but narrow notion of the First Amendment, focused on the rights of the speaker, especially corporate speakers. Until 1976, courts rarely if ever applied the

First Amendment to campaign finance laws. By 2010, claims of "free speech" were wielded to overturn campaign laws dating back decades at least. Nearly forgotten in the emerging jurisprudence were the interests of voters, of a workable government, or of democracy itself.

Even as the Court's conception of democracy has continued to narrow, new strategies and technologies are shaking and remaking the world of politics. New media create the possibility for positive change, from the role of low-cost social media, to the small donor phenomenon, to the possibility of real-time transparency in campaign spending. These trends can be magnified by reforms such as multiple matching funds for small contributions. But these shoots of reform could be washed away by the tide of big money in the wake of *Citizens United*.

We cannot ask courts to craft the institutional mechanisms for an effective democracy, but we can insist that courts allow those mechanisms to be created. In short, we must build a new jurisprudential movement, one that advances a vision of the Constitution as a charter for a vibrant democracy. This effort will call on the talents of the most powerful minds in law and the academy. The fight for democracy cannot be waged from an ivory tower: instead, such a movement can draw strength from a true dialogue between scholars and an active citizenry.

The Brennan Center for Justice at NYU School of Law is proud to play a leading role in launching such a movement. This volume and the symposium that produced it are among the first steps. We expect this thinking to play out in law reviews, briefs, and ultimately court decisions. For example, already many of these scholars have put their ideas into effect in amicus briefs in ongoing litigation, including the defense of public financing. These ideas do not advance in lockstep. Participants here disagree on many things (indeed, including the basic question of whether *Citizens United* was rightly decided). But all agree that constitutional interests are not hostile to our democratic values—instead, strengthening democracy is the very core of our constitutional enterprise.

As Justice Robert Jackson once wrote, the Constitution is not "a suicide pact." Similarly, the First Amendment is not a hostage note. Fealty to a narrow ideology of free speech ought not threaten democracy or workable governance. It is time to craft a constitutional vision that allows "we the people," directly and through elected representatives, to create our own democracy.

We are thrilled to publish this important volume with The Century Foundation. The newly created Brennan Center forged an important partnership with the Foundation nearly fifteen years ago, and we are glad to renew this collaboration now. We want to thank all of the contributors for pushing forward an ambitious jurisprudential movement, and all at The Century Foundation who helped make this volume happen, including Richard Leone for his leadership, and Greg Anrig, Jason Renker, Carol Starmack, Christy Hicks, and Laurie Ahlrich for their excellent work on this project.

MICHAEL WALDMAN, *Executive Director*
THE BRENNAN CENTER FOR JUSTICE AT NYU SCHOOL OF LAW

1

Introduction

*Monica Youn**

The modern jurisprudence of money and politics has long resembled a labyrinth. The U.S. Supreme Court's constitutional decisions in this area have erected seemingly unbreachable walls that block any straightforward path between acknowledged problems and proposed reforms. From the elevated vantage point of courts and scholars, these doctrinal walls might present some discernible pattern, but from the perspective of those who find themselves traversing this maze—lawmakers, reformers, candidates, fund-raisers, interest groups, and voters—these constitutional obstacles must seem at best arbitrary and at worst self-defeating. Well-intentioned policymakers who attempt to thread a constitutionally permissible route through this labyrinth may find themselves tracing a tortuous path and encountering unanticipated complications. The labyrinth's sheer complexity can exact a heavy toll: campaign finance policymaking

* I would like to recognize the work of my colleagues at the Brennan Center—this volume, as well as the symposium that generated it, can truly be considered a team effort. Burt Neuborne, Michael Waldman, and Susan Liss were instrumental in conceptualizing this symposium, recruiting participants, and ensuring that jurisprudential development is at the forefront of the Brennan Center's mission. Mimi Marziani and Mark Ladov played an invaluable role in editing this volume, while Ciara Torres-Spelliscy and Angela Migally contributed their deep expertise on campaign finance issues. Jeanine Plant-Chirlin arranged for the publication of this volume and shepherded us through the production process. Ali Hassan and Jafreen Uddin organized the symposium and ensured its success. NYU's *Review of Law and Social Change* co-sponsored the symposium with us and published many of the essays included in this volume.

may result in rules that are difficult to understand and implement, vulnerable to loopholes, and subject to perverse consequences.

Most notorious, perhaps, is the Supreme Court's 1976 decision in *Buckley v. Valeo.*[1] There, the Court drew a First Amendment bright line between contributions given directly to a campaign and expenditures made independently from the campaign: limits on the former were deemed constitutionally permissible, while limits on the latter were assumed to be unconstitutional. In the real world, this distinction has encouraged campaign money to flow to relatively unregulated outside groups, while candidates and political parties face restrictions on the contributions they can raise. The groups wielding monetary power cannot be voted in or out, and candidates can deny any responsibility for such outside spending. Thus, *Buckley's* legacy is a system in which money—and, consequently, power—is pushed to the political fringes, special interests wield disproportionate power over candidates and elected officials, and voters can hold no one accountable. For generations, legal thinkers have asked: is this really the result the First Amendment dictates? Despite these constant doubts, however, the contributions/expenditures distinction has become ever more deeply entrenched in the law.

In this convoluted doctrinal landscape, last year's decision in *Citizens United v. Federal Election Commission* arrived like a long-anticipated earthquake, leveling precedents and generating ongoing aftershocks. Even before the decision, the conservative majority of the Roberts Court had signaled its dissatisfaction with current campaign finance laws—"Enough is enough," pronounced Chief Justice John Roberts in the 2007 decision, *Federal Election Commission v. Wisconsin Right to Life,* rejecting an argument that federal restrictions should apply to campaign advertisements that did not advocate for the election or defeat of a candidate.[2] Three times prior to *Citizens United,* the Roberts Court considered campaign finance laws, and on all three occasions, the majority struck the regulation down. Thus, even before *Citizens United,* campaign finance law was suffering what election law expert Richard Hasen called "the death of a thousand cuts."[3]

Citizens United started as a little-noticed lawsuit regarding a ninety-minute video, *Hillary: The Movie.* The so-called documentary was harshly critical of Hillary Clinton, who was then a presidential primary candidate, arguing that she was unfit to be the commander-in-chief, unqualified for the presidency, and that "a vote for Hillary is a vote to continue 20 years of a Bush or a Clinton in the White House."[4] Citizens United—a nonprofit corporation that received some part of its funding from business corporations—wished to distribute the documentary on cable television as a "video-on-demand" in the period before the 2008 primary elections.

While *Hillary: The Movie* appeared to be simply just another salvo in the presidential campaign season, its production, timing, and planned release, in fact, were part of a coordinated and long-standing legal strategy to test the constitutional boundaries of federal campaign finance law, in particular the Bipartisan Campaign Reform Act (BCRA), popularly known as "McCain-Feingold."[5] Federal law barred corporations and unions from using general treasury funds to pay for "electioneering communications"—that is, broadcast campaign advertisements—or for federal communications that expressly advocated the election or defeat of a candidate.[6] Instead, corporations could engage in such election-related expenditures only by establishing and administering a "separate segregated fund" or political action committee (PAC).[7] Such a PAC could be funded only through contributions of the corporation's stockholders, employees, and their families, and were subject to generally applicable federal contribution limits. But, under the so-called *MCFL* exemption (named after the Supreme Court's decision in *Federal Election Commission v. Massachusetts Citizens for Life*),[8] federal electioneering communications restrictions did not apply to nonprofit ideological advocacy corporations that had no shareholders and that did not accept contributions from for-profit corporations or unions.

The corporate electioneering restriction had been an explicit feature of federal campaign finance law since at least 1947, and had been upheld against a facial constitutional challenge by the Supreme Court in its 2003 decision *McConnell v. Federal Election Commission.*[9] In that case, the Court reasoned that the existence of the PAC alternative gave corporations and unions a "constitutionally sufficient" alternative to participate in federal electoral politics.[10] The Court had also upheld a state law analogous to the federal electioneering communications restriction in its 1990 decision *Austin v. Michigan Chamber of Commerce*.[11]

In multiple ways, *Hillary: The Movie* was at the very margins of the coverage of the corporate electioneering communications restrictions. Whether or not the proposed video-on-demand release was, indeed, a "broadcast" advertisement, whether the *de minimis* amount of business corporation contributions disqualified Citizens United from being covered by the *MCFL* exemption, and whether a ninety-minute documentary could be considered an advertisement were all questions that could have been resolved narrowly, avoiding the constitutional issue.[12] Rather than resolving the case on narrow grounds, on the last day of the 2009 term, the Supreme Court vastly expanded the scope and consequences of the case by requesting expedited reargument on whether the Court's precedents in *Austin* and *McConnell* should be overturned, and whether the restrictions on corporate electioneering should be held facially unconstitutional.

Suddenly, this sleepy little case had the potential to transform federal politics as we know it. The political community sat up and took notice: forty-one *amicus* briefs were filed in the few short weeks of the Court's rushed briefing schedule. The end result was, of course, a sweeping decision, clearing the way for unlimited corporate spending in federal elections for the first time in the modern era.

This volume of essays is an attempt to map out the complex labyrinth that led to *Citizens United* and to explore where this decision may lead. The chapters in it arose from a symposium sponsored by the Brennan Center just nine weeks after the *Citizens United* decision was announced. The timing was somewhat fortuitous—although we knew the *Citizens United* decision was pending when we organized the convening, we had no way of knowing that the Supreme Court was on the verge of upending decades of settled constitutional doctrine. We were painfully aware, however, that the increasingly byzantine contours of campaign finance law had driven many of our greatest constitutional scholars out of the field, leaving the topic of money and politics to be largely the province of specialists. A fundamental reassessment was long overdue. Our goal, then, was to bring together the most incisive, innovative, and profound constitutional scholars of our time to take a fresh look at the age-old conundrum of money and politics.

Now, *Citizens United* has created an inflection point in constitutional law. Fundamental questions of money and politics have been brought to the forefront of constitutional debate: Should the First Amendment favor individual speech rights at the expense of other democratic values, or is the First Amendment itself premised on an ideal of deliberative democracy? Are elections a marketplace that the economically powerful can rightfully dominate, or should they instead be viewed as an institution designed to facilitate informed decision-making by voters? Should money be treated as speech, and, if so, when and to what extent? How do the First Amendment rights of corporations and other organizations compare to the rights of individuals? Does the insulation of judges from politics make them the ideal arbiters of the competing claims of campaigners, or does their inexperience lead them to constitutionalize a misguided view of the political process?

In responding to these and other basic questions, the contributors to this volume have outlined unexpected and productive avenues to pursue in examining the constitutional law of money and politics. The volume is divided into four parts. The first part explores the concept of "electoral exceptionalism," in which elections may be deemed to be exceptional realms of First Amendment activity—comparable to town hall meetings or public debates—in which ordinary rules regarding government regulation of speech may apply differently than in other spheres of public discourse. In Chapter 2, Robert Post points out that First Amendment coverage is not omnipresent—whether particular circumstances trigger First Amendment analysis at all depends, crucially, on an underlying account of the purposes and values advanced by the First Amendment. He argues that First Amendment coverage should be triggered whenever state regulations threaten communication that is essential to public discourse, but also that First Amendment doctrine should be formulated to safeguard essential processes of democratic legitimation. The question of First Amendment protection should turn on the assessing the justification for campaign finance regulation in light of its impact on public discourse. He suggests that reconciling campaign finance regulation with existing

First Amendment doctrine will require a reorientation, so that such regulations are conceptualized as efforts to preserve the institutional purposes of elections.

In Chapter 3, Richard H. Pildes introduces more fully the concept of "electoral exceptionalism," arguing that elections should be constitutionally viewed as specially bounded domains warranting distinct First Amendment rules. Pildes explains that particularized treatment of election-related speech would be consistent with existing First Amendment doctrine, which recognizes a variety of context-dependent principles. Pildes outlines a jurisprudential theory that treats elections as a bounded sphere of First Amendment concern.

In Chapter 4, Geoffrey R. Stone responds with fundamental questions raised by the electoral exceptionalism approach. He sets forth the parameters that govern the recognition of First Amendment exceptionalism in other areas, such as in schools or town hall meetings. He explores the difficulty of finding an appropriate analogy between such recognized First Amendment exceptions and elections, and lists an array of questions that must be answered before suspending our general skepticism of government efforts to regulate electoral speech.

The second part of the volume offers new perspectives on a fundamental issue: whether and to what extent money spent on speech equals speech itself. In Chapter 5, Deborah Hellman posits a fresh approach to determining when the spending of money should be equated with an underlying constitutional right. She explores case law in other arenas in which such spending is, and is not, deemed to be encompassed within the penumbra of a particular right. She ultimately concludes that spending can be constitutionally regulated when the state provides an adequate, alternative means of accessing the right in question.

In Chapter 6, highlighting the constitutional primacy of consent in legitimate democratic government, Frances R. Hill faults the *Citizens United* Court for ignoring the underlying First Amendment rights of corporate shareholders and members. She explores the textual and doctrinal foundations of considering consent a constitutional principle. She then considers methods to ensure consent and accountability for corporate political spending in the post–*Citizens United* world.

In Chapter 7, I explain that the Court's campaign finance decisions have embodied two competing conceptions of the source of First Amendment value in campaign spending: the volitional account ties such value to the intention of the spender, while the commodity account assesses such value from the point of view of the marketplace. Through this lens, I explain how the *Citizens United* opinion's "source-blind" approach represents a radical extension of the commodity account and question some of this approach's destabilizing ramifications.

The third part of the volume considers how political spending may lead to a corruption of our democratic polity. In Chapter 8, Samuel Issacharoff takes a hard look at the meaning of political corruption and finds that the concept has never been satisfactorily explored. He explains that the concept of "corruption" is really a concern with ensuring public—rather than private—outputs from the policymaking process of government once in office, rather than when candidates stand for election. He suggests a reorientation of campaign finance law using an approach that guards against "clientelism" and can combat the corrosive distortion of political decision-making.

In Chapter 9, Zephyr Teachout also challenges the narrow concept of corruption adopted by the *Citizens United* Court. She shows that, in fact, American courts have long been concerned by the distorting influence of money in the political sphere, and historically relied on such concerns to refuse to enforce private contracts. With this case law as a guide, she suggests looking beyond traditional campaign finance principles to enrich and expand the judicial tools available to combat political corruption.

In Chapter 10, Mark C. Alexander argues that the Supreme Court's money-in-politics jurisprudence has over-emphasized free speech values at the expense of key equality considerations. He urges the Court to recognize, for example, equality concerns implicated when elected officials spend more time fund-raising than legislating, or when power is concentrated in the hands of an elite group of fund-raisers.

The fourth part of the volume examines the extent to which the courts have assumed too great a role in the realm of political spending. In Chapter 11, Richard Briffault demonstrates that campaign finance jurisprudence has become overly judicialized, routinely privileging the judgment of courts over the opinion of elected officials. Given the numerous constitutional interests implicated, the normative judgments about how to order competing concerns, and the importance of empirical considerations, Briffault maintains that questions of campaign finance regulation are best resolved by public debate, with judicial intervention justified only to prevent clear constitutional abuses.

In Chapter 12, Burt Neuborne takes a historical long view, tracing our dysfunctional law of democracy to a fundamental disagreement among Justices Felix Frankfurter, William Brennan, and John Marshall Harlan. He pinpoints the ultimate problem with the Court's money in politics jurisprudence—its refusal to consider how particular decisions will affect democracy.

The chapters in this volume are intended to serve as a guide through the labyrinth of judicial decisions on money and politics and to mark some new paths forward. Whether *Citizens United* is the first step leading to a brave new world of deregulated campaigns or whether it is ultimately revealed as a constitutional dead end is, at this point, yet to be determined. But the scholarship presented here will be crucial to determining the ultimate legacy of this watershed decision—and of our constitutional democracy.

Part I

"Electoral Exceptionalism"

Do Elections Have Special Status under the First Amendment?

2

Campaign Finance Regulation and First Amendment Fundamentals

Robert Post

For many commentators, a key question in contemporary debates over campaign finance regulation is whether money constitutes speech for the purposes of the First Amendment to the Constitution.[1] It might be more productive instead to focus on the precise issue driving these debates—whether, and to what extent, the First Amendment should protect campaign financing during elections. In order to answer this question, we must distinguish First Amendment *coverage* from First Amendment *protection.*

Issues of First Amendment coverage concern the threshold circumstances in which we believe it appropriate to apply the specific tests associated with First Amendment doctrine. Sometimes state regulations must undergo the scrutiny of First Amendment tests, and sometimes not. The difference marks the boundary of First Amendment coverage. Issues of First Amendment protection, by contrast, concern whether particular regulations should or should not survive the scrutiny of First Amendment tests. Whether or not specific regulations should be struck down as unconstitutional turns on the scope of First Amendment protection, which is defined by the content of First Amendment doctrine.[2]

Whether money is speech is often conceptualized as a question of First Amendment coverage. Those who argue that money is not speech imply that campaign finance regulations should not trigger any First Amendment scrutiny at all. They argue that the rigors of

First Amendment doctrine should simply not apply to the regulation of campaign contributions.

The first generation of theorists to confront the question of First Amendment coverage included Supreme Court Justices Hugo Black and William Douglas, as well as Yale law professor Thomas Emerson.[3] They sought to define the scope of First Amendment coverage by distinguishing between *speech* and *conduct*. They argued that the application of First Amendment doctrine should be triggered when government seeks to regulate speech but not when government seeks to regulate conduct. This position, of course, requires a clear distinction between speech and conduct.

It turns out to be extremely difficult to make sense of this distinction. In ordinary usage, much conduct is communicative, and much speech does not trigger First Amendment coverage. The Court's most sustained effort to explicate this distinction was in *Spence v. Washington,*[4] in which the Court defined speech as a form of behavior that seeks to communicate a particular message in circumstances where there is an objective likelihood that the message will be understood.[5] *Spence* held that the application of First Amendment doctrine should be triggered whenever government attempts to regulate speech as so defined.[6]

The difficulty is that the so-called *Spence* test is not a plausible way to explain the scope of actual First Amendment coverage. Persons often attempt to communicate particularized messages that have an objective likelihood of being understood, and yet First Amendment doctrine will not be applied to control the regulation of their behavior. The terrorists who guided planes into the World Trade Center were trying to communicate a particular message, and their message was in fact quite plainly understood, as they knew it would be. Yet had these terrorists been captured and tried, they would not have been able to mount a First Amendment defense to a criminal prosecution. It is easy to conjure many more such examples.[7] The *Spence* test is too broad because, if applied literally, it would extend First Amendment coverage to all kinds of behavior that no one would conceive within the remotest boundaries of the First Amendment.

The *Spence* test over-extends the scope of First Amendment coverage in another way. Imagine a plane that crashes into a mountain because a faulty aeronautical chart has misidentified the geographical location of the peak. Few would argue that the chart maker should have a First Amendment defense if she is later sued by the crash victims. Yet the chart plainly meets the requirement of the *Spence* test. It intends to communicate a particularized message and is in fact successful. Taken literally, the Spence test would encompass written documents such as contracts, product labels, or prescriptions, all of which successfully communicate particularized messages, and all of which are regularly controlled by the state without the benefit of First Amendment coverage.

The distinction between speech and conduct is thus not helpful in assisting us to define the scope of First Amendment coverage. The fundamental error of such an approach lies in the assumption that the boundaries of First Amendment coverage can be determined by the presence or absence of factual properties of the world. A better approach to defining the scope of First Amendment coverage, and indeed to me the only possible approach, is to reverse this assumption. The scope of First Amendment coverage is determined by the application to the world of the values that we interpret the First Amendment to protect. We apply First Amendment doctrine to the regulation of conduct whenever that regulation threatens to undermine the purposes of the First Amendment. When the regulation of conduct does not threaten to impair First Amendment values, we do not apply First Amendment doctrine. The question of First Amendment coverage is thus not analytically distinct from the question of the substance of the First Amendment.

This account of First Amendment coverage implies that the question of whether money is speech is fundamentally misguided. The right question is instead whether regulations of particular financial transactions, like campaign contributions or expenditures, implicate First Amendment values. Phrased in this way, we are forced to confront the real issue: What do we wish to use the First Amendment to accomplish?

In order to think concretely about this issue, imagine a statute that bans newsprint in order to save trees. Although newsprint is not speech, the statute would nevertheless affect widely held First Amendment values because it would severely impact many great newspapers. Under the approach I am suggesting, a ban on newsprint would trigger First Amendment coverage because it would threaten to compromise First Amendment values. This of course leaves open both the nature of the First Amendment tests that the statute must satisfy and also the application of these tests to the statute. Both these issues involve the question of the scope of First Amendment *protection.*

To apply this reasoning to the case of campaign finance regulation, we should address the question of coverage by asking whether state regulation of campaign finances affects First Amendment values. In analogous circumstances, we would not hesitate to answer this question affirmatively. A statute prohibiting movies from selling tickets would certainly affect whatever First Amendment values are associated with cinema, as would a law setting price limits on novels. I would think that prohibiting campaign finance contributions and expenditures would sufficiently affect the First Amendment values associated with campaign speech as to merit First Amendment coverage.

But this conclusion leaves open the question of First Amendment protection. What kind of First Amendment tests should be applied to campaign finance regulations? The answer to this question depends upon the relationship between government campaign finance regulations and First Amendment values. To analyze this relationship, we need first to specify the nature of First Amendment values.

Some people argue that the First Amendment should be interpreted to protect the "marketplace of ideas," a concept first introduced to American jurisprudence by Justice Oliver Wendell Holmes in the early twentieth century.[8] Proponents of this theory hold that the First Amendment should protect the free exchange of ideas so that our knowledge of the world can be increased.

Although the marketplace theory has many adherents, I do not believe that it provides a plausible account of the First Amendment. When we actually look at institutions that seek to expand knowledge—institutions like scientific journals or universities—the ideal of the marketplace of ideas is not in evidence. Such institutions routinely evaluate speech and regulate it according to its merits.[9] If expanding the realm of knowledge were a fundamental First Amendment value, First Amendment doctrine would not preclude the state from penalizing ideas because of their truth or falsity. If for purposes of the First Amendment there is no such thing as a false idea, there can also be no such thing as a true idea. This perspective is incompatible with the aspiration to expand knowledge; institutions that actually produce knowledge routinely distinguish between true and false ideas. This strongly suggests that the cognitive ideals of the marketplace of ideas are insufficient to explain the nature of existing First Amendment doctrine.

A second value that is frequently attributed to the First Amendment is the protection of the "autonomy" of persons to define their own life. I find this theory also to be implausible. Every regulation of human conduct restricts the autonomy of individuals. For this reason the value of autonomy does not help us to understand the distinctive doctrinal tests of the First Amendment.

My own view is that the First Amendment protects speech in order to facilitate democracy. Democracy is a form of government in which the people govern themselves. Fundamental to democracy is the warranted belief that persons are free to participate in the formation of public opinion and that government is accountable to public opinion. I shall use the term *public discourse* to describe those communicative processes deemed essential to the free formation of public opinion. First Amendment coverage should be triggered whenever state regulations threaten adversely to impact forms of communication that are essential to public discourse, and First Amendment doctrine should be formulated to protect essential processes of democratic legitimation.[10]

This account of First Amendment values rather well explains the actual scope of First Amendment coverage and protection. First Amendment coverage tends to be triggered by government efforts to regulate the public sphere, within which public opinion is formed. And First Amendment protection is formulated so as to block efforts to regulate public discourse in ways that are viewpoint discriminatory. The reason for this kind of First Amendment protection is that viewpoint discriminatory regulation excludes persons from participating in the formation of public opinion on the basis of their ideas, and hence refuses to extend to such persons the democratic legitimation of public discourse. The prohibition against viewpoint discrimination does not reflect an equality among ideas, as the theory of the marketplace of ideas would suggest, but instead an equality among persons with regard to their right to make government democratically responsive.

Campaign finance regulation plainly seeks to constrain efforts to form public opinion and thus should trigger First Amendment coverage. But whether it should survive constitutional scrutiny is quite a different question. The question of First Amendment protection should turn on an assessment of the justification for campaign finance regulation in light of its impact on public discourse. There are a number of plausible justifications for campaign finance regulation that are consistent with standard First Amendment analysis. I shall close these short remarks by remarking on one such justification that is not usually theorized in the existing literature.

Public discourse is protected because democratic legitimation consists in making government accountable to public opinion. But public debate also serves the purpose of enabling public decision-making. Once a democracy has reached a decision about what to do, it must effectively implement its will. If we decide to create a social security system or a health care administration, we must also create government institutions that are authorized and empowered to realize these ambitions. The social structure of such institutions will be quite different from public discourse.

Public discourse is a social structure in which a democracy seeks to determine the content of its own ends. Public discourse therefore cannot be subordinated to any particular end, since any such end might be altered after sufficient discussion. Government organizations, by contrast, exist to achieve particular ends that have already been decided within public discourse. Government organizations must therefore be authorized to regulate speech as necessary to achieve their predetermined ends. Otherwise, the very function of public discourse will be frustrated.

It follows that government organizations cannot be structured so as to perennially to keep options open for deliberation. Government organizations must be structured so as to accomplish the ends for which they have been established. School systems must be empowered to educate students, court systems to dispense justice, and so on.[11] As a consequence First Amendment doctrine protecting speech within the managerial domain of organizations is very differently structured than First Amendment doctrine protecting speech within public discourse. Schools are authorized to regulate speech as is necessary to educate students; courts to regulate the speech of attorneys, witnesses, and jurors as is necessary in order to attain the ends of justice; and so on.

This insight poses a constitutional puzzle with regard to campaign finance regulation. On the one hand, campaign communications are quintessential efforts to shape public opinion in circumstances when public opinion truly matters. On the other hand, elections are themselves government institutions designed for the particular purpose of ensuring that government remains accountable to public opinion.[12] Campaign finance regulation can thus be conceptualized either as an effort to suppress public discourse, in which case it should face a heavy presumption of unconstitutionality, or as an effort to secure the effectiveness of elections, in which case First Amendment scrutiny should turn on whether particular campaign regulations are necessary for elections successfully to accomplish the purposes for which they have been established. Although in neither case would campaign finance regulations lie beyond the scope of First Amendment coverage, the appropriate form of First Amendment protection would very much depend on how we have decided to conceive the constitutional status of elections.

In many countries, elections are conceived as managerial domains. Even in the United States there are many ways in which we already regard elections as purposive institutions. For example, we prohibit people from saying, "I offer you twenty dollars in exchange for your vote," or from soliciting for votes on election day within one hundred feet of the entrance to a polling place.[13] These rules regulate speech during elections without raising fatal First Amendment concerns; they are regarded as necessary for elections to succeed in their assigned task, which is essential to democracy.

To regard campaign finance regulation as restricting public discourse is effectively to constitutionally prevent public control of campaigns. If we wish to reconcile campaign finance regulation with existing First Amendment doctrine and values, we shall need instead to conceptualize such regulations as efforts to preserve the institutional purposes of elections.[14] This reconceptualization of campaign finance regulations would require us to ask whether particular government rules are necessary for the successful functioning of elections. This perspective is not logically required, and we are required to adopt it by nothing apart from the growing fear that our elections are increasingly failing to fulfill their democratic task, and that as a consequence the successful legitimation of our constitutional government may be slipping from our grasp.

3

Elections as a Distinct Sphere under the First Amendment

*Richard H. Pildes**

The strongest legal argument, in my view, for justifying regulations of election financing, such as electioneering paid for out of a corporation's or union's general treasury funds, is the view that elections should be considered a distinct sphere of political activity. Elections are distinct from the more general arena of democratic debate, both because elections serve a specific set of purposes and because those purposes can, arguably, be undermined or corrupted by actions such as the willingness of candidates or officeholders to trade their votes on issues for campaign contributions or spending. Given this risk of corruption of the political judgment of officeholders, regulations of the electoral sphere—including how elections are financed—might be constitutionally permissible that would not otherwise be permissible outside the sphere of elections. This is the form of argument that must be accepted to justify measures such as ceilings on campaign contributions, disclosure of campaign spending, and limits on the role of corporate and union electioneering.

To begin to reveal the structure of this argument and to justify it, I want to start with a recent U.S. Supreme Court decision. A few years back, in *Arkansas Educational Television Commission v. Forbes*,[1] the Court held that at least one phase of the electoral process,

---

*Parts of this essay are abridged from Frederick Schauer and Richard H. Pildes, *Electoral Exceptionalism and the First Amendment*, 77 Tex. L. Rev. 1803 (1999). For assistance with this article, I thank Alex Mindlin.

a candidate debate, is special for First Amendment purposes. At issue was the decision of a state-owned television station to exclude from the congressional candidate debate it was sponsoring an independent candidate who had qualified for the ballot; the station included only the Democratic and Republican candidates. In essence, the case required the Court to decide whether state journalism was best characterized as the state or as private journalism. In the Court's view, the journalism categorization was more apt.[2] As a consequence of this characterization decision, the constraints of content and viewpoint neutrality that might otherwise bind agencies of the state were held not to apply to a public television station.

Yet the Court went on to add an intriguing qualification. According to *Forbes*, candidate debates play a special role in democratic politics.[3] Therefore, the Court decided, state-sponsored debates are subject to the requirement of viewpoint neutrality, even though the Court recognized that other public television programming, including political programming, could be as viewpoint-skewed as the station's management desired. The Court held that the First Amendment applied in one way to general activities of the state, another way to activities of state-owned media, and yet another way when state-owned media sponsored candidate debates as part of the electoral process.

My goal here is to explore the implications of the Court's holding that the First Amendment requires unique treatment of candidate debates because such debates play a special role in democratic politics. More broadly, I want to explore a possible extension of this principle: Is it possible that other aspects of electoral politics could also be the subject of special election-specific First Amendment principles because of their special role in democracy? Even if the current Court would not accept this extension of *Forbes,* is it nonetheless a consistent direction along which constitutional oversight of politics might logically proceed?

The Rhetoric of Exceptionalism

The position is one that Frederick Schauer and I have labeled "electoral exceptionalism." According to electoral exceptionalism, elections should be constitutionally understood as (relatively) bounded domains of communicative activity. Because of the defined scope of this activity, it would be possible to prescribe or apply First Amendment principles to electoral processes that do not necessarily apply through the full reach of the First Amendment. If electoral exceptionalism prevails, courts evaluating restrictions on speech that are part of the process of nominating and electing candidates would employ a different standard from what we might otherwise characterize as the normal, or baseline, degree of First Amendment scrutiny.

What Schauer and I call electoral exceptionalism surfaced in public debate and in First Amendment literature in the 1990s. Typically, it has been the foundation for an argument against *Buckley v. Valeo*.[4] This contra-*Buckley* argument asserts that, even though the principle that one may spend personal money to promote a cause is good First Amendment law in general, it does not apply when one is not advocating particular ideas or issues but instead seeking to elect a candidate to public office. Operationally, therefore, the most common version of electoral exceptionalism would permit restrictions on communicative activity in the context of elections that would not be permitted in other contexts.

Those with a penchant for oversimplification might say that electoral exceptionalism is an argument for weaker First Amendment protection in the context of elections. I describe this as an oversimplification, however, because in the context of arguments that campaign finance regulation would increase voter and candidate participation, decrease the influence of money compared to other sources of influence, or enhance voter confidence in democratic institutions, it is hardly clear that the values underlying the First Amendment would be more supportive of speaker (or candidate) immunity than they are of speaker (or candidate) participation. It is not self-evident that the values of democratic deliberation, collective self-determination, guarding against the abuse of power, searching for truth, and even self-expression are better served by treating government intervention as the unqualified enemy than by allowing the state a limited role in fostering the proliferation of voices in the public sphere,[5] or of increasing the importance of message and effort by decreasing the importance of wealth. Although it is plainly true that a negative conception of the First Amendment generally, and freedom of speech in particular, have held sway over the past several decades, both in the literature and in the case law, it may still be too early in the First Amendment day to assume that the possibility of a positive conception of the First Amendment, and thus of a positive but limited role for the state, have no claim to recognition as the legitimate carrier of the free speech banner.

Moreover, although the position we label electoral exceptionalism would ordinarily be associated with greater state intervention, and thus with what some commentators might characterize as weaker First Amendment protection with respect to elections, electoral exceptionalism could logically support the opposite result. Critics of campaign finance regulation might argue that state restrictions on communicative activity in the electoral process are especially risky, largely because the self-interest of potential governmental regulators would be greatest in precisely this sphere.[6] Consequently, this argument would continue, permissible restrictions in other or more "normal" contexts should be impermissible in the electoral context; if anything, the First Amendment ought to be even more absolute in this domain precisely because of its special characteristics.[7]

In sum, concluding that elections constitute a distinct domain for First Amendment purposes does not dictate what we would do within that domain. The primary goal of this essay is to explore the possibility of electoral exceptionalism, rather than to evaluate any particular laws or policies that could be applied to elections as a result.

Competing Conceptions of Rights

That there is some "normal" or "standard" conception of what First Amendment doctrine does is widely believed. This off-the-rack understanding of the doctrine, centrally informed by such icons of the First Amendment tradition as *Brandenburg v. Ohio,*[8] *New York Times Co. v. Sullivan, New York Times Co. v. United States*[9] (the Pentagon Papers case), *Cohen v. California,*[10] and *Texas v. Johnson,*[11] is thought to represent the essential form of First Amendment protection. Departures, generally in the direction of less rather than more stringent protection, are routinely denigrated as exceptions.[12] We often hear the argument from the Supreme Court and others that these and other cases establish something like a compelling interest standard for any regulation of speech,[13] that the compelling interest standard is practically unattainable,[14] and thus that any proposal for regulation of campaign-related speech or expenditures would be tantamount to carving out an exception from the First Amendment.

This view tends to be associated with an individualist conception of the purposes of the First Amendment. If the First Amendment protects rights intrinsic to essential attributes of individual personhood, autonomy, or dignity, such as the right to self-expression, it is easy to see how one might conclude that First Amendment "rights" should not depend in significant ways on the particular contexts in which they are asserted.

That many might think the First Amendment should be understood in this way comes as no surprise. Much of American constitutional law, not just the First Amendment, is cast in the language of protecting individual rights: rights to democratic participation, rights to equality, or rights to freedom of belief. Indeed, the most influential metaphor for the way constitutional rights are often thought to work is the imagery that legal philosopher Ronald Dworkin conjured up of rights as "trumps."[15] Dworkin argued that rights protect individual interests by excluding majoritarian preferences or judgments about the common good as a justification for limiting rights.[16]As Dworkin put it, "If someone has a right to something, then it is wrong for the government to deny it to him even though it would be in the general interest to do so."[17] This perspective is easily read to portray constitutional cases as entailing direct conflicts between individualistic interests (in liberty, autonomy, personhood, or dignity) and majority judgments about the common good—with constitutional rights trumping the latter to secure the former.[18]

There is, however, an alternative "structural conception of rights."[19] On this view, rights are a means of realizing various common goods, rather than being protections for individualist interests against collective judgments about those common goods. Rights do protect the interests of the rights holders, but not only those interests; the protections that rights bestow are not justified because they protect these individualistic interests, but because rights protect various spheres or domains from governmental intrusion on the basis of constitutionally impermissible reasons. Rights are not general trumps against appeals to the common good; instead, they are better understood as channeling the kinds of reasons that government can invoke when it acts in certain areas.

In this structural conception, rights function as linguistic tools that the law invokes in the pragmatic task of bringing certain issues before the courts for judicial resolution. Rights exclude government action within certain contexts in order to preserve the normative integrity of various domains, as constitutionally delineated. So, rights protect a certain conception of public education;[20] they protect a certain conception of religion and the boundary between religion and the state;[21] they protect a civil-service bureaucracy from the intrusions of partisan politics;[22] they define the appropriate structure of the sphere of democratic politics;[23] and they protect other spheres from state intrusion on the basis of impermissible purposes. Far from standing opposed to the pursuit of various common goods, rights are the tool through which constitutional law creates and preserves common goods, such as democratic education, politics, religion, public service, and other domains that help realize various social values. In other words, rights help create a constitutional culture by differentiating various domains from each other and precluding the state from acting on certain reasons in some of these domains, even if those same reasons could properly form the basis for state action in other domains.

This structural conception of rights is deeply rooted in the American idea of constitutionalism itself. This idea did not begin with philosophical conceptions of the person and reason out from there to rights. It was rooted in the experience of government, both English colonial administration and state governments after the Revolution.[24] American constitutional rights are better pictured, at least in origin, as reasoning "in" from judgments about government to constitutional barriers erected to avoid what past practice had made all too visible: the corrosive potential of government.[25] Rights were not designed to protect individuals in their atomistic interests in, for example, self-expressiveness;[26] rather, rights were designed to sustain a political culture in which "public liberty"[27] was enhanced by recognizing certain domains as relatively autonomous. This conception meant defining certain domains as off-limits to state action that rested on particular, impermissible purposes.[28]

Domains for First Amendment purposes are not empirical facts, nor brute conventions, that require no further acts of legal interpretation.

Instead, they are ongoing social practices, constituted in part by past legal understandings, whose meaning consists of critical reflection on those practices on the basis of standards that are at least partly internal to the practice itself.[29] Even when the claim is that a new domain ought to be recognized under the First Amendment, that claim is likely to be made on the basis of analogizing from existing legal understandings or from interpretations of the practice as it currently exists.

The critique of the individualist account of First Amendment rights offered here is one of existing practice that conceptualizes the First Amendment at too abstract a level of generality in relation to the social and economic practices the First Amendment seeks to regulate and evaluate. There is no general right of free speech.[30] There is no one general value or interest that free speech protects.[31] There is no realm of action of undifferentiated liberty called freedom of speech. When the Supreme Court, commentators, or participants in public discourse suggest otherwise, they are reifying free speech into an overly abstract conception. First Amendment public discourse has drifted toward too high a level of abstraction and generality—a level that cannot make sense of the actual cases themselves. Actual First Amendment practice depends upon a considerably more embedded understanding of speech, one that recognizes speech interests to be contingent upon the specific social context.

Elections as Bounded Spheres

With respect to elections and regulation of campaign finance, then, the question is not whether such regulation intrudes on some abstractly conceived individualistic interest in liberty or self-expression. It is whether the domain of electoral politics should be recognized as a domain distinct, for First Amendment purposes, from other domains, such as the general sphere of public discourse. Elections are already highly structured spheres, including regulations that would be impermissible in the general domain of public discourse. There are limits on what voters are permitted to express at the ballot box;[32] mandatory disclosure obligations on the identity of political speakers;[33] content-based regulations of electoral speech, ranging from mundane constraints such as electioneering near polling places[34] to more dramatic ones, such as selective bans on contributions from some speakers (for example, corporations[35]); and a series of other constraints.[36] Moreover, elections are already structured in many ways that could be conceived as impinging upon constitutional rights other than those in the First Amendment. For example, what considerations justify requiring that voting be viva voce, as in the late eighteenth century, or by open balloting, as it was through much of the nineteenth century, or by the secret balloting process that did not become widespread in America until the late nineteenth century? Any of these choices prefer some modes of electoral practices over others on the basis of judgments about "better" forms of democracy. Are the rights of self-expression, free speech, or the right to vote violated by any of these choices? We do not stop to consider that a serious question, though it could be. The justification of these structures is that they promote a "fairer" mode of representation, that they enhance the deliberative quality of choosing candidates and making policy, or that they improve the quality of voter decision-making. These are precisely the kinds of justifications that would be offered for some types of campaign finance reform.

The question of how to finance elections currently looms large as a unique problem in constitutional theory partly because we have come to suppress awareness of many background decisions previously made about other crucial elements of the electoral structure. In other words, elections are already extensively regulated, state-structured processes; this structuring is designed to achieve specific instrumental purposes. From a constitutional perspective, decisions about whether to structure the financing of elections are not so obviously different from other decisions that are currently far less controversial about how to structure elections. The argument from electoral exceptionalism would draw upon the understandings already embedded in the way elections are legally constructed.

Arguments that the First Amendment should recognize a distinct set of principles to evaluate speech regulations in the electoral context would draw upon the understandings already embedded in the way elections are legally constructed. To the extent values of individual self-expression play a role in the best constitutional understanding of various domains, they are one factor in the legal analysis, but always in relation to the social values that are argued to constitute distinct institutional domains.

The First Amendment as Unitary or as an Exception

In the First Amendment context, the argument that there is a general, "normal" conception of free speech rights that applies the same way in nearly all contexts—an argument associated with the individualist justification of constitutional rights—is long on rhetoric and short on substance. Even if we accept the claim that money is speech,[37] it does not follow that identifying a restriction as a restriction of speech necessarily puts us within the domain of the First Amendment. Almost all the law of contracts, warranties, labels, wills, deeds, trusts, fraud, and perjury, as well as much of antitrust law, securities law, and consumer law, is accurately seen as a regulation of speech in the literal sense of that word, yet exists without even a glimmer of First Amendment scrutiny. In most of these instances, the claim that the First Amendment is even relevant would generate little more than quizzical judicial disbelief.[38] Once we see that the overwhelming proportion of speech is not covered by the First Amendment, and the overwhelming proportion of speech regulation not touched by the First Amendment, we can see the rhetorical sleight-of-hand implicit in the standard talk of "exceptions" to the First Amendment.[39] In reality, the First Amendment itself might better be seen as an exception to the prevailing principle that speech may be regulated in the normal course of governmental business.

A more plausible but still unsound argument would recognize that, although the First Amendment does not cover all speech, subdivision within what the First Amendment does cover remains highly disfavored.[40] The argument for a unitary First Amendment within its otherwise circumscribed coverage appears to have a sound foundation in the modern American First Amendment tradition and in much of American legal theory generally.[41] Indeed, this argument could be put in a particularly strong form when applied to campaign finance regulation. This is political speech—the paradigm case for the First

Amendment,[42] so the argument goes—and at least with respect to political speech we should not go down the road of subdividing types of communicative activity.[43]

Yet, even here the argument against exceptionalism is fragile. For even with respect to political speech, the degree of that protection is more institution-dependent than many recognize. There is one form of protection for political speech on government property,[44] another for political speech on the broadcast media,[45] another for political speech in the public schools,[46] another for political speech by government employees,[47] and so on. What this suggests, therefore, is that the idea of a standard, normal, or off-the-rack conception of even political speech is an egregious oversimplification. Rather, the context of elections, like the contexts of billboards,[48] posters,[49] signs in windows,[50] schools,[51] colleges,[52] government employment,[53] polling places,[54] and so on, is just one of numerous settings in which political speech occurs. All regulations of political speech thus already are measured by domain-specific, institution-specific, sometimes media-specific, and generally context-specific First Amendment principles—rather than some undifferentiated, "general" First Amendment rule.

Instead, the argument against electoral exceptionalism must rely on the normative view that elections ought not to be treated differently from the larger and election-independent domains of First Amendment–protected communication. Thus, it might be argued, as the Supreme Court assumed in *Buckley* itself and numerous other cases,[55] that the form of advocacy that urges the election of one candidate over another is indistinguishable in First Amendment terms from the form of advocacy that advocates the round-earth over the flat-earth position, flat taxation over progressive taxation, pro-choice over pro-life, or socialism over social Darwinism.

The question, then, is whether some degree of government regulation in the service of enhancing the electoral process, based on the diverse justifications that have been offered for doing so, ought to be permissible. More particularly, the question is whether regulation should be permissible to remedy various perceived pathologies of current electoral discourse, even if that same degree of government intervention would be impermissible to remedy the parallel pathologies of non-electoral discourse in roughly comparable situations. Even more specifically, the question is whether such regulation ought to be permissible against the perceived distortions resulting from the undue influence of wealth, even if doing so would leave an imbalance in other sources of political influence. Accepting that position would require accepting the idea that elections can be demarcated, for First Amendment purposes, from the general domain of public discourse. This is both a normative question in First Amendment theory and a functional question of whether any regulatory approach can enforce this boundary with sufficient integrity.

Oddly, the Court in *Buckley* never confronted this issue in either of these terms.[56] There had been little academic development or sustained public debate of the First Amendment perspectives surrounding regulation of elections at the moment of the Court's momentous and baptismal engagement with these issues in *Buckley*. Thus, the Court assessed the Federal Election Campaign Act of 1974 by assimilating general principles of First Amendment adjudication that apply in the broad domain of public discourse without considering in any depth whether the kind of domain-specific analysis it applies in other areas of speech—including political speech—should apply to regulation of election-related spending.

Congress and the Court on Electoral Exceptionalism

In the Bipartisan Campaign Finance Reform Act of 2002 (BCRA), colloquially known as the McCain-Feingold Law, Congress essentially endorsed the concept of electoral exceptionalism. Title II of the act barred corporations and unions from using general treasury funds for broadcast communications that, in Congress's judgment, were intended to influence, or had the effect of influencing the outcome of federal elections. More specifically, Congress defined a specific window of time it treated as, in effect, "the election period," and then adopted special rules for corporate and union electioneering that applied only during that period. Thus, Congress defined as an "electioneering communication" any "broadcast, cable, or satellite communication" that

> (I) refers to a clearly identified candidate for Federal office; (II) is made within—(aa) 60 days before a general, special, or runoff election for the office sought by the candidate; or (bb) 30 days before a primary or preference election, or a convention or caucus of a political party that has authority to nominate a candidate, for the office sought by the candidate; and (III) in the case of a communication which refers to a candidate other than President or Vice President, is targeted to the relevant electorate.[57]

Corporate or union general treasury fund spending on these ads, in this period, was prohibited.

Although Congress did not use the language of electoral exceptionalism, it clearly acted on the basis of the principles and understandings that inform the concept of electoral exceptionalism. Congress created a bright-line rule that defined a unique period of time as the election period. Such a period is a familiar concept in English and European democracies.[58] In many of these systems, elections do not take place at previously established times; instead, the government in power calls for an election at a specified date in the future. At times, only a month transpires between the calling of the election and the election itself. During this election period, the processes of electoral competition are highly regulated. Candidates, for example, might have access to a certain amount of state-specified free media time, but not to additional access.

The United States has no natural election period, in a comparable sense, because it is known years in advance that the next election will take place on a specific date in the future. Nonetheless, Congress identified unique considerations that justified, in Congress's judgment, unique treatment of corporate and union electioneering in a period of time close to the actual election. Congress did not seek to ban or regulate corporate and union general treasury spending on political matters in general, or even with respect to candidates or potential candidates for office outside the sixty-day window (for general elections) and the thirty-day window (for primary elections).[59] Instead, Congress defined an election period and concluded that special considerations justified unique regulatory restrictions on corporate and union spending during that period. In particular, Congress concluded that such spending in the election period generated unique risks of corruption (or perhaps, the appearance of corruption) of those who would wield public power;

as a result, unique restrictions on spending during the electoral period were appropriate and, in Congress's view, consistent with the First Amendment. This is precisely the set of understandings reflected in the idea of electoral exceptionalism.

The Court too—initially—accepted and endorsed this notion of electoral exceptionalism. In *McConnell v. Federal Election Commission*,[60] the Court upheld the constitutionality of these provisions in BCRA. Although the Court did not directly use the language of electoral exceptionalism, it upheld the ban on corporate and union electioneering on precisely the understandings and principles that underlie the concept of legitimately distinct First Amendment understandings properly applying to the distinct spheres of elections. The Court held that a "compelling governmental interest" justified regulations of speech in the electoral sphere that would not be justified if the regulations applied to speech outside the electoral sphere.[61] Among the justifications that made for a compelling interest in regulating corporate and union electioneering communications were preserving the integrity of the electoral process, preventing corruption, and preserving confidence of citizens in government.[62] The Court did not develop these principles at great length, which might not be surprising, given the overall massive length of the *McConnell* opinions. But there is no question that in *McConnell* the willingness to recognize that First Amendment principles could properly be applied and understood differently in the context of elections than in the context of more general public debate rested on the Court's willingness to endorse, in essence, the concept of electoral exceptionalism.

In *Citizens United v. Federal Election Commission*,[63] however, the Court overturned this portion of *McConnell* (as well as part of the Court's earlier decision in *Austin v. Michigan Chamber of Commerce*[64]). In doing so, the *Citizens United* Court necessarily rejected the concept of electoral exceptionalism. Moreover, the Court came closer to engaging directly with that concept than it had in any of its previous cases, perhaps in part because the idea of electoral exceptionalism, endorsed in both BCRA and *McConnell*, had become more explicitly recognized by the time of *Citizens United*. Thus, the Court felt obligated to recognize that it had previously endorsed the principle that the First Amendment applied differently in a number of specific institutional contexts than it did in the general sphere of public debate. Citing the kinds of decisions discussed throughout this chapter, the Court acknowledged that it had applied the First Amendment differently in the context of public schools, prisons, the military, and the civil service. The Court recognized that otherwise impermissible speech restrictions could be justified when the government had a sufficiently strong "interest in allowing governmental entities to perform their functions." But the Court then rejected the argument that this same principle applied in what we might consider the distinct sphere of elections. The Court concluded that corporate electioneering "would not interfere with governmental functions"; it held that these other cases stood only for the principle that when government "cannot operate" without some restrictions on particular kinds of speech, then those restrictions are permissible. Thus, the Court directly rejected the idea of electoral exceptionalism and, in doing so, held unconstitutional BCRA's ban on corporate and union electioneering.

The argument for electoral exceptionalism, of course, has the same form as the argument for the speech restrictions that the Court has permitted in the other institutional contexts the Court identified. While *Citizens United* stated that the government simply could not operate in these other spheres without the speech restrictions, this is an overstatement. More accurately put, the Court had concluded that these other institutional environments would function better—would better serve the purposes for which we create these institutional structures, such as schools, prisons, the civil service, and the like—if the relevant speech restrictions were permitted. That is the same form of argument made for electoral exceptionalism: elections would better serve the purposes for which they exist if certain kinds of restrictions, such as those on corporate and union electioneering, were permitted. Elections are designed to empower a government that is generally accepted as legitimate and is motivated to act for the common good. If corporate and union electioneering undermine those purposes, is banning that electioneering justified in light of the accepted aims of elections? To take an extreme example, if so many citizens lost confidence in government, because they believed their votes made no difference and officeholders were effectively bought by massive corporate and union electioneering spending, that voter turnout dropped to 25 percent, would regulation of such electioneering then be justified in order to preserve the purpose of elections—including the purpose of enabling a government that was generally perceived to be legitimate?

Thus, the idea of electoral exceptionalism was accepted by a 5–4 Court in *McConnell*, then rejected by a 5–4 Court in *Citizens United*. But even if *Citizens United* remains stable law, the idea of electoral exceptionalism is not going away, for many of the proposed responses to *Citizens United* continue to be based on this idea. In Congress, the major response to date, the Disclose Act,[65] was an effort to require full disclosure of the sources of funding for corporate electioneering communications. But Congress did not seek to require disclosure of these sources for all corporate political spending; Congress limited the proposed law to spending in the electoral sphere, where candidate elections are involved.[66] Similarly, some have proposed a constitutional amendment to overturn the result in *Citizens United*. But some of these proposals, such as that put forward by scholar and political activist Lawrence Lessig, do not seek to regulate all corporate spending on political speech.[67] Instead, they limit their reach to spending in the sixty days before an election. Thus, the idea that elections themselves implicate distinct concerns, and should be regulated differently than the general sphere of public debate, persists even after *Citizens United*.

Finally, for reformers who seek to limit the influence of corporate or union money on government, there are only four directions the legal argument to justify limits like those in BCRA can take. Yet, each of the available alternatives has much more sweeping implications than the electoral exceptionalism argument. First, one can argue that corporations should not have First Amendment rights at all. Second, one can argue that "money is not speech," or more precisely, that the spending of money to communicate political ideas is not the kind of activity to which the First Amendment ought to apply. Third, one could argue, as Ronald Dworkin has, that political equality supports the principle that government can act to ensure that differential levels of wealth are not translated into differential levels of political influence.[68] But each of these arguments would require a far more dramatic transformation in First Amendment understandings than electoral exceptionalism; moreover each of these arguments would have significantly broader implications for speech outside of the electoral context. The argument from electoral exceptionalism is thus the narrowest argument that can be made to support regulations of corporate and/or union spending in the specific and limited context of elections.

Electoral Exceptionalism Revisited

That American free speech doctrine is unique is not controversial. Even after decades of American influence on the development of free speech principles throughout the world, no country has come close to following the American model to the full extent of its free speech libertarianism. Nations that few would be inclined to brand as totalitarian today—Canada, New Zealand, Germany, France, and contemporary South Africa, to name just a few—have free speech and free press principles less speaker-protective on important issues than those in the United States. In the libertarian extent to which it immunizes speakers and speeches from state regulation, the United States stands alone.

Americans debate whether this state of affairs is to be applauded or condemned, but there is little likelihood it will change. As long as American free speech doctrine and culture remain so intolerant of the regulation of speech, attempts to permit the regulation of electoral speech must confront the question of whether a distinct domain of electoral speech can be distinguished from the broader domain of public discourse.[69] If not, regulation of electoral speech would be constitutionally doomed even if *Buckley* were no longer the law. But if electoral speech can be seen as a relatively distinct domain, then it would be intellectually plausible to press for its regulation with less threat to the uniqueness of American free speech culture. The justification of a separate domain for electoral speech is thus a necessary task for any potential regulator of campaign speech who recognizes the futility of wholesale changes in the American approach to freedom of speech and freedom of the press.

As I have argued here, justifying this special domain seems to me a less daunting task than it has to many others. First Amendment doctrine is not a monolith to which the separate treatment of electoral speech would be a dangerous exception. Rather, recognition of the multifariousness of speech and of the multifariousness of the regulatory environments in which it exists points the way to seeing that developing distinct principles for electoral speech would not be appreciably different from the structure of existing First Amendment doctrine. If there are arguments against electoral exceptionalism, they cannot be arguments against exceptionalism per se, because exceptionalism in the First Amendment is the rule and not the exception.

The task here has thus been narrow but necessary. I have not undertaken the task of asking whether any particular regulation of campaign finance would be a good idea. But if such regulation would be desirable as a policy matter, its permissibility would depend on the ability to develop First Amendment principles permitting such regulation while still prohibiting regulations that some would see as somewhat similar in non-electoral environments. Even this narrower agenda was not the project here, for the positive case for election-specific principles would again require recourse to numerous institutional and empirical features of campaigns and elections that I have not taken up in this context.

Yet even if I have avoided the issue of the desirability of campaign finance reform as a policy question, and avoided the issue of the positive case for election-specific First Amendment principles, I have confronted directly the primary impediment to both of those tasks: the argument that election-specific First Amendment principles are inconsistent with essential features of the First Amendment itself. Most forms of regulating our privately financed electoral system ultimately rest, explicitly or implicitly, on the argument that certain threats to democracy arise in unique form in the electoral sphere—particularly the risk that the judgment of candidates and officeholders will be corrupted by the role of money in their attainment and maintenance of office—and that these risks justify regulation of the electoral sphere that would not be permitted in the more general sphere of public debate over issues and policy. Because that idea is central to any regulatory effort in this area, I have tried to draw that idea out clearly and show the kind of justifications on which it rests. None of the argument is meant to endorse any specific form of regulation. But acceptance of the idea of electoral exceptionalism is a necessary predicate to most forms of regulation of election financing.

4

"Electoral Exceptionalism" and the First Amendment

*Geoffrey R. Stone**

The Supreme Court's recent decision in *Citizens United v. Federal Elections Commission*[1] reignited debate over whether the First Amendment should be understood as incorporating a principle of "electoral exceptionalism."[2] *Citizens United* invalidated restrictions on corporate and union "electioneering communications"—a category of communications defined by their potential influence on federal elections.[3] Before considering the argument that the U.S. Supreme Court in *Citizens United* should have upheld these restrictions by invoking a doctrine of electoral exceptionalism, we need some sense of what might be meant by such a principle.

In the usual First Amendment case, it is necessary (1) to determine what type of issue is presented, (2) to decide what standard governs that particular issue, and (3) to apply that standard to the facts to determine whether the challenged restriction of speech is constitutional. For example, suppose a law prohibits the use of any loudspeaker in a residential neighborhood after 8:00 P.M. This is a content-neutral regulation of speech. It therefore is constitutional if the state interest is sufficient to outweigh the restrictive effect of the law. Because the law has a relatively modest impact on speech and a reasonable justification, the law will be upheld.[4]

*This chapter also appears in NYU's *Review of Law and Social Change* 35, no. 3 (2011). Reproduced by permission.

Or, suppose a law prohibits the use of any loudspeaker in any place at any time. This, too, is a content-neutral regulation of speech, so the same standard will apply. But because this law has a more significant impact on speech and applies in circumstances in which the justification is more attenuated, this law will be invalidated.

Finally, suppose a law prohibits the use of any loudspeaker by anti-war speakers in a residential neighborhood after 8:00 P.M. This is a viewpoint-based restriction, which triggers a very different standard. Because viewpoint-based laws are thought to threaten core First Amendment values, this law is presumptively unconstitutional and will be upheld only if it is necessary to serve a compelling state interest, a test that clearly cannot be satisfied in this situation.[5]

The point of all this is simple. As a general rule, the task of a court is to determine what standard applies in any given situation, and then to apply that standard fairly and consistently to the facts. I do not mean to suggest, by the way, that this is like "call[ing] balls and strikes."[6] Deciding what the appropriate standard should be is often quite complex, knowing how to classify particular situations can be maddeningly difficult, and applying the appropriate standard to particular circumstances often demands considerable judgment. What is clear in principle, however, is that this general approach ordinarily applies to all First Amendment issues.

What, then, is electoral exceptionalism? Suppose a law prohibits the use of any loudspeaker in a residential neighborhood after 8:00 P.M., except that candidates for public office are permitted to use a loudspeaker until 10:00 P.M. within thirty days of an election. This law provides a special dispensation for electoral speech. One way to understand electoral exceptionalism is to ask whether the First Amendment *allows* government to give special benefits to electoral speech. At least as a first cut, this seems quite sensible.

Alternatively, suppose a law prohibits the use of any loudspeaker in a residential neighborhood after 8:00 P.M., and this law is challenged by a political candidate on the grounds that, even though the law generally is constitutional, it should be held unconstitutional as applied to political candidates within thirty days of an election. Here, the claim of electoral exceptionalism is not that the First Amendment allows the government to give special benefits to electoral speech, but that it *requires* the government to do so. Although both of these positions seem plausible, because electoral speech is at the very heart of the First Amendment and therefore might well merit special benefits, neither of these situations implicates what the proponents of electoral exceptionalism mean by the term.

What advocates of the term mean by electoral exceptionalism is illustrated by the following situation: Suppose a law prohibits the use of any loudspeaker in a residential neighborhood after 8:00 P.M., except that political candidates may not use a loudspeaker at all in a residential neighborhood within thirty days of an election. Here, the law restricts electoral speech *more* than other speech. This might seem perverse because, as the Supreme Court has observed, the First Amendment "has its fullest and most urgent application precisely to the conduct of campaigns for political office,"[7] but that is precisely what the proponents of electoral exceptionalism mean by the term. It is not about giving electoral speech *more* protection than other expression, but about giving it *less* protection. As Frederick Schauer of the University of Virginia Law School and Richard Pildes of New York University School of Law have argued, the "most common version of electoral exceptionalism would permit restrictions on communicative activity in the context of elections that would not be permitted in other contexts."[8]

Now, in the hypothetical I just posited, there are two possible arguments for the constitutionality of the law. First, the government might argue that electoral speech in this context poses special harms that justify the restriction of electoral speech, but not other speech, even though the same constitutional standard applies. For example, the government might argue that political candidates often run amuck in the days leading up to an election, and that to ensure reasonable peace and quiet in residential neighborhoods it is necessary to exclude them entirely from using loudspeakers during those thirty days. If this is the government's argument, then it is simply asserting that, applying the ordinary standards of First Amendment review, it has a legitimate interest in banning electoral loudspeakers within thirty days of an election that is more weighty than its interest in banning other uses of loudspeakers, and that the restriction is constitutional for that reason. That is not what the proponents of electoral exceptionalism mean by the term.

Second, the government might argue that elections are so distinctive as a context for speech that the same First Amendment standards that govern other types of speech should not apply to electoral speech. That is, the government might insist that it should have special leeway to regulate electoral speech, in ways it could not restrict other speech, in order to promote the electoral process. On this view, the loudspeaker ban would be permissible, not because the government can satisfy the ordinary standards of First Amendment review, but because a more deferential approach is appropriate when the government regulates electoral speech than when it regulates other forms of expression. This is what the proponents of electoral exceptionalism mean by the term. Does this make any sense?

Exceptionalism and First Amendment Doctrine

There are several instances of "exceptionalism" in First Amendment doctrine in which a particular restriction of speech would be unconstitutional under ordinary First Amendment standards, but is constitutional because the Court applies a different standard in response to the distinct circumstances of the situation. For example, the government ordinarily cannot constitutionally prohibit individuals from discussing politics, but a public high school can discipline a student who insists on discussing politics instead of mathematics in class. In light of "the special characteristics of the school environment," the Court has held that freedom of speech in that setting can be restricted if it would "'materially and substantially interfere with the . . . operation of the school.'"[9]

The argument for electoral exceptionalism proceeds along similar lines. That is, the argument posits that although the government generally cannot prohibit speakers from expressing their views, it should be able to do so when the speech takes place in the context of an election. To test this proposition, we must assume that under ordinary standards of First Amendment jurisprudence a particular restriction of speech would be unconstitutional, and then ask whether the fact that the speech takes place in the context of an election justifies applying a less stringent standard of review. To reiterate, the claim of electoral exceptionalism is not that the government interests in the electoral context are sufficiently weighty to justify otherwise unconstitutional restrictions of speech. Instead, it is that the very fact that the speech takes place in the context of an election that warrants diluting the standard of review.

At first blush, of course, one reasonably might think that the electoral setting would, if anything, justify even *greater* protection for speech. After all, such speech is most fundamentally what the First Amendment is about. But the electoral exceptionalism argument is precisely the opposite—that the government should have greater authority to *restrict* speech in the electoral context than otherwise. This may seem to stand the First Amendment on its head, but the situation is not so simple. In the mathematics class hypothetical, for example, the school constitutionally could discipline the student for talking politics, even though that speech lies at the very heart of the First Amendment.

In the context of a case like *Citizens United*, then, the issue may be posed as follows: Assuming *arguendo* that, under generally applicable First Amendment standards, the government constitutionally could not forbid corporations and labor unions from endorsing or opposing policy positions as part of general public debate, can it nonetheless forbid them from endorsing or opposing political candidates during the course of an election? Again, for the sake of clarity, I must emphasize that the question is not whether the government's interests in the electoral situation are more weighty than in the general public debate situation, so that its electoral restrictions would pass muster under generally applicable First Amendment standards, but, rather, whether there is something unique about the electoral context that justifies the application of a *less speech-protective* standard of First Amendment review.

Established Examples of Exceptionalism

In fact, the Supreme Court has recognized a number of exceptional speech environments in which generally applicable First Amendment principles do not apply. I already have noted one of them: public schools. Another is the courtroom. We accept all sorts of limitations on free speech in the courtroom that we would never accept in general public discourse. For example, in the courtroom the government bars speech that consists of hearsay, that it deems unduly "prejudicial," and that it judges to be "irrelevant." We would scoff at the suggestion that such limitations would be appropriate in general public debate.[10]

In such exceptional environments, the Court has concluded that the ordinary assumptions of the First Amendment are inapplicable. Both the classroom and the courtroom have very distinctive purposes. If the generally freewheeling principles of public discourse were to govern in those environments, they would not be able to serve their most basic purposes. Imagine the educational process if students could talk in class about whatever topic happens to interest them, as they can do in a park or a car or online. Or, imagine the judicial process if lawyers and witnesses enjoyed the same degree of free expression they have in general public discourse. Evidentiary rules governing hearsay, privilege, relevancy, and the like would all go by the boards. Thus, in these exceptional environments, the Court has recognized that the fundamental assumptions of free speech are inapplicable, not because the government interests in regulating the speech satisfy the ordinary standards of First Amendment review, but because these environments simply could not function if the usual rules of free speech applied. Thus, the law recognizes what we might call educational and judicial exceptionalism.

This concept is not limited to schools and courtrooms. The Court has extended the same basic idea, for example, to prisons[11] and the military. In these environments, too, the Court has recognized that the basic assumptions of First Amendment theory cannot apply sensibly if prisons and the military are to function as intended. The Court therefore has held that the government can exercise greater authority to regulate speech in these settings than in general public discourse. The Court has recognized, for example, that "the military is, by necessity, a specialized society separate from civilian society," and that a military unit "is not a deliberative body."[12] Thus, although "members of the military are not excluded from the protection granted by the First Amendment, the different character of the military community and the military mission requires a different application of those protections."[13] As in the education and judicial contexts, the Court gives the government a relatively high degree of deference in reviewing speech restrictions governing soldiers and prisoners. There is therefore military and prison exceptionalism.

One characteristic that classrooms, courtrooms, the military, and prisons have in common is that traditionally and functionally they are so lacking in the essential prerequisites for free expression that it would make no sense to apply to them the same First Amendment rules that protect general public discourse. Put simply, prisons, the military, classrooms, and courtrooms do not, by their very nature, reflect or embody the fundamental premises of free expression, nor could they realistically serve their intended functions if they were subsumed within the general "marketplace of ideas." Indeed, there is a real danger that if we insisted on applying the ordinary standards of the First Amendment to such settings, we ultimately would wind up *diluting* the protection the First Amendment offers speech in general public debate. So there is even a good First Amendment reason for recognizing school, prison, military, and courtroom exceptionalism.

The principle of exceptionalism goes much further. The Court, for example, applies this approach to regulations governing the speech of public employees.[14] For example, although a newspaper or blogger has a constitutional right to disseminate information obtained from leaked classified documents (at least in the absence of a clear and present danger of grave harm to the national security), the public employee who leaked the information can be punished under a much more lenient standard.[15] The general standards of First Amendment review do not apply to public employees, because the government could not perform its basic functions if its employees had the same free speech rights relative to their employment that they and other citizens enjoy in general public discourse. The Court, in other words, has recognized what we might call public employee exceptionalism.

There are still other examples, more closely tied to the electoral process. In town hall meetings and legislative sessions, government can impose more restrictive regulations of speech than in general public discourse. The number of speakers, the order of speakers, eligibility to participate, the topics to be discussed, and the length of time one may speak all are subject to restriction in ways that never would be permissible in a public park or in newspapers or online. Here, too, the Court has recognized that even though the activity in such settings is at the core of the First Amendment, the need to enable these entities to achieve their essential functions justifies a significant departure from general free speech standards.

Similarly, presidential press conferences, electoral ballots, polling places, and candidate debates all can be regulated in ways that clearly would be unconstitutional if applied to general public discourse.[16] No one has a First Amendment right to speak out of turn at a presidential press conference, no one has a First Amendment right to be on the ballot without meeting reasonable qualification requirements, candidates can be required to comply with time limits and to stick to the topic in government-sponsored candidate debates, and government can restrict speech near polling places. In all of these situations, the Court recognizes that the application of the otherwise generally applicable First Amendment standards would wreak havoc on the ability of these institutions to serve their most essential functions. These all are settings in which the very principle of free speech, as ordinarily understood and applied, is incompatible with the underlying assumptions and realities of the institution. First Amendment exceptionalism, in other words, is commonplace.

Limits on Exceptionalism

Of course, there must be a limit to these exceptions, or they would swamp the First Amendment. Focusing on these examples should not lead to the erroneous conclusion that general First Amendment principles are the exception rather than the rule. In fact, these exceptions constitute only a small fraction of the overall free speech regime. They are, indeed, exceptions.

If the First Amendment is to remain robust, it is important for these exceptions to be well-founded and carefully bounded. Each exception should be based on a clear and convincing understanding of both its rationale and its boundaries. The question, then, is whether elections are more analogous to general public discourse or to speech in schools, courtrooms, the military, candidate debates, and legislative proceedings. My law school professor Harry Kalven, one of the most influential First Amendment thinkers of the twentieth century, used to tell his students that "law is the process of choosing among competing analogies." That is a good description of what is called for here, if we are to determine in a principled and persuasive manner whether there should be an electoral exception to the general First Amendment standards of review.

Viewed from this perspective, the two closest analogies to elections (by which I mean not just the process of voting, but the much larger process by which we deliberate about who our elected officials should be) would seem to be ballots and candidate debates. In deciding which candidates and which issues will be on the ballot, the government is not bound by the same standards that apply in general public discourse. Everyone seems to agree that, subject to certain important limitations, the government can determine by reasonable means eligibility for being on the ballot.[17] But the First Amendment does not cede to the government any similar authority to determine the issues or candidates we may discuss in general public discourse. Why does the First Amendment not give everyone the right to put his or her favored candidates or issues on the ballot with the same freedom with which we can decide what candidates or issues to discuss in public debate? The answer is clear. What works in public debate would produce utter chaos on a ballot. If the ballot is to serve its essential function, it must be reasonably uncluttered, coherently organized, and limited in length. If people want to promote certain candidates and issues for inclusion on the ballot, there are procedures to achieve that goal, and so long as they do not unreasonably or discriminatorily block access to the ballot, the ballot itself can be deemed outside the ordinary marketplace of ideas. The ballot, in other words, is like the classroom or the courtroom.[18]

Government-sponsored candidate debates are similar. One could, of course, imagine such debates following the ordinary rules of public discourse, in which there are no time limits on how long or how much individuals may speak, no equal time requirements, no moderator to keep speakers focused on particular issues, and no limit on the number of participants. But, of course, an event following such procedures would not be what anyone would recognize today as a candidate debate. Although there is plenty of room for such a free-for-all in the marketplace of ideas, for a candidate debate to achieve its essential purpose it must be much more closely regulated. Indeed, it is precisely those regulations, which otherwise would violate the First Amendment, that make candidate debates useful.

Is an election similar to a ballot, a candidate debate, a courtroom, a classroom, or a prison, for these purposes? I see several difficulties with the argument for electoral exceptionalism. First, the other exceptions that I have identified all have relatively clear boundaries. For the most part, it is possible to recognize exceptions for schools, prisons, public employees, courtrooms, ballots, and candidate debates without running the risk of spilling over in dangerous ways to more general public discourse. Of course, there are always issues of ambiguity at the margin, but for the most part in these situations it is not all that difficult to tell the difference between a courtroom and a blog, or a candidate debate and a newspaper editorial, or a prison and a public park. But what is the boundary between free speech about public issues and free speech in the context of elections? Is criticism of an officeholder's policy during the course of an election part of public debate, or is it electoral speech? As demonstrated by the McCain-Feingold legislation[19] and the Court's decisions in *McConnell v. Federal Election Commission*[20] and *Federal Election Commission v. Wisconsin Right to Life*,[21] it is exceedingly difficult to draw a line between election speech and public issue speech.

It is possible to define electoral speech as speech about issues relevant to a pending election, or speech about issues relevant to a pending election within a certain defined period of time before the final vote, but those definitions clearly bleed over into general public discourse. It also is possible to define electoral speech as speech that expressly endorses or opposes a clearly identified candidate or that expressly mentions any candidate by name, but even these definitions create serious concerns about both line-drawing and stifling important public discourse.[22] Although laws defining the boundaries of electoral speech are not impossible to draw, they are inevitably much less well-defined than speech in courtrooms, in prisons, in the military, or in town hall meetings.

Second, in the other contexts, the exceptional institutions—schools, trials, prisons, legislative bodies, public employment, the military, and so on—exist independently of any desire of government to regulate speech. That is, we did not create such institutions in order to regulate speech. They exist and have long existed as schools, prisons, trials, and the military without regard to any desire to restrict free expression. Significant restrictions on speech in such settings were built into the very fabric of their structure and always have been assumed to be essential to the very existence of such institutions.

Elections are more complicated. Although elections have existed for a long time, and there always have been laws governing such matters as eligibility to vote, the timing of elections, and eligibility for inclusion on the ballot, speech about the merits of competing candidates and policies traditionally has not been regulated any more than public discourse generally. Indeed, although the basic ground rules of elections have long been established by law, electoral speech historically has been regarded as largely indistinguishable from general public discourse. Unlike the situation with respect to courtrooms, schools, prisons, public employees, candidate debates, and the military, historically we have not thought of elections as institutions in which extensive government regulation of speech is either natural or inevitable.

This is relevant in several ways. Tradition often plays an important role in First Amendment doctrine, especially when it comes to upholding speech restrictions that have stood the test of time. This is perhaps most evident when it comes to recognizing categories of "low" value speech, where the Court has been quite reluctant to recognize new categories of low-value speech that traditionally have not been regulated.[23]

Tradition is also relevant in the other direction. When government traditionally has tolerated free speech, the Court has been especially reluctant to allow the government to change the rules. This is illustrated by the public forum doctrine and by the insistence that criminal trials generally remain open to the public.[24] This cuts against recognizing a new category of exceptional speech that would empower the government to restrict free expression in the electoral context, where traditionally it has been allowed to flourish largely free of government intervention.

Moreover, the very fact that government suddenly wants to regulate speech that traditionally has been left to the marketplace of ideas inevitably gives rise to suspicion that the reason for suddenly seeking to regulate speech that historically was unregulated derives not from anything inherent in the electoral process, but instead from a desire to manipulate that process for political gain. After all, if there is any arena in which the risk of government manipulation of free expression is at its peak, it must be in the regulation of electoral speech. In such circumstances, it is hard not to wonder why a process that worked well enough in the past without regulation suddenly demands government control. Of course, there may be a good answer to that question. It is possible that circumstances have changed, and that the enormous influx of money into the political process has profoundly altered the continued vitality of past processes. But in the absence of a tradition of extensive regulation of political speech in the electoral process, the risk of partisan manipulation cannot be ignored.

Third, in the contexts in which the Court has recognized exceptions to general First Amendment standards, the exceptions usually are thought to be justified not only by tradition, but also by considerations that are inherent in the effective functioning of the institution. It is hard to imagine town meetings, presidential press conferences, candidate debates, classrooms, and courtrooms without limitations on who may speak, about what subjects, in what manner, for how long, and in what order. Because these settings are time-constrained, it is necessary to have some mechanism to allocate the opportunity to speak in a manner that serves the central mission of the institution. If one speaker could use up all or a disproportionate share of the available time the very purpose of the institution could not be achieved. There is no similar rationale for constraining speech in the electoral context. As a practical matter, there is limitless opportunity for free expression in the electoral process, just as there is in public debate generally, so there is no resource constraint that would justify government interference with the right of all speakers to speak to their hearts' content.

Another consideration that is inherent in most of the traditional exceptions to general First Amendment standards is the need to maintain order, without which the institution could not function. A classroom, a courtroom, a candidate debate, a legislative session, and a ballot could not serve their essential functions if people could speak in those settings as much as they want, whenever they want, without some sort of regulatory control of their expression. Indeed, without such control, chaos would reign. There is no similar rationale for restricting speech in the context of election campaigns. As a general rule, election campaigns are no different from ordinary public discourse in this regard. In these settings, there may be some measure of chaos, but that sort of chaos is inherent in the very idea of a free market in ideas.

Fourth, all of the recognized exceptional situations involve speech that is closely allied to government activity. That is, all of these institutions are deeply embedded in government action. Schools, trials, presidential press conferences, candidate debates, prisons, the military, public employees, and election ballots all are government functions. The government always has greater control over its functions than over private activities. Thus, although the government has special authority to regulate speech in public schools, government-sponsored candidate debates, government courtrooms, and on government election ballots, it has no similar authority to interfere with free speech in private school classrooms, privately sponsored candidate debates, private arbitrations, or ballots in privately run elections.

The government constitutionally cannot discipline a student in a private school for discussing politics rather than mathematics; it constitutionally cannot require equal time for all candidates in a privately run candidate debate; it constitutionally cannot forbid the lawyers in a private arbitration from invoking hearsay in their closing arguments; and it constitutionally cannot dictate the content of a ballot in an election to choose the officers of a private organization. In other words, a common feature of all of the recognized exceptional situations is that they involve activities run by the government itself. This is not, and has never been, the case with elections. Government determines the basic framework for elections, including time, place, and manner, but it has never (until recently) claimed the right to structure private speech in an election campaign the way it structures speech in a public school, a government-sponsored candidate debate, or a courtroom. Traditionally, the public discourse in a political campaign has been thought to be as much a part of the marketplace of ideas as public discourse generally.

A Case for Exceptions?

Having covered the basic concepts of exceptionalism, I now want to recognize the argument that the exceptions I have discussed should be understood in terms of a much broader and more open-ended judgment: these speech-restrictions are constitutional, even though they do not satisfy the ordinary standards of First Amendment review, because they enable these institutions to function effectively. On this view, the justifications for such restrictions need not be couched in terms of tradition, time constraints, maintaining order, or the connection of the institution to the government's "ownership" of the institution. Rather, exceptions to general First Amendment standards might be thought warranted *whenever* it would improve the functioning of a particular activity or institution.

Under this approach, an exception for regulations of speech in the electoral context might be thought warranted as long as the government asserts that its regulations will improve the electoral process. That argument, however, might prove too much. If the government can regulate speech in the electoral context without meeting the ordinary requirements of the First Amendment merely because the government maintains that such restrictions will improve the process, then there is nothing to prevent it from seeking a similar exception when it claims that speech restrictions would improve public debate more generally. That claim quickly collapses into the notion that a regulated marketplace of ideas is better than a free marketplace of ideas. That may or may not be right, but it is surely incompatible with well-established First Amendment jurisprudence.

A somewhat narrower argument, put forth by Frederick Schauer and Richard Pildes, is that the First Amendment should not be understood as a negative constraint on government interference with speech, but as a positive premise for government regulation designed to enhance "the values of democratic deliberation, collective self-determination, guarding against the abuse of power, searching for truth, and even self-expression."[25] In their view, "it is not self-evident" that these values "are better served by treating government intervention as the unqualified enemy than by allowing the state a limited role in fostering the proliferation of voices in the public sphere" or otherwise improving the quality of electoral discourse.[26]

This is a perfectly plausible position, but it never has commanded much support in the judicial understanding of the First Amendment, and with good reason. As Schauer and Pildes concede, critics of this position maintain that, if anything, we should be especially wary of government restrictions in the electoral context, "because the self-interest of potential government regulators would be greatest precisely in this sphere."[27] Although Schauer and Pildes dismiss this argument, in my judgment the critics of electoral exceptionalism are quite right to emphasize this concern.

This is not to say, of course, that government regulation of electoral speech is per se impermissible. Rather, it is to say that such regulation must stand up to the ordinary standards of First Amendment review. A variety of regulations of electoral speech have satisfied those standards, including, for example, limitations on political contributions, disclosure requirements, government subsidies of political speech, restrictions on ballot access, regulation of speech near polling places, and rules governing candidate debates.[28] But the idea that the government should be able to restrict speech in order to improve speech—without meeting the ordinary standards of First Amendment review—is and should be foreign to the basic premise of the First Amendment, at least in the absence of a compelling justification for recognizing an exception to those general standards.

In this respect, it is worth comparing government regulation of a government-sponsored candidate debate to government regulation of electoral speech more generally. In the candidate debate, the government can decide how many and which candidates may participate (as long as it does so in a reasonable manner that is not designed to favor or disfavor particular candidates because of the government's approval or disapproval of their views[29]), it can insist that all candidates have equal time, it can select the moderator, and it can determine the subjects to be addressed, the order in which the candidates will speak, the amount of time available to answer each question, whether questions will be taken from the audience, and so on. All this is permissible for the reasons suggested above, and such rules make perfect sense, given the realities of candidate debates.

Under the approach advocated by the proponents of electoral exceptionalism, analogous rules should be constitutional in the much broader context of electoral speech, and courts should accord the government a similar degree of deference when it regulates general electoral speech as when it regulates government-sponsored candidate debates. There is certainly some appeal to this argument, *if* one assumes that government officials have the wisdom, integrity, and impartiality to structure electoral discourse on our behalf and that the need for government intervention and structuring in the debate context carries over to the much larger and traditionally more freewheeling context of electoral discourse—but presumably not to public discourse more generally. This, in my view, is a very hard sell. It invites an analogical stampede that well could enable a narrow doctrine of exceptionalism to swallow the First Amendment.

What If Exceptionalism Were Accepted?

For the sake of argument, though, let us briefly consider the questions that might arise if we were to accept the logic of electoral exceptionalism. It was, of course, the Court's decision in *Citizens United* that ignited the current interest in this question. This is ironic, because only seven years earlier, in *McConnell*,[30] the Court—*without any reliance on any notion of electoral exceptionalism*—upheld the very restrictions on corporate and union speech that it later invalidated in *Citizens United*. The only thing that had changed in the intervening years was the makeup of the Court—Justice Samuel Alito, who joined the majority in *Citizens United*, had replaced Justice Sandra Day O'Connor, who had joined the majority in *McConnell*. Moreover, there is no reason whatever to believe that the justices in the majority in *Citizens United* would have reached a different result in a legal domain that included a concept of electoral exceptionalism. What was "wrong" with *Citizens United*—assuming the decision was "wrong"—was not the Court's failure to invoke electoral exceptionalism, but its failure to uphold the law even under the generally applicable standards of First Amendment review.

Let us consider, though, how we might frame possible regulations of speech in the electoral realm if we accepted the proposition that elections are analogous to classrooms, trials, candidate debates, and town meetings. Suppose, for example, Congress enacted legislation making it a crime for any individual independently to spend more than

$1,000 of his own money in an effort to elect a political candidate. In *Buckley v. Valeo*, the Court held that such a restriction violated the First Amendment.[31] But, in *Buckley*, the Court applied the ordinary standards of First Amendment review, and thus concluded that the government's interest in equalizing speech was not sufficiently important to justify the infringement of individual freedom. Would electoral exceptionalism lead to a different outcome?

If we think of candidate debates or town meetings as appropriate analogies, then the law invalidated in *Buckley* might well be upheld. At least two principles govern speech in candidate debates and town meetings that would seem to support this outcome. First, we accept equal time regulations in those settings for reasons that are similar to the reasons offered in defense of the legislation invalidated in *Buckley*—that is, we want a fair contest, in which each side has an equal opportunity to make its case, and if this is appropriate in town meetings and candidate debates, why not in electoral speech more generally? Second, we would be appalled at the suggestion that we should sell time to the highest bidder in a government-sponsored candidate debate or a town meeting. Such a practice would undermine our deepest assumptions about a fair discussion of the issues. Why, then, should the government not take the same approach in its regulation of general electoral speech? On this view, accepting the premise of electoral exceptionalism might, for better or worse, lead to a different result than the one reached in *Buckley*.[32]

Many other questions could arise if we embraced the idea of electoral exceptionalism. For example:

- Can the government constitutionally make it a crime for any person knowingly to make a false statement in the electoral context (as it does in trials)?
- Can the government constitutionally prohibit any person to make any statement based on hearsay in the electoral context (as it does in trials)?
- Can the government constitutionally prohibit any person to make any unduly prejudicial statement that might inflame or mislead voters (by analogy to trials)?[33]

- Can the government constitutionally require the media to provide equal time to all political candidates (by analogy to candidate debates)?
- Can the government constitutionally limit each person to one "unit" of speaking in the electoral context (by analogy to one person/one vote)?
- Can the government constitutionally forbid convicted felons to speak in the electoral process (by analogy to voting)?
- Can the government constitutionally forbid candidates without a certain level of support to participate in the electoral process (by analogy to ballots and candidate debates)?
- Can the government constitutionally forbid candidates and their supporters from airing more than a fixed number of minutes of campaign ads (by analogy to candidate debates and town meetings)?
- Can the government constitutionally forbid candidates from discussing issues other than those specified by the Federal Election Commission (by analogy to classrooms, town hall meetings, and candidate debates)?

These are just a few of the issues that would naturally arise in a realm of electoral exceptionalism. Each of these restrictions clearly would be unconstitutional under the ordinary standards of First Amendment review because the First Amendment, as interpreted and understood, demands a high level of skepticism about supposedly well-intentioned government efforts to restrict free speech. But each of these restrictions arguably would improve the overall quality of deliberative democracy. Should we lower the general standards of First Amendment review in order to cede the government that power? This is an important question. But the implications need to be understood much more fully before we embrace that conclusion.

Part II

Money and Rights

When Does Spending Equal Speech?

5

Money and Rights

*Deborah Hellman**

Many campaign finance laws restrict the ability to give or spend money. U.S. Supreme Court decisions treat such laws as restrictions on "speech" that are therefore subject to heightened judicial review. Our campaign finance doctrine focuses on the connection between restrictions on giving and spending money, and the ability to exercise the right to freedom of speech. The Court has reasoned that, because money facilitates speaking or incentivizes speaking and can itself be expressive, restrictions on giving and spending money should be treated as restrictions on "speech" for purposes of constitutional analysis. This manner of framing the inquiry is overly narrow and has limited the perspective of both the Court and commentators.

The Court is surely right that money is useful to the exercise of First Amendment rights. But this is not because money has a unique connection to speaking. Rather, money facilitates the exercise of the right to free speech, as it does the exercise of many other constitutionally protected rights. For example, it is difficult to obtain an abortion without money. While the right to abort a pre-viable fetus thus likely includes the right to pay a doctor to perform this service, other constitutional rights would not be thought to include the right to spend money to effectuate them. In another article, "Money Talks But It Isn't Speech," I develop these claims.[1] There, I argue that we ought to view restrictions on giving and spending money in politics through a wider

*This chapter also appears in NYU's *Review of Law and Social Change* 35, no. 3 (2011). Reproduced by permission.

lens. When assessing the constitutionality of campaign finance laws, we should ask: When do constitutional rights include a penumbral right to give or spend money to exercise the right effectively?

Some rights likely include a penumbral right to give or spend money. Abortion exemplifies this sort of right because women cannot terminate pregnancies without spending money for a doctor's services in most instances. In the case of other rights, notably voting and sexual intimacy, we would likely conclude the opposite. The right to vote does not include the right to buy or sell votes, and the right to sexual intimacy with the partner of one's choosing does not include the right to engage in prostitution.

These insights lead to the conclusion that the fact that money facilitates or incentivizes the exercise of a right is insufficient on its own to show that a right includes the penumbral right to give or spend money. The final section of "Money Talks" articulates a theory that begins to answer the question of when rights include a right to spend money and when they do not. Briefly, I argue as follows: if the exercise of a constitutional right depends on a good that is distributed via the market, as abortion services are, then a right that depends on that good must include the right to spend money to effectuate it. If a right depends on a good that is not distributed via the market, as votes are not, then the right at issue ought not to include the right to spend money to effectuate it.

This chapter continues the project of exploring the connection between money and rights. The overarching question is the same: When do constitutionally protected rights include a penumbral right to spend or give money to effectuate them? In "Money Talks," I drew on shared intuitions about how hypothetical cases *might* be resolved by courts. In this chapter, I turn from the normative to the descriptive, looking at how the Supreme Court and some lower courts have begun to answer this question. This analysis has two goals. First, I hope to encourage courts and scholars to explore the relationship between money and rights.[2] Second, I hope to deepen, and to complicate, our overly narrow approach to campaign finance issues by situating them within the broader question of the relationship between money and rights. Restrictions on giving and spending on political activity raise general questions about when constitutionally protected rights include the right to give and spend money to effectuate them.

This chapter proceeds as follows. First, I provide two different answers to the question of how money relates to rights. In what I term the *integral strand* cases, a constitutionally protected right is treated as including the right to spend money to effectuate the underlying right. In what I term the *blocked strand,* a constitutionally protected right is not treated as including a concomitant right to spend money to effectuate the right. When faced with a new right, a court therefore must decide whether it falls into the integral or blocked strand. Then, I illustrate this point by describing how both the Fifth and Eleventh Circuits are wrestling with precisely this question in their application of *Lawrence v. Texas*, the 2003 decision that struck down laws against homosexual sodomy. Next, using the cases discussed, I offer an account of why the Supreme Court and other courts treat some rights as following the integral approach and some the blocked approach. Then, using this theory, which I term *adequacy theory,* I suggest that some of the cases described may be incorrectly decided. I then explain the ways in which the theory that underlies the case law is consistent with the normative vision I advocate in "Money Talks."

Two Strands

The Integral Strand and the First Amendment: The *Buckley* Answer

In *Buckley v. Valeo*,[3] the Supreme Court addressed the relationship between the right to spend money and the First Amendment right of free speech in connection with political campaigns. There, the Court held that the right to spend money on political expression was protected by the right of free speech because money facilitates, indeed may even be necessary to, the effective exercise of the right to participate in political debate.[4] In a key passage defending its view, the Court explained that "virtually every means of communicating ideas in today's mass society requires the expenditure of money."[5] Because money is necessary for effective political speech, the Court argues that the right to spend money must be protected as part of the free speech right in this context.[6] The right to spend money on political speech is therefore treated as part of the penumbra of the First Amendment right.[7]

While campaign finance doctrine has waxed and waned in its willingness to tolerate restrictions on the use of money in politics, the doctrine has remained faithful to this basic claim. The right to spend money on political speech is to be treated as part of the right of free speech itself, such that laws that limit this right to spend receive strict scrutiny.[8] In fact, in the most recent campaign finance case, *Citizens United*, the Court treats this approach as so obvious and entrenched that it provides neither supporting argument nor citation to *Buckley*.[9]

The Integral Strand outside of the First Amendment: *Carey v. Population Services International*

The view that a constitutionally protected right should be seen to include a concomitant right to spend money to make the underlying right effective is not unique to *Buckley*'s treatment of the relationship between money and political speech. One prominent example of this approach can be seen in the development of the right of procreative liberty. The right to procreative liberty was first recognized by the Court in *Griswold v. Connecticut*,[10] where the Court invalidated a state law restricting the *use* of contraceptives as applied to married couples.[11] There, the Court held that the state law at issue was particularly offensive to the privacy of the marital relationship protected by the Constitution because "in forbidding the *use* of contraceptives rather than regulating their manufacture or sale, [the law] seeks to achieve its goals by means having a maximum destructive impact upon that relationship."[12] Seven years later, in *Eisenstadt v. Baird*,[13] the Court, relying on an Equal Protection rationale, extended the protection offered in *Griswold* to unmarried couples as well.[14] Because Baird's appeal concerned his conviction for giving away contraceptives to a group of college students, the Court never addressed whether the procreative liberty right protected by *Griswold* included a right to buy and sell contraceptives in the commercial marketplace.[15]

Carey v. Population Services International[16] most closely addresses the question whether the procreative liberty protected by the Constitution includes the right to buy and sell contraceptives. There, the Court considered whether a New York law permitting only pharmacists to distribute contraceptives violated the Constitution.[17] The Court in *Carey* treated *Griswold* as having defined a constitutionally protected right to make decisions about childbearing, rather than as grounded in a narrower right to merely *use* contraceptives.[18] The Court then drew an analogy to the line of cases following *Roe v. Wade* that invalidated various restrictions on a woman's right to abort a pre-viable fetus.[19] Just as these laws made it too difficult for a woman to exercise her right to choose abortion, so too the restriction on who can sell contraceptives at issue in *Carey* made the right to procreative choice too difficult to exercise and thus similarly constitutionally problematic.[20] For the Court in *Carey*, the restriction on who could sell contraceptives was similar in kind (if different in degree) to an outright ban on sale.[21] The Court explained that, because a ban on the purchase or sale would limit a person's access as much, if not more, than a ban on use, prohibiting the commercialization of contraceptives burdens the right to procreative liberty in a constitutionally cognizable way.[22] Thus, *Carey* has come to stand for the proposition that the constitutionally protected right to determine whether to procreate includes the right to buy and sell contraceptives. The right to spend money to obtain contraceptives is part of the penumbra of the right to procreative liberty because a person is unlikely to have access (or adequate access) to contraceptives without buying them.

The Blocked Strand and the First Amendment: The *Stanley* Approach

Buckley's analysis of the relationship between money and free speech is not the only approach found within First Amendment doctrine. In *Stanley v. Georgia*,[23] the Court adopted the opposite view. There, the Court held that the constitutionally protected right to read and possess obscene materials in the home does not include a penumbral right to spend money to buy this material, nor a related right to sell it.[24]

In *Stanley*, the Supreme Court held that the conviction of a man for possession of obscene materials in his home violated both the First and Fourteenth Amendments on the grounds that the "mere private possession of obscene matter cannot constitutionally be made a crime."[25] However, both *Stanley* itself and subsequent decisions of the Court emphasized that the articulation of this constitutionally protected right does not entail a right to buy or disseminate obscene materials. The Court made clear that this holding does not disturb prior decisions upholding convictions for selling obscene materials.[26] As the Court emphasized, "the States retain broad power to regulate obscenity; that power simply does not extend to mere possession by the individual in the privacy of his own home."[27] In other words, the right to read or possess obscene materials in one's home does not include a penumbral right to buy or to sell these materials.

Following *Stanley*, several cases pushed on the viability of this distinction. How could a latter-day Stanley obtain these materials to read privately in his home unless he could buy them and unless someone else has a right to sell them?[28] Nonetheless, the Court repeatedly refused to extend the right to possess obscene material in the home to cover a right to sell, buy, or distribute this material.[29] For example, in *United States v. Reidel,* the Court emphasized that *Stanley* "does not require that we fashion or recognize a constitutional right in people like Reidel to distribute or sell obscene materials."[30] This line of cases established that the First Amendment right protected in *Stanley* does not include the right to spend money to effectuate this right.

The Blocked Strand outside of the First Amendment: Due Process and Procreative Liberty

Just as both the integral and the blocked approach to the relationship between money and rights are represented in First Amendment case law (in *Buckley* and *Stanley* respectively), so too both strands are represented in case law exploring the scope of other constitutionally protected rights. This section begins with an example for the blocked strand in the context of due process and then moves on to discuss the blocked strand in the context of procreative liberty.

Due Process. In *Walters v. National Association of Radiation Survivors*,[31] the Supreme Court addressed the question of whether the Due Process Clause of the Fifth Amendment protects an individual's ability to spend his own money to retain private counsel. There, the Court held that, so long as the state has provided an adequate alternative dispute resolution system, due process is not violated by a statutory restriction that effectively prohibits hiring a private lawyer.[32] In other words, the right to due process protected by the Fifth Amendment of the Constitution does not, at least in all cases, protect the right to spend one's own money to hire a lawyer.

In *Walters*, two veterans groups, along with individual veterans, challenged a federal law that limited the amount that a veteran could pay an attorney to represent him in his claim for veteran's benefits to $10.[33] The Court agreed with the challengers that this limit effectively denied veterans the right to hire private counsel to represent them in their claims for benefits.[34] Nonetheless, the Court upheld the law despite claims that the fee limit violated the Due Process Clause of the Fifth Amendment and the First Amendment rights of veterans.[35]

Justice William Rehnquist, writing for the Court, found that due process was not violated by the restrictions on paying for private counsel because the alternative process afforded by the statute provided an adequate means to be heard.[36] The Due Process Clause was implicated because the state sought to deprive veterans of constitutionally important property interests.[37] The Court thus was required to determine if the process provided to veterans satisfied the constitutional guarantees of due process.[38] What is striking about the *Walters* Court's analysis is that Rehnquist draws no attention to the fact that the cost of additional procedural safeguards—to wit, allowing veterans to hire and pay private attorneys—would be paid by the individuals bringing the challenge, not by the government. As Justice John Paul Stevens points out in his dissenting opinion, "we are not considering a procedural right that would involve any cost to the Government. We are concerned with the individual's right to spend his own money to obtain the advice and assistance of independent counsel in advancing his claim against the Government."[39]

Nonetheless, the Court upheld the restriction on the use of private funds to hire lawyers for three reasons.[40] First, the government's interest in ensuring that the benefits awarded are not shared with lawyers, though paternalistic, was justifiable.[41] Second, if veterans hired private attorneys, a more adversarial and complex process might develop, which in turn might press all veterans to hire a lawyer.[42] Finally, and most importantly, the process provided by the Veterans' Administration sufficiently safeguarded the interests of veterans.[43] This last point seemed most important to the Court. The Court reviewed data demonstrating that veterans do nearly as well without lawyers as with them.[44] The Court emphasized that the scheme set up by the statute provided veterans with non-lawyer representatives, noting that there was insufficient evidence that some cases are too complex to be handled adequately by the non-lawyer representatives.[45] In other words, the fact that the government provided an adequate alternative system of dispute resolution was essential to the Court's decision that the due process right at issue was not violated by the restriction placed on using one's own money to hire counsel.

This case thus stands for the proposition that the due process guaranteed by the Constitution does not require that benefits claimants have an unfettered right to use their own money to hire a lawyer. No constitutional problem exists when the state has established a dispute resolution system that provides sufficient process but forbids hiring of private lawyers.[46]

Procreative Liberty. Procreation occurs increasingly in contexts that require money. Fertility treatments are big business. Paying doctors to harvest eggs, mix eggs and sperm together outside the body, and implant fertilized embryos in women have become more and more common. One such method, surrogacy, and in particular paid contract surrogacy, has been controversial at least since the well-known case of Baby M.[47] In the years since the New Jersey Supreme Court refused to enforce a surrogate parenting agreement, states have passed laws addressing the legality and enforceability of these contracts.

States have adopted a myriad of approaches. Some have permitted both paid and unpaid surrogacy, and have enforced contractual agreements exchanging gestational services for pay. Others have permitted both paid and unpaid surrogacy but, like New Jersey, refused to enforce these agreements. Still others have permitted only unpaid surrogacy, forbidding or criminalizing payments to a surrogate that exceed reimbursement for actual medical expenses.

If procreative liberty is a constitutional right, and the ability to procreate via surrogacy is a protected part of that right, may a state forbid paid contract surrogacy? In 1992, the Court of Appeals of Michigan decided *Doe v. Attorney General*,[48] which addressed this question. In this case, infertile couples and prospective surrogate mothers asked the court for a declaratory judgment that the Michigan Surrogate Parenting Act violated the plaintiffs' constitutional rights.[49] The plaintiffs asserted that "if the Surrogate Parenting Act were interpreted as being an outright ban on surrogacy contracts for pay, the statute would deny them their constitutionally protected privacy rights and would offend the Due Process and Equal Protection Clauses of the state and federal constitutions."[50] The case is interesting because the Michigan court found that would-be parents and surrogates have a protected liberty interest in procreating via surrogacy.[51] Nonetheless, the Michigan court upheld the ban on paid surrogacy.[52]

In this case, the court found that the law restricts the underlying right at issue—here, the right to procreate via surrogacy.[53] However, the court also found that this "intrusion into plaintiffs' right to procreate in the surrogacy context" is outweighed by the compelling interests offered by the legislature on behalf of the law.[54] This formulation of the court's resolution of the case would thus seem to suggest that the liberty interest at stake in the right to procreate via surrogacy *does* include the right to pay a surrogate or to receive pay for being a surrogate, even though the constitutional right itself is not violated because there are compelling governmental interests that justify restrictions on paid surrogacy.

If this interpretation were correct, the case would still be an important exemplar of a decision in which a court finds that a prohibition on spending money in connection with the exercise of a constitutional right does not ultimately violate the right. However, there is good reason to think that the court really does not believe that the right to spend or accept payment for surrogacy is part of the protected liberty interest at stake in the first instance. If so, the case stands for a stronger proposition: the procreative liberty interest protected by the Constitution does not always include the right to spend or receive money.

The Michigan court cites three reasons to forbid paid surrogacy, each of which it finds compelling. First, the state has a compelling interest in "preventing children from becoming mere commodities."[55] Second, "the best interest of the child is also an interest that is sufficiently compelling to justify government intrusion."[56] Finally, "a third compelling state interest is that of preventing the exploitation of women."[57]

I begin with the second: protecting the best interests of children. Here, the court cites the effect on children of knowing "of the purchase and sale aspect of one's birth"[58] and the harm to children of custody battles that might ensue. While these are surely real and important concerns, the court's emphasis on them belies its claim that couples and prospective surrogates have a protected liberty interest in procreating via surrogacy. The court notes in this part of the opinion that surrogacy contracts do not look to the child's interest in determining who should raise the child, and in that respect are contrary to the child custody law of the state.[59] Of course, the same could be said about decisions by biological parents or mothers to continue pregnancies. We respect the procreative liberty of women and couples to have and raise their biological children whether or not they would make the best parents for these children. Therefore, the fact that paid surrogacy does not attend to the best interests of children should not be sufficient to restrict procreative liberty. The treatment of this justification as a "compelling" interest to restrict the asserted liberty interest in procreating through paid surrogacy suggests that the Michigan court does not, in fact, treat this liberty interest as constitutionally protected.

This argument is strengthened when we compare whether the court is likely to say the same thing about unpaid surrogacy. These eleemosynary agreements also "focus exclusively on the parents' desires and interests,"[60] so that the child's best interest is not a primary consideration. The Michigan court's perception of a great difference between paid and unpaid surrogacy arrangements suggests that it is not really the fact that the agreements are made to benefit the parents or surrogate that is the problem.

The first and third reasons offered by the court focus on the likely effects of payment itself on children and women in the context of surrogacy.[61] In particular, the court emphasizes that paid surrogacy risks making children into commodities and risks exploiting women by turning them into "breeding machines."[62] These reasons are offered by the court as compelling reasons to restrict the protected liberty of couples to pay a surrogate to gestate a child.[63] What is odd about them in this context is that they are reasons that go directly to the liberty asserted in the first place. The risk of commodifying children and women's procreative labor is not a risk that just happens to accompany paying a surrogate to gestate a child. Rather, for those who believe that paid surrogacy inappropriately commodifies children and women's procreative capacity, it does so because paying for children and procreative labor is to value them in the wrong sort of way.[64] If this is correct (and I am making no claim about that), then it is hard to see how one has a protected liberty interest in doing this that is then *outweighed* by the negative consequences. Rather, if one believes that buying children and women's reproductive capacity values these things in the wrong sort of way—as the judge appears to believe in this case—then it is hard simultaneously to argue that the constitutionally protected procreative liberty gives one a right to enter into paid surrogacy arrangements.

This Michigan case found that couples and prospective surrogates have no right to enter into paid surrogacy arrangements. The right to engage in unpaid surrogacy is protected, however, as an aspect of procreative liberty. The court reaches this decision by finding that there is a protected liberty interest in procreating via surrogacy but that this interest is outweighed in the context of paid surrogacy by compelling governmental interests. However, I question whether what the court does in fact comports with what it says. While the court describes its holding in this manner, the reasons it offers suggest that the court's decision might be better captured by saying instead that while one has a protected liberty interest in procreating via surrogacy, one does not have a protected liberty interest in procreating via surrogacy for pay.

A Live Debate between the Integral Approach and the Blocked Approach

It is not clear whether most constitutionally protected rights include a penumbral right to spend money to effectuate them or not. In part, this is likely due to the fact that neither courts nor commentators have identified this as a question that must be answered. Nonetheless, we see a debate over precisely this question in the lower federal courts as they wrestle with the implications of the holding of *Lawrence v. Texas*.[65] Does *Lawrence* entail a right to buy sex toys?

The Fifth and Eleventh Circuits have both considered the implications of *Lawrence v. Texas* in challenges to the constitutionality of state laws that ban the buying and selling of sexual devices.[66] The circuits differ with regard to how they define the right articulated in *Lawrence*[67] and whether *Lawrence*'s failure to use the language of fundamental rights is significant.[68] However, both the Fifth and Eleventh Circuits view *Lawrence* as providing constitutional protection for the right to possess and use sexual devices.[69] Both courts were then faced with the question of whether the right to possess sex toys (derived from *Lawrence*) includes a concomitant right to buy or sell these devices.

In *Williams v. Attorney General of Alabama* and the subsequent appeal heard as *Williams v. Morgan*, the Eleventh Circuit found that *Lawrence* protected the use of sexual devices in private and not the public, commercial sale of such devices.[70] The court emphasized the significance of the distinction between use and sale, stressing that "plaintiffs here continue to possess and use such devices," a liberty not threatened by the statute.[71] Prohibitions on sales of sexual devices are constitutionally permissible as "states have traditionally had the authority to regulate commercial activity they deem harmful to the public."[72] Thus, the Eleventh Circuit, consistent with *Stanley* and *Walters*, follows the blocked approach and finds that recognition of a constitutionally protected right—here to possess or use sexual devices privately—does not entail a concomitant right to buy or sell these devices.[73]

In *Reliable Consultants v. Earle*, the Fifth Circuit adopted the opposite view. As in the *Williams* cases, the court in *Reliable* explored the implications of *Lawrence* for laws banning the sale of sexual devices, here asking whether the statute at issue "impermissibly burdens the individual's substantive due process right to engage in private intimate conduct of his or her choosing."[74] Drawing on the decisions in *Carey* and *Griswold*, the Fifth Circuit found that restrictions on sale unconstitutionally burden the right to use sexual devices privately.[75] The Fifth Circuit explained its view in this way: "An individual who wants to legally use a safe sexual device during private intimate moments alone or with another is unable to legally purchase a device in Texas, which heavily burdens a constitutional right."[76]

After *Lawrence*, both the Fifth and Eleventh Circuits thought it necessary to address the implications of that decision for challenges to laws banning the sale of sexual devices. The Eleventh Circuit followed *Stanley* and the blocked approach, adopting the view that the right to use sex toys privately does not give rise to a right to buy or sell them. The Fifth Circuit followed *Carey* and the integral approach, adopting the view that the right to use these devices privately entails a right to buy or sell them.

Generating a Theory

Some rights include a penumbral right to give and spend money to effectuate the underlying right. Some rights do not. Which are which, and why? By looking at the cases that fall into each category and especially at the *reasons* provided by the Supreme Court for why a given right includes or does not include a penumbral right to spend money, the outlines of a theory emerge. The state may forbid spending money to exercise a right where the state provides an adequate alternative means of securing, effectuating, or providing access to the right in question.

We see this theme most clearly in *Walters*. In *Walters*, the Supreme Court upheld a law that prohibited spending more than $10 to secure private counsel in veterans' benefit claims, precisely because the Court found that the alternative system for resolving benefits claims provided adequate process.[77] While the Court acknowledges that the district court found some small advantage in having a lawyer in these cases, the Supreme Court concludes that "the evidence adduced before the District Court as to success rates in claims handled with or without lawyers shows no such great disparity as to warrant the inference that the congressional fee limitation under consideration here violates the Due Process Clause of the Fifth Amendment."[78]

Admittedly, this decision rests in part on the Court's understanding that due process is "a flexible concept."[79] However, the Court's decision to apply that flexible approach not only to determinations about whether the state has provided a process that meets the Fifth Amendment's due process guarantee, but also to state-imposed restrictions on the ability of people to expend private resources, is telling.

Access and the adequacy of alternatives also explain the Court's view that the right to use contraception includes within its ambit the right to purchase contraceptives recognized in *Carey*. In explaining why the restrictions at issue in *Carey* violated the constitutionally protected right to make decisions about child bearing, the Court explains: "this is so not because there is an independent fundamental 'right of access to contraceptives,' but because such access is essential to exercise of the constitutionally protected right of decision in matters of childbearing."[80] Because one must be able to purchase contraceptives, and do so with relative ease, in order to adequately exercise one's constitutionally protected choice regarding childbearing, laws restricting or limiting the sale of contraceptives violate due process.

Buckley v. Valeo itself also focuses on whether there is adequate ability to exercise the underlying right. The First Amendment right of free speech includes the right to spend money on political speech because "virtually every means of communicating ideas in today's mass society requires the expenditure of money."[81] It is because money is necessary to political expression, in the Court's view, that restrictions on the ability to spend on political campaigns constitute a restriction on speech. Moreover, the *Buckley* Court's acceptance of contribution limits can too be traced to adequacy. Part of the Court's reasoning was that "a limitation on the amount of money a person may give to a candidate or campaign organization thus involves little direct restraint on his political communication, for it permits the symbolic expression of support evidenced by a contribution but does not in any way infringe the contributor's freedom to discuss candidates and issues."[82] In other words, the Court found that limitations on contributions still allowed for adequate alternative means of showing political support.

The theory that emerges from these cases is this: where alternative methods for effectuating the right exist (*Walters*, *Buckley*-contributions), the state may restrict the ability to spend money to effectuate the underlying right. Where there are no adequate alternatives, the state must permit individuals to use private funds to effectuate the underlying right (*Carey*, *Buckley*-expenditures).[83]

Adequacy Theory Suggests Some Cases Are Wrongly Decided

The theory that emerges from the case law suggests that legislatures may restrict one's liberty to spend money in connection with rights where, as in *Walters*, an adequate alternative means of securing the right is provided. Conversely, legislatures may not restrict one's liberty to spend money in connection with rights where, as in *Carey*, no alternative means of gaining access to a good used to exercise a right exists. Applying this theory to *Stanley* and that part of *Buckley* dealing with expenditures suggests that the Court may have its First Amendment cases backwards.

Stanley and the cases that follow it held that a person has a constitutionally protected right to read obscene material at home but no constitutionally protected right to buy or sell this material.[84] This group of cases exemplifies the blocked approach. Adequacy theory suggests that *Stanley* belongs in the blocked strand if, and only if, there is an adequate alternative means for Stanley to procure the obscene material without spending money to buy it. Short of creating it himself, it is hard to see how this is so. While one *could* make the argument that homemade pornography is a sufficient alternative to the store-bought kind, this rationale plays no role in the case law. Thus the adequacy theory suggests either that the right to read obscene materials at home includes the right to buy and sell this material or that *Stanley* itself was wrongly decided. If one accepts that obscene materials are of low value and thus are outside of the First Amendment's protection, it is hard to see why a prosecution for possessing such materials in the home should be protected. While the home does enjoy a special status in constitutional law,[85] still one can be prosecuted for otherwise illegal actions (like violence against family members or drug use) notwithstanding the fact that these actions take place in the privacy of the home. Indeed, the Court has refused to extend the rationale of *Stanley* to the context of child pornography,[86] thereby implicitly recognizing the inter-relationship of use and sale. Thus, either *Stanley* belongs in the integral strand or it should be overruled.[87]

Conversely, the focus on adequacy suggests that *Buckley* and its progeny erred in holding that the right to engage in political speech entailed a concomitant right to spend money on such speech. The relevant question is whether adequate alternative means for engaging in political expression exist. Where adequate alternatives do exist, the right to free speech may not include the right to spend money. Public funding of campaigns is the obvious example to consider. Just as *Walters* recognizes that the publicly provided non-lawyer representatives made it the case that the right to due process did not include the right to spend money on a lawyer, so too adequate public funding of political campaigns should make it the case that the right of free speech does not include the right to spend money on political speech. Currently, public funding of campaigns is not robust. However, were the Court to embrace the analysis provided here, legislatures would have good reason to enact better-funded public financing systems in the future.

The focus on adequacy that, I argue, underlies the division of cases between the blocked and the integral approach makes an explicit appearance in at least one other campaign finance case in a way that is suggestive. In *Randall v. Sorrell*,[88] the Supreme Court struck down a provision of Vermont's campaign finance law that restricted contributions to state candidates on the grounds that the contribution limits were too low.[89] The *Randall* Court followed *Buckley* in finding that contribution limits are generally constitutionally acceptable; they burden speech, but the infringement on this right is justified by the compelling interest in preventing corruption or the appearance of corruption. However, the specific limit must also be narrowly drawn. There is some "lower bound."[90] If there is too little money available for political activity, "effective [campaign] advocacy" will be compromised.[91] This word—*effective*—is used by the *Randall* Court several times. The Court worries that "the critical question concerns . . . the ability of a candidate running against an incumbent officeholder to mount an effective *challenge*."[92] Similarly, in commenting on the fact that the Vermont law includes, in its definition of a "contribution," services donated by volunteers, the Court finds fault with the law because "the Act may well impede a campaign's ability effectively to use volunteers."[93]

In other words, the adequacy of the system for providing access to the right (here, the ability to participate in politics) is the central factor to use in assessing whether a legislature may limit the ability of people to use their own money to effectuate the right. Where the system established by limiting contributions does not provide adequate access to the right, then the law that limits the use of private funds is constitutionally infirm. While *Randall v. Sorrell* applies this focus on adequacy to contribution limits and not expenditure limits, the approach underlying the Court's treatment of the relationship of money and rights more generally suggests that this question ought to guide analysis of when and whether expenditure limits violate the First Amendment right to free speech as well.

The Descriptive and the Normative

I recognize that this descriptive account—that a state may restrict the right to spend money in connection with constitutionally protected rights as long as there are adequate alternative ways to access the right—does not explain all the cases as well as it could. Rather, I propose it as the best reconstruction of what appears to underlie the sorting of cases we see in our law. Because neither the Supreme Court nor lower courts have focused on providing an answer to the question of when and why constitutionally protected rights include a concomitant right to spend money, it is not surprising that the case law is only suggestive of an underlying explanatory theory.

In my prior article, "Money Talks But It Isn't Speech," I argue, as mentioned earlier, that the elected branches of government ought to be left to determine which goods are to be distributed via the market and which should not. For example, in our society, we currently distribute most goods via the market, but notably not all. Babies, organs, the vote, and other goods are distributed via non-market principles. Where a constitutional right depends for its exercise on a good that is distributed via the market, the right should be understood to include a concomitant right to spend money to exercise the underlying right. Conversely, where a constitutional right depends for its exercise on a good that is distributed via non-market principles, that right should not be understood to include a concomitant right to spend money.

The descriptive account of the case law offered here and the normative account offered in "Money Talks" are consistent, if somewhat different in emphasis. The focus on adequacy of access to constitutionally protected rights described in this chapter entails that the state cannot cut off one very important way of getting access to a right—that is, using money—unless there is an alternative available method of gaining access to the right. There is likely to be such an alternative when the good used in connection with the right is distributed through non-market means. For example, because condoms are distributed via the market, individuals must be able to buy them to secure their constitutionally protected right to procreative choice. By contrast, the non-lawyer advocate used to ensure due process in *Walters* is provided via a non-market mechanism. So long as this advocate is adequate, the restriction on the ability to use one's own money to hire a lawyer does not violate due process protections.

Conclusion

This chapter contributes to the project of looking at campaign finance laws through a wider lens. Rather than asking only whether laws that restrict giving and spending money in connection with campaigns violate the First Amendment, we should instead ask the more general question: When do constitutionally protected rights give rise to an attendant right to give or spend money? Specifically, this chapter contributes to that project by exploring what the Supreme Court and other courts have said about this issue already. These cases suggest two conclusions. First, restrictions on the ability to use money to effectuate rights are not always forbidden. Sometimes they are and sometimes they are not. If this is correct, then courts and commentators must develop an account of when rights generate an attendant right to give or spend money and when they do not.

Second, one part of that theory may involve the notion of adequacy. It is not enough to say—as the Supreme Court does in *Buckley*—that money facilitates the exercise of a right. Money would facilitate the right to representation and thus due process of law in *Walters*, yet the ability to spend money on counsel is permissibly restricted. Where an adequate alternative system—as we see in *Walters*—provides a way to effectuate the right in question, restrictions on the ability to spend money on the underlying right appear to be permissible.

6

Nonparticipatory Association and Compelled Political Speech: Consent as a Constitutional Principle in the Wake of *Citizens United*

Frances R. Hill[*]

In *Citizens United v. Federal Elections Commission,* the U.S. Supreme Court put nonparticipatory association and compelled political speech at the heart of campaign finance jurisprudence.[1] The Court held that corporations can use their general treasury funds to finance independent expenditures that expressly advocate the election or defeat of clearly identified candidates for public office.[2] The majority opinion concludes that "the Government may not suppress political speech on the basis of the speaker's corporate identity."[3] This principle applies to all types of corporations, associations, and organizations. The majority found that "no sufficient governmental interest justifies limits on the political speech of nonprofit or for-profit corporations."[4] The Court held that prohibitions on the use of general treasury funds constituted government censorship akin to content discrimination by the government.[5]

In its zeal to abolish distinctions between natural persons and corporations in campaign finance law, the Court amplified the political speech rights of corporations and constrained the associational and political and speech rights of the shareholders and members who form

* This chapter also appears in NYU's *Review of Law and Social Change* 35, no. 3 (2011). Reproduced by permission.

and fund corporations. This approach to corporate political speech begs the question of who is speaking when a corporation speaks, and whose First Amendment rights are at issue. Under the Court's holding, the corporation has rights under the First Amendment to use its general treasury funds to finance independent expenditures. But what happens to the First Amendment rights of the individuals who have affiliated themselves with corporations? Do individuals have rights of political speech as members of corporations?

A corporation may be considered an entity controlled by its managers or as an aggregate of the persons who have affiliated themselves in some way with the corporation. The strong form of the entity theory of a corporation is that the entity itself has First Amendment rights. The strong form of the aggregate theory is that the corporation derives its First Amendment rights from its members and shareholders. The operational question is who plays a role in deciding how the corporation will use its general treasury funds for political speech. Under an entity theory, corporate managers decide. Under an aggregate theory, members and shareholders play some role in these decisions.

Citizens United is based on an entity theory of a corporation, and thus denies the constitutional significance of members' and shareholders' consent to the corporation's political speech. The majority, in an opinion authored by Justice Anthony Kennedy, briskly dismisses any compelling state interest in "protecting dissident shareholders from being compelled to fund corporate political speech."[6] The majority reasons that recognizing the rights of dissident shareholders would give the government the authority to restrict the corporation's political speech. The majority finds "little evidence of abuse that cannot be corrected by shareholders 'through the procedures of corporate democracy.'"[7] Nonetheless, the majority offers no thoughts on what procedures of corporate democracy it might find most appropriate in the context of an election campaign.

Reading Justice Kennedy's dissent in *Austin v. Michigan Chamber of Commerce* suggests that the majority has no interest in this question because it finds claims relating to member and shareholder consent constitute a burden on the First Amendment rights of the associations considered solely as entities. In *Austin*, Justice Kennedy expressly rejected the claim that protecting dissident members was a sufficient compelling state interest.[8] He concluded that "allowing government to use the excuse of protecting shareholder rights to stifle the speech of private, voluntary organizations undermined the First Amendment."[9] Justice Kennedy expressed the strongest possible form of the entity theory of association by claiming that members' rights erode the rights of corporations. Similarly, Justice Antonin Scalia's dissent in *Austin* denounced the statute that required that the Chamber of Commerce finance its independent expenditures with the funds in its political action committee (PAC) rather than its general treasury funds. Deriding the statute as "a paternalistic measure to protect the corporate shareholders of America,"[10] Justice Scalia set forth at some length a theory that joining an association means giving up individual views and rights.[11] He casually rejected any concern about "association-induced trauma."[12]

Yet, political speech of individuals is unquestionably protected under the First Amendment. Nothing in *Citizens United* disputes this. *Citizens United* unintentionally raises the question of what First Amendment rights of political speech individuals are accorded when they affiliate with, invest their money in, or make contributions to various types of corporations. The strong form of the entity theory tacitly embraced by *Citizens United* suggests that individuals lose their individual rights as political speakers once they join an association. In contrast, the aggregate theory of association relies on participation by members. Individuals retain their rights as political speakers when they join organizations. Indeed, they join organizations to amplify their voices.

In his concurring opinion in *Austin,* Justice William J. Brennan agreed with the dissents that political speech is at the core of the First Amendment, but he extended this reasoning to the members and shareholders of the corporations and not just the entities. He found that "just as speech interests are at their zenith in this area, so too are the interests of unwilling Chamber members and corporate shareholders forced to subsidize that speech."[13] He insisted that the Michigan statute should be understood as "preventing both the Chamber *and other business corporations* from using the funds of other persons for purposes that those persons may not support."[14] He also noted that the PAC option "protects dissenting shareholders of business corporations that are members of the Chamber to the extent that such shareholders oppose the use of their money, paid as dues to the Chamber out of general corporate treasury funds, for political campaigns."[15] Justice Brennan's articulation of the aggregate theory raises questions about participation in organizations. What do enhanced political speech rights for organizations mean for the political speech rights of members?

Individuals join associations for many reasons. They invest in business corporations to earn income. They join a chamber of commerce to share views about business with other persons with similar interests. They join advocacy organizations to persuade other people of the virtues (or not) of opera, guns, cats, trees, literacy, or a seemingly infinite array of other issues and causes. They may wish to lobby city councils, county commissions, state legislatures, or Congress on these issues. They may not want to lobby at all, only to persuade others to join them in private voluntary efforts on behalf of these causes. They may wish to pool their money with that of other members of the organization to support or oppose a candidate for public office—or they may not. Even if a candidate supports the organization's cause, some members of the organization may not support the candidate because of his or her positions on other issues.[16] What role do members of organizations have in determining how their money will be used for activities in which both they and the corporation have protected rights of political speech? This question has always been difficult because of the attenuated jurisprudence of association in constitutional law. *Citizens United* extended these difficulties into the area of political speech in elections campaigns.

Citizens United has changed a great deal about the terms of association. Before *Citizens United,* federal election law prohibited the use of general treasury funds for independent expenditures that expressly supported or opposed the election of clearly identified candidates for public office.[17] In effect, federal election law operated as a term in corporate articles or bylaws protecting shareholders or members from managerial discretion in using corporate assets to support political candidates through independent expenditures. *Citizens United* removed this implicit term from corporate organizing documents and thereby extended to political speech the marked disparity in rights that already existed between corporate management and shareholders.[18] Members or shareholders will now find that the money they contributed or invested is being used to finance political speech with which they may not agree.

Citizens United is a very broad case about the control of corporations and their resources and the use of those resources to influence campaigns, election outcomes, and the operation of the government. The opinion is based on First Amendment speech claims, an entity theory of association in the guise of a discussion about the use of general treasury funds, the express rejection of any limits on the speech rights of the entity, and the refusal to find constitutional significance in any rights of shareholders or members to participate in deciding how to use general treasury funds for political speech by the corporation. In *Citizens United* the Court has used the First Amendment to support nonparticipation in associations and compelled subsidization of political speech. This use of the First Amendment is inconsistent with the speech clause of the First Amendment, with the participatory language of the association clause of the First Amendment, and with the constitutional principle of consent that makes the people of the United States the source of government legitimacy.

Consent as a Constitutional Principle

The Constitution begins with consent, stating, "we the people of the United States . . . do ordain and establish this Constitution for the United States of America."[19] The purposes to which the people consented are public purposes—"to form a more perfect Union" and "to establish justice, insure domestic tranquility, provide for the common defense, promote the general welfare, and secure the blessings of liberty to ourselves and our posterity."[20] Consent is the foundation of the government as it operates to achieve these purposes.

This affirmation and assertion of consent in the first sentence of the Constitution invoked the language of the Declaration of Independence, which describes governments as "deriving their just powers from the consent of the governed."[21] Just as the colonists grounded the legitimacy of their rebellion on the consent of the people, the drafters of the Constitution grounded the legitimacy of their revised plan of self-government on the consent of the people. Ratification of the Constitution through conventions in each of the states was intended to provide evidence of consent and hence the legitimacy of the new government.[22]

The Declaration of Independence not only based the legitimacy of government on consent but also affirmed the right of the people to continue to consent or not as they saw fit. Among the "self-evident truths" enumerated in the Declaration of Independence was the assertion "that whenever any Form of Government becomes destructive of these ends, it is the Right of the People to alter or to abolish it, and to institute a new Government, laying its foundation on such principles and organizing its powers in such form, as to them shall seem most likely to effect their Safety and Happiness."[23]

Consent is a principle of active and continuing participation for the purpose of addressing questions of government legitimacy. In his important and provocative study of consent and the Constitution, Stanford law professor Larry Kramer claims that the people of the United States were quite aware of their role in founding and shaping their government:

> Americans of the Founding era reveal how they understood their role in popular government in ways that we, who take so much for granted, do not. The United States was then the only country in the world with a government founded explicitly on the consent of its people, given in a distinct and identifiable act, and the people who gave that consent were intensely, profoundly conscious of the fact. And proud. This pride, this awareness of the fragility and importance of their venture in popular government, informed everything the Founding generation did.[24]

Kramer emphasizes the continuing role of the people in interpreting and implementing the Constitution.[25] He finds that, when the drafters of the Constitution referred to "the people," they were referring to actual living, participating, debating, disputing, contentious people and "not conjuring an empty abstraction or describing a mythic philosophical justification for government."[26] The Constitution provided for initial ratification,[27] for ratification of amendments,[28] and for convening another constitutional convention.[29] The text of the Constitution thus expressly embraces a principle of continuing consent.[30] Amar describes the Constitution as "a democratic and intergenerational project."[31]

Elections are perhaps even more important expressions of the principle of continuing consent. Elections establish that consent is a foundational constitutional principle applicable to the ordinary operation of government on a continuing basis. As Justice Brennan explained some twenty-five years ago, the Constitution is a document that should be understood in terms of "contemporary ratification."[32]

The idea that voting is an expression of consent that constitutes the continuing legitimacy of government is most apparent when the legitimacy of government is most centrally challenged. After the Civil War the Court enforced federal statutes defining voting fraud as a federal crime and, in the process, articulated a concept of constitutive voting.[33] The Court explained this reasoning in *Ex parte Yarbrough*, which involved a federal criminal prosecution against private persons who had violently attacked a freed slave who was eligible to vote.[34] The Court reasoned that

> It is as essential to the successful working of this government that the great organisms of its executive and legislative branches should be the free choice of the people as that the original form of it should be so. . . . In republican governments, like ours, where political power is reposed in representatives of the entire body of the people, chosen at short intervals by popular elections, the temptations to control these elections by violence and corruption is a constant source of danger.[35]

In the early twentieth century, as primary elections began to replace private meetings of party bosses as mechanisms of candidate selections, the White Primary cases addressed such questions as whether primaries are elections and whether the constitutional protections accorded voters under the Fourteenth and Fifteenth Amendments applied to primary elections.[36] In the end, the Court resolved these questions by treating elections as mechanisms of consent through participation and treating consent as a core principle establishing the legitimacy of government.[37]

More recently, the Court in *Baker v. Carr* struck down electoral districts that weighed the votes of various voters differently.[38] In so doing, the Court extended the principle of consent and affirmed its central role in defining legitimate government. Equality mattered and vote dilution mattered because elections were part of the process of ensuring and affirming the legitimacy of government.[39]

Yet, while the Court was exploring the role of elections as a mechanism of consent in legitimate democratic government, it did not extend the principle of consent to campaigns and campaign finance. In the wake of *Citizens United,* this oversight has become untenable; conceptualizing campaigns and campaign finance without taking account of consent as a constitutional principle results in impermissible burdens on the First Amendment rights of association members. If contributions and expenditures are made by individuals, those individuals can be assumed to have consented to their own actions. If, as *Citizens United* has now provided, an organization makes independent expenditures using the organization's general treasury fund, the presumption of consent by members cannot be made without consideration of the terms of association.

The focus on consent in this article does not mean to suggest that consent is the only constitutional principle important to understanding the relationship between campaign finance and government legitimacy. In his discussion of the nature of the Constitution and the enterprise of judging constitutional issues, Justice David Souter emphasized that the Constitution embraces a multiplicity of desirable values not all of which are simultaneously achievable.[40] As he notes, "the Constitution is a pantheon of values, and a lot of hard cases are hard because the Constitution gives no simple rule of decision for the cases in which one of the values is truly at odds with another."[41] Justice Souter rejected what he labeled the "fair reading model," which he described as "the notion that all of constitutional law lies there in the Constitution waiting for a judge to read it fairly."[42] Justice Souter chose the interpretation of the First Amendment in the Pentagon Papers case as an example of the limits of the fair reading model and of the importance of understanding the role of competing constitutional values. Justice Souter rejected First Amendment literalism and absolutism as the basis of the Court's decision, stating that "the court did not decide the case on the ground that the words 'no law' allowed of no exception and meant that the rights of expression were absolute."[43] According to Justice Souter, "the court's majority decided only that the government had not met a high burden of showing facts that could justify a prior restraint."[44] He concluded:

> Even the First Amendment, then, expressing the value of speech and publication in the terms of a right as paramount as any fundamental right can be, does not quite get to the point of an absolute guarantee. It fails because the Constitution has to be read as a whole, and when it is, other values crop up in potential conflict with an unfettered right to publish. . . . The explicit terms of the Constitution, in other words, can create a conflict of approved values, and the explicit terms of the Constitution do not resolve that conflict when it arises.[45]

The same approach applies to understanding the First Amendment in the context of campaign finance. In this case, too, "no law" does not mean exactly, literally, and absolutely "no law" because the First Amendment speech clause is necessarily read as part of the First Amendment, which includes the assembly clause, and as part of the Constitution, which includes among its fundamental principles the principle of consent.

Association and Consent

If one takes the text of the Constitution seriously, as anyone must, it is quite surprising that the majority in *Citizens United* felt that it could simply ignore the association clause of the First Amendment. The First Amendment association clause reads "Congress shall make no law respecting . . . the right of the people peaceably to assemble, and to petition the Government for a redress of grievances."[46] The association clause focuses on the "right of the people to assemble." This suggests an aggregate theory of association in which the people who associate are active participants.

The Court interpreted the association clause in terms of consent and participation in a series of cases involving the rights of certain NAACP chapters, officials, and members in the face of various efforts to impede their rights to associate.[47] The Court in *Bates v.*

City of Little Rock reasoned that "like freedom of speech and a free press, the right of peaceable assembly was considered by the Framers of the Constitution to lie at the foundation of a government based upon the consent of an informed citizenry—a government dedicated to the establishment of justice and the preservation of liberty."[48] In their concurring opinion, Justice Hugo Black and Justice William O. Douglas observed that "freedom of assembly includes of course freedom of association; and it is entitled to no less protection than any other First Amendment rights."[49] In *NAACP v. Alabama ex rel Patterson,* the Court noted that "effective advocacy of both public and private points of view, particularly controversial ones, is undeniably enhanced by group association, as this Court has more than once recognized by remarking upon the close nexus between the freedoms of speech and assembly."[50] The Court further observed that "it is immaterial whether the beliefs sought to be advanced by association pertain to political, economic, religious or cultural matters."[51]

The association clause of the First Amendment recognizes the right of people to assemble peaceably "to petition the Government for a redress of grievances." In short, people participate in governance. They have a voice in the operation of government and, through this voice, determine the legitimacy of government. The association clause of the First Amendment is consistent with the Preamble in treating ordinary people as the source of legitimate government. Nothing in the text of the First Amendment on its face supports the idea that, once people assemble, they allow the assembly to co-opt their own voices.

Unfortunately, the Court has reinterpreted the NAACP cases to produce a jurisprudence of expressive association that negates participation and consent by members. Even the expressive association cases did not begin with strong assertions of an entity theory of expressive rights under the First Amendment speech clause. Indeed, the first cases began with an affirmation of women's right to join the Jaycees[52] and the Rotary Club.[53] Although the Court found that both of these organizations were expressive associations, it also found that extending full membership to women would not burden this right.[54] When the Court confronted the issue of an openly gay former Eagle Scout who wanted to serve as an assistant scoutmaster, however, the Court deferred entirely to the unsupported claims of the Boy Scout managers that permitting an Eagle Scout to serve in this capacity would conflict with a policy against homosexuality.[55] In *Boy Scouts of America v. Dale*, the Court held that the First Amendment right of association took precedence over the rights of nondiscrimination set forth in a New Jersey state statute. *Dale* represented the ascendance of an entity theory of nonparticipatory association in the Court's First Amendment jurisprudence, an ascendance that has continued with *Citizens United*.

In *Citizens United* the Court embraced without analysis a theory of association that ignores the association clause of the First Amendment and grounds its reasoning solely on the speech clause. The question then becomes who controls the speech of the organization. The only answer that the Court considers is that the organization managers exercise absolute control over all aspects of organizational operation.

Now that the Court has rejected distinctions among corporations in terms of their right to engage in political speech, all corporations are potentially expressive associations. *Citizens United* has extended the expressive association jurisprudence of managerial control to all corporations.[56] The result of nonparticipatory association is compelled political speech and compelled subsidization of political speech.

Association Membership and Compelled Political Speech

Individuals have broad but not absolute rights of political speech under the First Amendment. Once an individual affiliates with an association, the situation becomes far more complex and problematic. *Citizens United* exacerbates this complexity. For all its rhetorical flourishes about combating government censorship of political speech, *Citizens United* embraces both compelled political speech and nonparticipatory association.

The Court has given limited attention to compelled speech or compelled subsidization of speech, and the cases that it has decided provide little enlightenment in the cases of political speech by association members. Yet here, too, the Court in the past decade has begun to introduce substantial doubts about the rights of association members into precedents that historically upheld rights of participation and consent.

The most straightforward compelled speech cases are those involving government attempts to compel individuals to speak. The Court rejected efforts by state governments to require that individuals salute the flag or display a state motto on their car's license plates.[57] While this is not the pattern of compulsion at issue here, these cases established the importance of voluntarism as a component of speech. The Court found that a legitimate state interest was not advanced by coerced public expression and that individuals could not be penalized for refusing to obey statutes that compelled them to speak.

The Court has also decided a number of cases involving claims by union members that their dues should not be used to finance political speech with which they disagree. The cases dealing with the rights of union members and the rights of nonmembers in agency shops present the closest analogy to the compelled speech at issue here.[58] The fundamental issue in these cases was to balance the right of the union to collect dues from members and payments in lieu of dues from nonmembers to avoid a "free rider" problem, while at the same time prohibiting compulsory political speech and compelled subsidization of political speech.

Abood v. Detroit Board of Education involved a teachers union.[59] Teachers who objected to the use of union dues for political activities brought suit against both the school board and the union that was the sole collective bargaining representative of public school teachers in Detroit. The teachers claimed that the requirement that they contribute funds to the union for political speech that they did not support was an impermissible burden on their First Amendment rights. In ruling for the teachers, the Court held that "the fact that the appellants are compelled to make, rather than prohibited from making, contributions for political purposes works no less an infringement of their constitutional rights."[60] The Court based its decision on the absence of consent by the teachers to the political expenditures.[61] The Court made it clear that its decision did not deprive the union of the First Amendment right to engage in political speech but that it protected the rights of those who associated in the union to avoid compelled speech, citing Thomas Jefferson as saying that "to compel a man to furnish contributions of money for the propagation of opinions which he disbelieves, is sinful and tyrannical."[62]

Abood provided guidance on the specificity of consent. Simply being a member of the union or simply being a nonmember who benefited from the union's collective bargaining on his or her behalf did not establish the requisite consent to the use of some part of their dues for political speech with which they did not agree. Political speech requires specific consent by the members. Affiliation does not provide the required consent.

The Court revisited the issue of consent to political expenditures in *Davenport v. Washington Education Association.*[63] The Court held that a nonmember who pays an agency shop fee must be given an opportunity for affirmative consent to the use of any portion of this fee for political activities. Writing for the majority, Justice Scalia rejected the union's claim that the agency fees were union funds because they were paid under government compulsion.[64] Justice Scalia concluded that a limitation on how the union can spend agency funds in the form of the state law requirement that the union obtain the affirmative consent of the nonmembers to use some part of the agency fees for political purposes is not a restriction on the union's First Amendment right of political speech but "is a condition placed upon the union's extraordinary *state* entitlement to acquire and spend *other people's* money."[65] Justice Scalia concluded that "the union remains as free as any other entity to participate in the electoral process with all available funds other than the state-coerced agency fees lacking affirmative permission."[66] Justice Scalia noted that requiring an affirmative authorization is not burdensome to the nonmember who wishes to do so.[67]

Justice Scalia observed that the holding might be different had the complaint been made by a union member.[68] In this case, a union might well be able to rely on *First National Bank of Boston v. Bellotti* and the other campaign finance cases because the member dues became the union's money when these dues were not paid in response to government compulsion. This comment is, of course, *dicta* for purpose of *Davenport* but it is quite suggestive in the context of a post–*Citizens United* challenge by a corporate shareholder or association member. The concept of a general treasury in *Citizens United* suggests that

Davenport would apply only in the very limited circumstances of an agency shop fee paid by a nonmember to the collective bargaining agent. Other funds would be treated as union funds because they had been transferred to the organization voluntarily even if they had not been transferred for purposes of supporting the organization's political speech.[69]

Justice Scalia also suggested that the outcome might be different in the case of a private sector union.[70] He observed that the distinction between the use of agency fees for collective bargaining activities and for political speech "is arguably content based," which would support strict scrutiny under the First Amendment.[71] Justice Scalia nevertheless stated that the majority was not taking the position that it was necessary to distinguish between public-sector and private-sector unions.[72] This hint that *Communications Workers of America v. Beck* might be overruled in some future case suggests that Justice Scalia finds a burden on political speech arising from contributions to a corporation only where the government compelled the contribution. If this becomes the law and *Beck* is overruled, the scope of the concept of the general treasury would be expanded and the scope of managerial discretion consistent with the jurisprudence of expressive association would know no bounds in the private sector. In other words, compelled speech jurisprudence would have been transformed to fit into the pattern established in *Citizens United*. Political speech by associations would not require consent by members. *Dale, Davenport,* and *Citizens United* would have become an unholy trinity of nonparticipatory association and compelled political speech at the core of the First Amendment.

Consent in Operation:
Crafting Remedies to Nonparticipatory Association and Compelled Political Speech

In *Citizens United,* the Court put nonparticipatory association and compelled political speech at the core of its First Amendment campaign finance jurisprudence. Short of developing a jurisprudence of participatory association based on the text of the First Amendment association clause, what forms of mitigation might be developed based on treating consent as a constitutional principle? This chapter suggests two categories of remedies: voting on corporation policies, and permitting members to allocate contributions to activities other than financing independent expenditures. Voting on policies means allowing members to give or withhold consent to uses of general treasury funds. Permitting members to allocate their contributions to particular activities means allowing members to exclude their dues or contributions from being spent from the general treasury for particular purposes.

These two types of remedies are not equally suited to all types of corporations. The differences among types of corporations will be considered here, with reference to three types of entities—single purpose nonprofits, multipurpose nonprofits, and taxable business corporations.

The Court in *Citizens United* appears to assume that general treasury funds "belong" in some way to the organization. The question here is whether that is an adequate assumption in the context of political speech at the core of the First Amendment. This assumption fits comfortably with an entity theory of association, but it fits less comfortably with an aggregate theory. Considering remedies based on consent either to the use of general treasury funds or to the inclusion of funds in the general treasury highlights the operational issues that become important if consent is taken seriously as a constitutional principle.

Voting on corporate policies raises questions of specificity of consent. Should members vote on whether to use general treasury funds to finance independent expenditures, or should members be able to vote on the specific candidates that the organization proposes to support or oppose? These questions are more difficult than the mechanics of voting, given the widespread use of online voting procedures. It may seem paradoxical to some that business corporations could adopt these consent procedures more readily than could most nonprofit organizations. However, business corporations already have shareholders with voting rights attached to their stock. Nonprofits generally have no members with voting rights. It would be difficult for a nonprofit to determine who should vote on the use of their general treasury funds for purposes of financing independent expenditures unless nonprofit organizations changed their organizing documents to provide for voting members. This would be a major change in the governance of most nonprofit organizations.

In the absence of members with any form of voting rights, nonprofits might claim that their supporters have already consented to their use of general treasury funds for independent expenditures because contributors have voluntarily chosen to make contributions, presumably based on their desire to support particular causes. This was the Court's argument in *Federal Election Commission v. Massachusetts Citizens for Life.*[73] As discussed above, the nature of the voting decision makes the assumption of inferred consent problematic even in the case of a single-issue organization like Massachusetts Citizens for Life. It does not work at all in the case of a multipurpose entity such as the Chamber of Commerce in *Austin.* The expressive association cases, especially *Dale,* replace a presumption or inference of consent with managerial control based on the asserted rights of the association itself and without regard to any right of the members or contributors.

Remedies based on allocating contributions to particular purposes would permit contributors to express or withhold consent to the use of general treasury funds to independent expenditures. In nonprofit fund-raising, it is common for very large contributions to be made pursuant to a grant agreement specifying the uses. If the organization fails to use the contribution for the purpose specified in the grant agreement, the contributor can bring a breach of contract claim seeking return of the money contributed.[74] This would, of course, be a very cumbersome procedure in the case of smaller contributions.

One workable mechanism in the case of smaller contributions is to create a fund to be used solely for the exempt entity's exempt purpose, excluding independent expenditures. The *Massachusetts Citizens for Life* Court suggested that contributors could earmark their contributions for particular uses.[75] The Court noted that this approach might be particularly useful when a contributor wanted to support a cause but did not wish to do so through support of candidates for public office. It is possible that having a separate fund for activities other than independent expenditures might merely free up other funds for independent expenditures, but it does give individuals who wish to support the organization's other activities a mechanism for doing so. A fund mechanism, however, would not solve the issue of consent in a business corporation. There is no structure that would permit a designation of the purchase price for a particular use at the time of a stock purchase or the purchase of corporate debt.

Without considering consent mechanisms operating inside organizations, ordinary people will be deprived of their right to amplify their voices during election campaigns. They will be deprived of their rights under the association clause of the First Amendment. The association clause does not give each individual absolute rights, but it does give some right of participation without compelled speech.

Considering these kinds of remedies to the problems of nonparticipatory association and compelled political speech can contribute to the larger project of considering the meaning of the association clause as part of the First Amendment and as part of the Constitution. Treating consent as a constitutional principle is an essential component of this larger project. Without active participation and well-considered consent by ordinary people, there can be no claim that the government is legitimate. Political speech is not an end in itself. It is an essential means to the end of legitimate government grounded in the continuing consent of ordinary people.

7

First Amendment Fault Lines and the *Citizens United* Decision

*Monica Youn**

As the dust settles from the 2010 midterm elections, it is clear that the current U.S. Supreme Court majority has transformed the landscape of federal politics, and has done so in service to a reified conception of corporate speech rights under the First Amendment.[1] How much of the widely reported flood of stealth corporate spending in this election cycle[2] was directly attributable to the Court's decision in *Citizens United v. Federal Election Commission*[3] may never be known, due to the lack of comprehensive federal campaign finance disclosure laws, but the majority's sweeping endorsement of the First Amendment status of corporate political expenditures certainly issued an open invitation for such a spending blitz.

Although *Citizens United* has provoked a firestorm of criticism, relatively few have engaged Justice Anthony Kennedy's majority opinion on the terms of First Amendment *value*—that is, the degree to which a particular corporate spending decision should be deemed to warrant First Amendment protection.[4] Instead, most constitutional scholars criticizing the opinion have focused on the non–First Amendment interests and other constitutional principles that the Court failed to accord adequate weight.[5]

* I am grateful for the comments provided by Frances Hill, Samuel Issacharoff, and Burt Neuborne and for editorial assistance by Leah Morfin, Daniel Craig, Danielle D'Onfro, and Lauren Wroblewski. This chapter originally appeared in 5 Harv. L. & Pol'y Rev. 135 (2011). Reproduced by permission.

But one overlooked aspect of campaign finance doctrine is the degree to which the constitutional case law in this area has been shaped by competing accounts of the source of First Amendment value—that is, what imbues particular uses of money with First Amendment significance. After all, it may be settled law that political spending is, under some circumstances, entitled to First Amendment protection, but few would argue that money is always speech. Most uses of money—paying taxes, purchasing consumer goods, financing a corporate takeover—are treated as inert for First Amendment purposes so that regulation of such forms of spending does not ordinarily raise First Amendment concerns. Meanwhile, other forms of spending, including campaign expenditures, are treated as having the highest degree of First Amendment significance. And even within campaign finance doctrine, a hierarchy of First Amendment value obtains so that campaign expenditures are deemed to be of high First Amendment value, while contributions to a candidate or party are considered to be relatively low-level speech[6]—a framework initially established in *Buckley v. Valeo*[7] and applied by generations of courts. Accordingly, First Amendment value is deemed to attach to some uses of money in campaigns but not others, and to attach in varying degrees depending upon the type of spending at issue.

This chapter argues that, in answering the recurring central question of campaign finance doctrine—the question of whether political spending can be treated as speech and, if so, when and to what degree—the Court has employed two competing accounts of First Amendment value. Under the first of these theories, which I call the *volitional account*, the source of First Amendment value is the volitional impulse of the spender: the spender voluntarily dedicates an expenditure to a particular expressive purpose, thus generating First Amendment value in that particular expenditure. Under the second theory, which I call the *commodity account*, the market is the source of First Amendment value, which is quantified externally through market measures, such as dollar value, rather than through such individualistic and subjective measures as volition or intensity. The first part of this chapter explains that the *Buckley* Court's differential treatment of contributions and expenditures is partially grounded on differing accounts of the source of First Amendment value. *Buckley*'s so-called proxy speech rationale, justifying the marginal

First Amendment value accorded to contributions,[8] is predicated on the assumption that the source of First Amendment value is the volition of the spender. By contrast, the elevated First Amendment status accorded to campaign expenditures is based on a commodity account of First Amendment value.

The problem, of course, is that the two theories coexisting in the *Buckley* decision are in considerable tension: the volitional theory creates a hierarchy of value among different categories of spending based on how directly such spending advances the expressive intention of the spender, while the commodity theory treats each dollar of political spending as of presumptively equivalent value to any other dollar of political spending, regardless of any nexus with expressive intention. This constitutional fault line between the volitional and commodity accounts of First Amendment value would become increasingly unstable as the various permutations and innovations of modern campaign financing were tested in the courts. The second part of this chapter traces this constitutional fault line through the subsequent campaign finance case law as these two competing accounts of First Amendment value are embodied in various elements of campaign finance doctrine. Although the commodity rationale occasionally emerges, the volitional account appears to be the more prevalent in the Court's analysis of First Amendment campaign finance doctrine, until this year's *Citizens United* decision.

Citizens United marks a new high point for the commodity account and, moreover, presents a major extension of that theory by setting forth a "source-blind" approach to the regulation of money in politics that forbids the state from differentiating among different sources of political spending.[9] Under this theory, the First Amendment value of spending is assessed purely by reference to its commodity value. Under a fully commodified conception of speech, speakers drop out of the picture—the only constitutionally relevant interest is that of speech "consumers" to consume as large a quantity of speech as can be made available. The source-blind approach adopted in *Citizens United* appears to be profoundly at odds with the volitional account of First Amendment value underlying much of campaign finance doctrine—the volitional approach requires an inquiry into the degree to which a funding source can be deemed to advance the volitional impulse of the spender; the source-blind approach would seem to forbid such inquiry. The third part of the chapter outlines some of the destabilizing ramifications of this source-blind approach as a First Amendment theory that excludes any volitional considerations. In the conclusion, I argue that this fully commodified conception of speech fails, since the economic marketplace cannot be considered an adequate proxy for the marketplace of ideas that is the First Amendment's ultimate ideal.

Buckley v. Buckley: The Volitional Approach and the Commodity Approach

Contributions: The Volitional Approach

The Supreme Court's 1976 decision in *Buckley v. Valeo* is widely despised, and central to its unpopularity is its core holding that the First Amendment confers differential status upon contributions and expenditures. This distinction has been criticized with equal vehemence by both sides—those who argue that to treat the expenditure of funds as speech distorts the First Amendment beyond recognition, and those who argue that denying full First Amendment protection to contributions impermissibly restricts speech. The product of compromise, the contribution/expenditure distinction has survived less as settled doctrine than as détente: the demarcation line where both sides lay down their arms out of exhaustion, rather than as a result of negotiated surrender.

As explained below, the differential treatment of contributions and expenditures in this regard can best be understood as the result of the Court's application of two different theories of First Amendment value. The Court takes a volitional approach in its analysis of contributions, adopting a theory that treats individual volition as the source and requirement of the First Amendment value of political spending, while applying a commodity rationale for expenditures, which treats First Amendment value as externally quantifiable.

The *Buckley* Court begins by noting that both "contribution and expenditure limitations operate in an area of the most fundamental First Amendment activities," and explains that "discussion of public issues and debate on the qualifications of candidates are integral to the operation of the system."[10] But, the *Buckley* Court goes on to treat the two forms of campaign spending very differently—contributions are accorded only "marginal" First Amendment value, while expenditures are entitled to full First Amendment protection.

The Court bases its holding that contributions have only marginal First Amendment value on an argument known as the proxy speech rationale: that "the transformation of contributions into political debate involves speech by someone other than the contributor."[11] In an often-cited passage, the Court explains:

> A contribution serves as a general expression of support for the candidate and his views, but does not communicate the underlying basis for the support. The quantity of communication by the contributor does not increase perceptibly with the size of his contribution, since the expression rests solely on the undifferentiated, symbolic act of contributing. At most, the size of the contribution provides a very rough index of the intensity of the contributor's support for the candidate. A limitation on the amount of money a person may give to a candidate or campaign organization thus involves little direct restraint on his political communication, for it permits the symbolic expression of support evidenced by a contribution but does not in any way infringe the contributor's freedom to discuss candidates and issues. While contributions may result in political expression if spent by a candidate or an association to present views to the voters, the transformation of contributions into political debate involves speech by someone other than the contributor.[12]

As is evident from the passage above, a fundamental assumption of the proxy speech rationale is the truism that "freedom of speech presupposes a willing speaker"[13]—that is, money as speech must be *volitional*, or voluntarily dedicated to the purpose of expression. Money takes on First Amendment value only because it "serves as a general expression of support for the candidate and his views."[14] Accordingly, the First Amendment takes no notice of dollars sitting in a bank account, no more than it does of paint filling up a tube. It is only the spender's act of donating that is expressive, not the dollars themselves. Unlike a painting, novel, or any other durable type of First Amendment expression, a contribution, under *Buckley*'s reasoning, ceases to express anything of the spender's intent once the act of contributing has taken place, although the recipient is, of course, able in turn to dedicate the funds to her own expressive purpose. Thus, contributions, like proxy speech, are of lesser First Amendment value because the expressive value of the contribution to the contributor is extinguished in the transaction, even though the recipient's future use of the funds could accrue First Amendment significance.

In applying this volitional approach to the First Amendment treatment of political spending, the Supreme Court adopts a proxy speech analysis that features three significant attributes. The first attribute is that such First Amendment value is *non-monetizable*—as the Court points out, the expressive value of a contribution is *symbolic*, so that the quantity of expression it represents has no objective relationship to the amount of money in the contribution. As the Court explains, "At most, the size of the contribution provides a very rough index of the intensity of the contributor's support for the candidate."[15] After all, my $100 contribution might entail a substantial sacrifice on my part, in terms of my personal financial budget, and I might spend $100 only on the candidates and causes about which I care most passionately, although I might be willing to give smaller contributions to causes about which I feel less urgency. Once, however, my $100 contribution is removed from the context of my personal financial calculus, there is no longer any relationship between the amount of money and the intensity of my support. The $100 that represents a major financial commitment for me might be a mere token for a wealthier individual, disbursed as a matter of course to a great number of low-priority candidates and causes.

Second, under the proxy speech rationale, such money-as-speech is *liquid*—a sum of money intended to fund an expression of support for a candidate can be contributed to that candidate's campaign, can be donated to a third-party association that supports that candidate,[16] or can be spent by the supporter herself on communications in support of the candidate. As the *Buckley* majority explains:

> The overall effect of the Act's contribution ceilings is merely . . . to compel people who would otherwise contribute amounts greater than the statutory limits to expend such funds on direct political

expression, rather than to reduce the total amount of money potentially available to promote political expression.[17]

The *Buckley* Court treats these alternative channels as a constitutionally acceptable substitute for the original form of the intended spending.

Finally, under the proxy speech rationale, the First Amendment value of political spending is *intransitive*—the speech value a spender may assign to money does not automatically pass from one person to another in any given transaction. Thus, I might give $100 to a political candidate or party, and that contribution is expressive and carries First Amendment value. However, once that $100 leaves my account, it does not retain the same quantity or intensity of First Amendment value that I had assigned to it. After all, the candidate or political party who receives it may spend the funds on an expressive purpose—such as broadcasting a campaign advertisement—or a non-expressive purpose, such as renting office space, paying travel expenses, or hiring legal counsel. Even if the candidate does spend the funds on an expressive purpose, the expression is that of the candidate, not of the original spender.

Expenditures: Enter the Commodity Rationale

As noted above, in its analysis of contributions, the *Buckley* Court had confronted questions regarding the creation and retention of First Amendment value in otherwise constitutionally inert funds. By contrast, the Court takes the First Amendment value of such spending as a given with political expenditures. But notably, in holding that campaign expenditures are subject to the highest degree of First Amendment protection, the Court never straightforwardly endorses a First Amendment "freedom to spend" or otherwise directly equates speech and money.

Instead, the Court assumes a direct correlation between campaign expenditures and volitional speech. The Court remarks, for example, that the "plain effect" of the expenditure ceiling is "to prohibit all individuals . . . and all groups . . . from voicing their views 'relative to a clearly identified candidate' through means that entail aggregate expenditures of more than $1,000 during a calendar year."[18] In an expenditure, volition is not deemed exhausted because whatever transactions occur are assumed to be part of the speaker's original intent. For example, a spender may hire a producer to create an advertisement, but that transaction is not deemed to extinguish the volitional impulse of the spender: the advertisement is still considered the spender's speech so long as the spender retains ultimate control over the advertisement. Thus, rather than being deemed proxy speech, an expenditure is treated as a direct expression of the speaker's views (that is, one in which no transaction occurs in which the volitional impulse of the donation could be exhausted).

In addition, the Court bypasses the question of whether the First Amendment value of an expenditure is context-dependent (that is, tied to a particular organization or structure). Although the Court recognizes that political expenditures are liquid to some extent, the Court holds that the expenditure ceiling is impermissible since it forecloses multiple channels of advocacy, leaving an individual who wishes to spend more than the limit no lawful outlet to advocate for the election (or defeat) of a federal candidate. As the Court puts it, "The Act's dollar ceilings restrict the extent of the reasonable use of virtually every means of communicating information."[19] Thus, it is unnecessary for the Court to decide whether the First Amendment value of an expenditure is tied to any particular organizational context, since it holds that the expenditure ceilings limit *all* organizational contexts.

As I have just explained, it is possible to treat two of the attributes of proxy speech—its intransitivity and its liquidity—as simply inapplicable to direct political expenditures while still remaining consistent with a volitional account of First Amendment value. Where the *Buckley* Court's analysis is incompatible with a volitional theory is in its assumption that the First Amendment value of an expenditure has a direct correlation with its dollar value—in essence, that it is indeed monetizable or quantifiable. A purely volitional account of First Amendment value cannot account for the differential treatment of contributions and expenditures. After all, a contributor presumably feels the same level of "intensity" regarding a $100 contribution in support of a particular candidate as she does about a $100 expenditure. To put it another way, the Court's observation about contributions—"at most, the size of the contribution provides a very rough index of the intensity of the contributor's support for the candidate"[20]—would seem to apply with equal accuracy as a description of an expenditure.

Instead, only a separate theory of First Amendment value can adequately account for this differential treatment of contributions and expenditures. In its analysis of expenditures, the Supreme Court employs a commodity approach to First Amendment value that differs markedly from the volitional reasoning it had applied to its analysis of contributions. Under such a theory, an expenditure, as soon as it is made, enters the marketplace and is assigned an objective value that is not dependent on its volitional content. Accordingly, the *Buckley* Court suggests that the expenditure limits raise constitutional concerns because such a restriction "necessarily reduces the quantity of expression by restricting the number of issues discussed, the depth of their exploration, and the size of the audience reached."[21] Thus, the Court concluded that "expenditure ceilings impose direct and substantial restraints on the quantity of political speech."[22] Under a commodity rationale, any law that reduces the amount of communication—measured by dollar value—existing in the marketplace is a presumptive First Amendment violation.

In sum, the volitional theory and the commodity theory coexist, albeit somewhat uneasily, in the *Buckley* opinion. This uncomfortable cohabitation has continued as campaign finance doctrine has developed in the decades since.

The Post-*Buckley* Case Law: Dormancy and Dominance

Bellotti: The Commodity Approach's Former High-Water Mark

Two years after the *Buckley* Court employed the commodity account of First Amendment value, the Supreme Court, in a 5–4 decision, elevated this rationale to its former high-water mark in *First National Bank of Boston v. Bellotti*—one that persisted for over thirty years, until the *Citizens United* decision pushed the commodity rationale to even greater heights.

The *Bellotti* case concerned a constitutional challenge to a Massachusetts statute that broadly prohibited business corporations from making any direct or indirect expenditures for the purpose of "influencing or affecting the vote on any question submitted to the voters, other than one materially affecting any of the property, business or assets of the corporation."[23] Notably, unlike the federal corporate expenditures restriction at issue in *Citizens United*, the Massachusetts statute did not provide any means, such as a political action committee (PAC) or similar segregated fund, for the corporate point of view to be communicated to the general public. Thus, the Massachusetts statute arguably banned not simply a funding source, but also a viewpoint—the corporate position on certain ballot questions—making such issues subjects "about which corporations may never make their ideas public."[24]

In *Bellotti*, the Court was thus presented with an opportunity to rule on the question of whether corporations have "free speech rights." Under a volitional theory, to say that corporations "have" the same First Amendment rights as natural persons would be to say that the volitional impulse of a corporation is as valid a source of First Amendment value as the volitional impulse of an individual—that either is equally capable of imbuing otherwise inert funds with constitutional significance. To make such an argument would necessarily involve the Court in a philosophical question: What does it mean for a corporation to have volition or intentionality to express itself?

Rather than facing this question squarely, the Court sidestepped it, explaining that the First Amendment protects societal interests that might be broader than those of the party seeking vindication:

> The proper question therefore is not whether corporations "have" First Amendment rights and, if so, whether they are coextensive with those of natural persons. Instead, the question must be whether [the challenged law] abridges expression that the First Amendment was meant to protect. We hold that it does.[25]

While the *Buckley* Court had focused on the intention of the spender—whether her spending was intended to convey a message, and, if so, whether this message survived the transaction—the *Bellotti* Court focuses entirely on the *hearer*. Indeed, referring back to the deliberative goals of the First Amendment, the Court measures First Amendment value entirely from the perspective of the audience, referring to "the inherent worth of the speech in terms of its capacity for informing the public."[26] Such worth, according to the Court, "does not depend upon the identity of its source, whether corporation, association, union, or individual."[27]

But how is such a statement reconcilable with the holding of *Buckley*, which set up a hierarchy of First Amendment value depending on the directness with which a particular donation conveyed the volitional impulse of the spender? In order to hold that such value is not source-dependent, does not the Supreme Court have to answer the question that it claims it is not answering: whether corporations are equally capable of generating First Amendment value as individuals? In order to extricate itself from this bind, the *Bellotti* Court limits its inquiry to whether the First Amendment protects communications with a corporate source *at all*. The Massachusetts statute's total restriction on ballot issue communications with a corporate source enabled the Court to treat the source restriction on corporate funding as identical to a viewpoint restriction—the corporate point of view. The equation of source and viewpoint made possible by the all-encompassing nature of the Massachusetts restriction makes this a much easier case from a First Amendment perspective—since viewpoint restrictions are almost never constitutional—and allows the Court to avoid the more difficult question of the relative First Amendment value of corporate versus individual expression.

By avoiding the more difficult constitutional question, the *Bellotti* Court reaches a somewhat unstable compromise between the volitional and commodity approaches. The commodity approach answers a threshold question: Is the First Amendment implicated by a particular communication? Only once that threshold question is answered need a court reach questions regarding the relative value of particular types of political spending, and the *Bellotti* Court never ventures beyond this threshold.

MCFL, Austin, and *McConnell:* First Amendment Volition and Corporate Political Spending

As the Burger Court gave way to the Rehnquist Court, the Court faced renewed challenges to restrictions on corporate political spending. In three cases—*Federal Election Commission v. Massachusetts Citizens for Life, Inc.* (*MCFL*),[28] *Austin v. Michigan Chamber of Commerce*,[29] and *McConnell v. Federal Election Commission*[30]—the Court assessed the constitutionality of restrictions on corporate independent expenditures, which was the same topic the Court later considered in *Citizens United*. In upholding the constitutionality of the expenditures restriction in these three cases, the Court largely avoided the commodity account of First Amendment value, which underlies the *Buckley* Court's overturning of the federal expenditures ceiling. Instead, the Court in these three cases seemed to import volitional reasoning into the expenditures arena.

The net result was a compromise that survived for over twenty years, until *Citizens United*—namely that when restrictions on corporate political expenditures lack a volitional nexus, they pass constitutional muster.

In a 5–4 decision in *MCFL*, the Court struck down the federal corporate expenditure restriction as applied to nonprofit ideological advocacy corporations that had no shareholders and that did not accept contributions from for-profit corporations or unions. The Court based its holding on the fact that "individuals who contribute to appellee are fully aware of its political purposes, and in fact contribute precisely because they support those purposes."[31] Accordingly, the Court reasoned that such nonprofits "have features more akin to voluntary political associations than business firms, and therefore should not have to bear burdens on independent spending solely because of their incorporated status."[32] Rather than treating such political expenditures as liquid—so that a state could constitutionally require that one organizational form be used rather than another—a plurality of the Court ruled that the separate segregated funds requirement imposed a "substantial" restriction on speech, at least for ideological nonprofits.[33] Thus, for expenditures, the *MCFL* Court deemed First Amendment significance to attach to the organizational structure through which they are spent, while viewing contributions as liquid—the expressive intention could be diverted to other organizations and forms of spending without imposing a burden on speech.

While treating the First Amendment value of political expenditures as monetizable—having a direct correlation with the amount spent—for ideological nonprofits, the *MCFL* Court emphasized that no such assumption should apply to the treasury funds of business corporations. Thus, the *MCFL* Court reasoned that, at least for political (as opposed to business) organizations, "relative availability of funds is after all a rough barometer of public support."[34] The Court, however, distinguished the treasuries of business corporations as lacking such a volitional nexus:

> The resources in the treasury of a business corporation, however, are not an indication of popular support for the corporation's political ideas. They reflect instead the economically motivated decisions of investors and customers. The availability of these resources may make a corporation a formidable political presence, even though the power of the corporation may be no reflection of the power of its ideas.[35]

Indeed, the Court identified the corporate expenditures restriction for business corporations as "meant to ensure that competition among actors in the political arena is truly competition among ideas."[36] But although the *MCFL* Court reasoned that the treasury funds of a business corporation are not directly related to any expressive intention of shareholders, the structure of the Court's decision suggested that strict scrutiny should apply to all political expenditures—whether by business corporations or by ideological nonprofits. Although the narrow holding of *MCFL* was limited to ideological nonprofits, the Court's analysis treated all corporate political expenditures as *prima facie* entitled to the highest level of First Amendment protection.

Four years later, *Austin* expanded on *MCFL*'s reasoning, explaining that business corporate expenditures risk a "distortion" of our political discourse because the immensity of corporate treasuries bears no relation to the popular support for the ideas advanced therewith.[37] Although the *Citizens United* majority later overruled *Austin* as an "aberration,"[38] its holding in fact closely followed the reasoning of the *MCFL* Court. In *Austin*, the Court considered a Michigan statute that, like the federal corporate expenditure restriction, prohibited corporations from using treasury funds for independent expenditures in support of or in opposition to state candidates.[39] As under federal law, corporations could make such expenditures only through a separate segregated fund.[40]

Notably, although *Austin* dealt with political expenditures, it treated such expenditures in a manner more consistent with *Buckley*'s treatment of political contributions—as low value, proxy speech. Specifically, the Court first treated such expressive value as non-monetizable: corporate treasuries risk a "distortion" of the political process because their accumulated funds "have little or no correlation to the public's support for the corporation's political ideas."[41] Second, the Court treated the volitional impulse of shareholders as liquid: the PAC requirement was held not to be a "ban" on the viewpoints expressed, but instead was deemed a means to ensure that "the speech generated accurately reflects contributors' support for the corporation's political views."[42] Third, the Court treated the shareholder's volitional impulse as intransitive: the political spending of the corporation was not deemed to advance the volitional impulse of the shareholder without a specific dedication by the shareholder of such funds for political uses. This treatment of the corporate expenditures as non-monetizable, liquid, and transitive would seem to indicate that the *Austin* Court deemed such expenditures to be low-value First Amendment speech. But rather than holding that such corporate expenditures had low First Amendment *value*, the *Austin* Court employed the nonmonetizable, liquid, and transitive nature of corporate expenditures as support for the state's asserted interest in the expenditure restrictions.

McConnell follows upon the reasoning in *Austin* thirteen years later, further strengthening the congruence between the law on political contributions and for-profit corporate expenditures. Indeed, in its discussion of the corporate expenditures restriction, the *McConnell* Court quotes at length from the decision in *Federal Elections Commission v. Beaumont*, a case regarding the ban on corporate *contributions*:

> The PAC option allows corporate political participation without the temptation to use corporate funds for political influence, quite possibly at odds with the sentiments of some shareholders or members, and it lets the government regulate campaign activity through registration and disclosure without jeopardizing the associational rights of advocacy organizations' members.[43]

Like the relatively marginal First Amendment value of political contributions, the First Amendment value of corporate expenditures is deemed to be nonmonetizable and liquid. This value is undiminished, even though the PAC requirement places both spending limits and organizational requirements on such corporate political spending. Once again, corporate political speech is treated in a manner similar to the treatment of low-value speech, but the Court imports these volitional arguments into a state-interests rationale.

Citizens United and the Ascendancy of the Commodity Account

At the advent of the Roberts Court, the campaign finance case law had developed two nearly mirror-image categories of political spending: contributions having First Amendment value that is non-monetizable, liquid, and intransitive; and expenditures possessing First Amendment significance that is monetizable, organizationally rooted, and transitive. The doctrine applying to contributions and that applying to expenditures both employed volitional rhetoric, but reached nearly diametrically opposed results. Under a volitional theory, the Court had been primarily concerned with the development and refinement of First Amendment hierarchies—contribution versus expenditure, direct versus proxy, ideological versus for-profit—in which First Amendment value was assessed with respect to the spender's original expressive intent. At the same time, the commodity account that the *Buckley* Court had partially endorsed and that the *Bellotti* Court had applied as a threshold question of First Amendment value had remained largely dormant throughout the development of the campaign finance case law.

The Commodity Approach in Ascendance

Citizens United represents a change of direction away from the volitional theory that was prevalent in the rhetoric and reasoning of previous Court majorities and towards the ascendancy of the commodity conception of First Amendment value. Indeed, while the volitional account and the commodity account had coexisted—albeit uneasily—over decades of campaign finance doctrine, the *Citizens United* majority articulates a radical version of the commodity account—a source-blind approach that would appear inconsistent with the volitional account, at least if applied to contributions as well as expenditures. In contrast to the doctrinal hierarchies of the volitional rationale, the *Citizens United* majority's view of speech commodities is flattened out: the majority opinion simply does not concern itself with inquiring into the source of First Amendment value, much less whether political spending maintains the volitional intent of a particular contributor. Instead, the majority adopts—and thereby constitutionalizes—a source-blind conception of First Amendment value: "the worth of speech 'does not depend upon the identity of its source, whether corporation, association, union, or individual.'"[44]

Under the *Citizens United* majority's account of First Amendment value, an expenditure on political communication, in the instant that it is made, is commodified; it enters into the economic marketplace and receives a market value. Such a market value is measured not from the perspective of the generator of the communication—the speaker or spender—but by the marketplace, which assigns an objective and quantifiable value to the communication, which is correlated to its monetary worth. The First Amendment terrain that the Court envisions is one of preexisting speech commodities with values corresponding to the economic marketplace. In the Court's view, each dollar of political spending is a quantum of presumptively equivalent First Amendment value, and any attempt to differentiate between these quanta would involve the state in impermissible discrimination.

Is *Citizens United* on a Collision Course with *Buckley*?

The *Citizens United* Court's seemingly simple source-blind doctrine has potentially sweeping implications for the law of campaign finance reform, at least if taken literally. After all, most federal and state campaign finance laws are predicated upon a system of source and amount restrictions that make distinctions among funds from corporations, political action committees, political parties, and individuals. Moreover, much of campaign finance jurisprudence is predicated on the framework set forth in *Buckley* that contributions, as proxy speech, are entitled to lesser First Amendment protection than political expenditures. Notably, while the *Citizens United* Court distinguishes the First Amendment case law on contributions, it does so only on the grounds that contributions have been held to have a definite nexus with "*quid pro quo* corruption," a nexus that the Court holds is absent as to independent expenditures.[45] The Court does not mention the better-known holding of *Buckley*, the proxy speech rationale, deeming contributions to have only marginal First Amendment value. Can *Buckley*'s contribution/expenditures rationale long survive if one half of the doctrine—contributions—necessitates hierarchical distinctions based on spender volition, while the other half of the doctrine—expenditures—expressly forbids any such inquiry and deems any hierarchical treatment constitutionally suspect?[46] As demonstrated below, the assumptions the *Citizens United* majority makes about the nature of corporate political spending are directly in conflict with the volitional assumptions underlying *Buckley*'s core holdings.

First Amendment Monetization: Money as Speech. First of all, as explained above, the *Buckley* Court's proxy rationale treated the First Amendment value of political contributions as non-monetizable—that is, the amount of such contributions bore no direct correlation to the First Amendment value of the funded expression. Conversely, the First Amendment value of political expenditures was deemed to be directly correlated with the amount of money expended. But, in *MCFL*, *Austin*, and *McConnell*, the Court had specifically disclaimed the application of this approach to spending by business corporations, reasoning that corporate treasury funds could not be deemed a "barometer" of popular support because corporate funds did not represent an exercise of political volition by shareholders. *Citizens United* overturns this distinction, rejecting *Austin* and *McConnell*'s "distortion" rationale directly, and rejecting *MCFL*'s "barometer" distinction by implication. The majority opinion derogates the "distortion" rationale as simple equalization[47]—the attempt to discriminate against corporate sources simply because they, unlike ordinary citizens, have access to "immense aggregations of wealth that are accumulated with the help of the corporate form."[48]

But, as explained above, such bald equalization was never the driving force behind the "distortion" rationale. Indeed, the *Austin* Court had explicitly recognized that "the mere fact that corporations may accumulate large amounts of wealth is not the justification for [the expenditures restriction]."[49] Instead, the *Austin* and *McConnell* Courts reasoned—in terms reminiscent of the volitional approach—that funds that "have little or no correlation to the public's support for the corporation's political ideas" risked distorting the political process.[50] But under the *Citizens United* Court's commodity account of First Amendment value, the First Amendment values of all political expenditures are treated as monetizable, whether or not they have any nexus with the expressive volition of an actual person.

First Amendment Illiquidity: The Rigidity of the Corporate Form. *Buckley* took a liquid approach to the First Amendment value of political contributions. If the expressive volition of the contributor could not express itself fully through contributions to a candidate or political party, such volition could be diverted to other channels—independent expenditures or political organizations—without substantial diminishment. As the case and statutory law developed, PACs were deemed a constitutionally sufficient outlet for the expressive volition of political spending. Nonetheless, Justice Kennedy's opinion treats the First Amendment value of corporate political spending as absolutely illiquid, finding the requirement that corporations spend through PACs as the simple equivalent of censorship. For Justice Kennedy, that requirement constitutes an "outright ban." But, given that generations of Courts had held that the PAC alternative gave constitutionally sufficient room for the expression of the "corporate point-of-view," it is unclear on what evidence Justice Kennedy bases this novel characterization.

First Amendment Transitivity: Avoiding Corporate Personhood. The source-blind approach adopted by the *Citizens United* Court allows the Court to sidestep the issue of transitivity and, with it, perhaps the most mystifying question in the First Amendment treatment of corporate political spending: whose speech are we talking about? Is it that of management, the shareholders, or the corporate "person" itself? Although *Citizens United* was widely reported in the press as granting First Amendment rights to corporations, the majority opinion notably lacked a full-throated defense of the concept of corporate personhood. The majority never outright says that corporate political expenditures represent an expression of the political opinions of the corporation—after all, a corporation no more "has" political opinions than it has a favorite color. But under a volitional theory, value is generated in otherwise constitutionally inert funds only through an exercise of political volition. What is the source of the First Amendment value of spending from corporate treasuries?

In *Buckley*, the Court had treated expressive volition as *intransitive*, at least with regard to political contributions; the speech of a "proxy," such as a party or candidate, is not deemed to advance the volitional impulse of the contributor. But when dealing with corporate political spending, who is the relevant speaker whose volitional impulse should be taken into account? One option is that the communication expresses the "volition" of the corporation. But to take this option would require the Court to hold directly that a corporation is a First Amendment "person" and is an equally legitimate source of "volition" as a natural person. Thus far, the Court has been unwilling to argue this point directly, instead following *Bellotti*'s avoidance of this issue.[51]

The other option would be that a corporate communication could derive its First Amendment value from the shareholders' initial dedication of the funds to a communicative purpose. This explanation, however, lacks plausibility, at least for business corporations. It is difficult to argue that a shareholder's purchase of shares conveys any volitional impulse that would imbue these funds with First Amendment value. Similarly, it is hard to conceptualize a business corporation as an "association" in the First Amendment sense, so that any volitional impulse of the shareholder could be deemed subsumed in the expression of the corporation. In any case, if the First Amendment value of a corporate political expenditure derived from the will of the shareholders its value would seem to be more akin to the marginal value accorded to contributions or other "speech by proxy" than to the heightened First Amendment value accorded to direct political expenditures.

Instead of deciding between these two options and settling the question of whose speech is at issue, Justice Kennedy's opinion simply avoids the issue. Under the source-blind, fully commodified view of speech adopted by the majority, speakers are almost absent from the picture—there are only speech commodities and speech consumers, and the only relevant values are the values of the economic marketplace.

Conclusion: Quantity without Quality?

The *Citizens United* majority opinion posits a radically simplistic vision of the First Amendment as applied to money in politics. In the Court's view, all speech commodities are of equivalent First Amendment value—whether they represent the political conviction of an individual or the profit-maximizing impetus of a business corporation. Thus, a court need not grapple with difficult questions of relative First Amendment value—the *quality* of the speech at issue. Instead, the court's only determination is a mechanical assessment of *quantity*. The majority's reasoning takes the following form:

1. Political speech is a First Amendment good.
2. Therefore, more speech is better than less speech.
3. Therefore, any law restricting speech is a prima facie violation of the First Amendment.

Money enters into the equation only as it pertains to speech quantity:

1. Money, in the form of political spending, can lead to the creation of speech.
2. Therefore, more money results in more speech.

3. Therefore, any law restricting political spending is a *prima facie* violation of the First Amendment.

Under this source-blind vision, whether a campaign advertisement is funded by an individual, a group of individuals, or a corporation makes no difference to the First Amendment value of such an advertisement. Indeed, for the state to distinguish among such advertisements based on source is to engage in impermissible discrimination.

One can readily understand the surface appeal of such a source-blind approach—it holds out the illusion of neutrality to judges to whom inquiries into First Amendment value seem uncomfortably close to content—or even viewpoint-based discrimination. But the source-blind approach is highly troubling because its veneer of neutrality conceals a deeper and more fundamental inequality. As the Supreme Court remarked in *Buckley*, "sometimes the grossest discrimination can lie in treating things that are different as though they were exactly alike."[52] Just as there would be nothing neutral about a race event that pitted a human runner against a race car, there is nothing neutral about a free market of ideas that requires individuals to outspend corporate treasuries in order to make their ideas available to the electorate.

The difference between individual and corporate election spending does not merely inhere in the aggregate amounts of money available to each—nor even in the relative advantages each enjoys in terms of the ability to amass and spend capital. Instead the difference inheres most fundamentally, and irreducibly, in the First Amendment value of the political spending of each. The volitional approach taken by the *Buckley* Court and by subsequent generations of courts was one effort to account for *quality* as well as quantity in confronting the vexed question of First Amendment value. Grappling with this question, as this chapter has tracked, embroiled the Court in fine distinctions and in doctrinal quandaries. But to abandon the question of First Amendment value is no solution—it is to put our politics and our constitutional values on the auction block.

Part III

Corruption and Democracy

Can Political Spending Undermine Our Republic?

8

On Political Corruption

*Samuel Issacharoff**

Lurking beneath the surface of all debates on campaign finance is a visceral revulsion over future leaders of state groveling for money. The process of fund-raising is demeaning to any claim of a higher calling in public service and compromises candidates, policies, donors, and anyone in proximity to the bleakest side of the electoral process. The intuition is that, at some level, money must be corrupting of the political process, and that something must be done to limit the role of money. The same logic dictates that less money is better than more money, and that successful reform must bring down the cost of modern electoral campaigning.

It is the logic of constricting the effects of money that has defined the modern era of campaign finance reform, an era that began after the Watergate scandals and is now completing its fourth decade. Time and again, the impetus behind the reform effort has been to depress the amount of money spent in campaigns and thereby limit the associated moral stain. So long as a stench attaches to money and by extension those who seek to direct political outcomes with money, the cause of campaign reform takes the high road. If money is the root of all evil, the logic runs inescapably to reducing the amount of money in the system.

* An earlier, longer version of this piece appeared in *The Harvard Law Review.* Reprinted by permission of the Harvard Law Review Association and William S. Hein Company from *The Harvard Law Review*, Vol. 124, pages 118–142.

With these efforts at limitation comes the inevitable result that some speakers will be handicapped in expressing their views, and that the total quantity of speech will be curtailed. For a persistent minority of justices on the U.S. Supreme Court, the claim that money is not speech lends constitutional cover to the search for a way to squeeze money out of politics. In turn, it is this attempt to restrain the amount of money in the system that runs headlong not only into the teeth of the constitutional concern of the majority of the Court, but also into the brute fact of the increased scale and complexity of campaigning for contested office.

This restrictive aspect of the reform agenda is ultimately both its strength and its constitutional liability. Constitutionally, it is the efforts to limit the spending of political campaigns—if not directly speech, then certainly "speechy enough"[1]—that have occasioned a long line of losses for reform efforts, with *Citizens United* but the last in an almost unbroken streak. In its approach to money and politics, *Citizens United* continues the troubled tradition of *Buckley v. Valeo* in drawing the divide between political contributions and expenditures. The former gives rise to potential regulation in order to combat a poorly specified corruption of the political process—a concept to which I return below—while the latter is seen as the domain of expressive liberties that the state may not seek to restrict.

Academic commentary has long had a field day with the core contributions-versus-expenditures rationale of *Buckley*. The division between a system that limits contributions but leaves expenditures unchecked runs afoul of the animating logic of the 1974 campaign finance amendments, and is in fact a regulatory structure created by the Court.[2] Even persistent majorities of the Court have rejected the *Buckley* divide between contributions and expenditures, with only a divide over which way to topple *Buckley* serving to shore up a frayed body of law.[3] Whether framed as the incoherence[4] of doctrines or simply as a doctrinal approach that proved not workable over time,[5] critics scored easy hits on the Court's attempt to muddle through the difficult issue of money and politics.[6]

I want to take *Citizens United* as a launching point to accept the Court's long-standing invitation to use the contribution side of the divide as a vehicle to shore up the vulnerabilities of democracy. My inquiry begins with the contested terrain over the nature of political corruption. Once the Supreme Court announced in *Buckley* that the concern over corruption or even its appearance could justify limitations on money in politics, the race was on to fill the porous concept of corruption with every conceivable meaning that advocates could muster. As with the elusive term "diversity" after *Buckley*'s contemporary, *Bakke v. Board of Regents*,[7] a thin constitutional reed transformed the lexicon of political debate. My argument is that, by altering the corruption concern and moving it away from efforts to depress political expenditures, there may be some measures that both satisfy constitutional scrutiny and address the financial vulnerabilities of democracy. A reorientation toward corruption in the outputs of policymaking suggests effective solutions compatible with the Court's strong constitutional stance in *Citizens United*.

What Is Corruption?

The Majority View: "Quid Pro Quo" Corruption

Prior to *Citizens United*, the Court had struggled between two competing sources of potential corruption resulting from the financing of political campaigns. A fairly consistent majority position, beginning in *Buckley v. Valeo*, focused on the capacity for the corruption of candidates who aimed to ingratiate themselves to their wealthy backers. Such corruption was defined in terms of actual quid pro quo arrangements, while allowing more expansively for the potential dispiriting influence of the appearance of such arrangements.[8]

Under the logic of this majority view, such arrangements corrupt the political process because they are surreptitious deals that bypass the mechanisms of political accountability. Thus, the Court fastened on the distinction between coordinated and uncoordinated activity in the electoral context as the defining line for what *Buckley* deemed could be regulated: "the absence of prearrangement and coordination undermines the value of the expenditure to the candidate, and thereby alleviates the danger that expenditures will be given as a quid pro quo for improper commitments from the candidate."[9]

Most clearly, in *First National Bank v. Bellotti*, the Court held that a banking corporation could not be prohibited from spending money in opposition to a ballot initiative because such initiatives do not have candidates and there could accordingly be no risk of any quid pro quo corruption.[10] Over Justice Byron White's dissent on the undue influence wielded by corporations, Justice Lewis F. Powell retreated to the liberty arguments of the First Amendment: "The fact that advocacy may persuade the electorate is hardly a reason to suppress it: The Constitution protects expression which is eloquent no less than that which is unconvincing."[11]

The Minority View: The Distorting Influence of Wealth

An alternative view on the Court has approached corruption as a distortion of political outcomes resulting from the undue influence of wealth.[12] According to this view, the source of corruption was large expenditures capturing the marketplace of political ideas;[13] the corrupted entities were, at bottom, the voters who could only succumb to the entreaties of money. Corruption itself is poorly defined in this view, and appears to be a problem that is merely "derivative" of broader societal inequalities.[14] As formulated in *Austin v. Michigan Chamber of Commerce*, the only case to adopt squarely the "distortion of electoral outcomes" view of corruption, the inequities born of wealth are compounded by the unnatural ability of corporations to amass wealth more readily than individuals,[15] although the logic extends to all disparities in electoral influence occasioned by differences in wealth.[16]

The animating logic behind this approach to corruption is the equality protections of democracy on the political process; this equality rationale provides a doctrinal justification for restricting expenditures.[17] The claim that money is not speech has been absolutely critical to distance the proposed governmental restrictions from traditional First Amendment concerns, particularly as the proposed restrictions were often justified on the basis of the content of the speech, or even the viewpoint of the speaker. Wealth, particularly corporate wealth, allowed those with "'resources amassed in the economic marketplace' to obtain 'an unfair advantage in the political marketplace.'"[18]

Although generally disregarded, *Austin* held precariously to life, especially in the hearts of reform advocates.[19] Justice David

Souter, in *Nixon v. Shrink Missouri Government PAC*, sought to retool the approach by tying the undue influence argument to the appearance of corruption: "Leave the perception of impropriety unanswered, and the cynical assumption that large donors call the tune could jeopardize the willingness of voters to take part in democratic governance."[20] Most centrally, in *McConnell v. Federal Election Commission*, the case that upheld most of the Bipartisan Campaign Reform Act (BCRA)[21] against constitutional challenge, the Court adopted a highly deferential view of congressional authority and allowed disproportionate electoral influence to stand in for corruption in upholding campaign limitations.[22] Ultimately, however, *Austin* could not be reconciled with the core analytic structure of *Buckley*. If the prohibition of wealth-based distortions of politics were the ultimate aim, then drawing a constitutional line between contributions and expenditures would make no sense. To distort political outcomes requires distorting appeals to the voters, something that of necessity occurs on the expenditure side of the ledger.

Citizens United and the Triumph of "Quid Pro Quo" Corruption

Citizens United closed the circle on the *Buckley* scenario. In expressly overruling *Austin*,[23] the Court has now struck down anything categorized as an expenditure limitation (unless found to be coordinated with a candidate and thereby a way of circumventing contribution limitations),[24] while at the same time upholding virtually all contribution limits, except in the rare case where they are so low as to threaten the viability of the ensuing political debates.[25] Ultimately, *Citizens United* rejected a claimed governmental interest in "equalizing the relative ability of individuals and groups to influence the outcome of elections,"[26] and refused to allow the concern over the "undue influence" of money to serve as a form of corruption that justifies regulation.[27] For Justice Anthony Kennedy, only the risk of explicit quid pro quo corruption appears to survive as a basis for regulating campaign finance.[28] Corruption proved not as malleable as *Austin* might have indicated.

The Corruption of Politics

Refocusing Corruption on the Problem of Clientelism

Any system of privately financed campaigns invites strategic use of money to influence public officials. So far, the debates at the Supreme Court have asked only whether the candidates are corrupted through illicit quid pro quo arrangements, or per the dissents, whether electoral outcomes are distorted as a result of concentrated corporate and private wealth. The case law has set off on a multi-decade search for a workable definition of just what is corrupt as opposed to benign when aspiring public officials solicit money to further their ambitions.

An alternative take on the problem of corruption of the political process would suggest that both of these definitions miss the mark. Each is concerned with the improper influences on the selection of candidates for office. While the influence of the well-heeled may be a concern, and while the prospect of out-and-out corruption is a serious issue, there is an alternative concern, perhaps the more serious problem, that looks not to inputs into who holds office, but to the outputs in terms of the policies that result from an elected class looking to future support in order to retain the perquisites of office. On this view, the underlying problem is not so much what happens in the electoral arena but what incentives are offered to officeholders *while in office*. While the question of holding office remains key, the focus shifts to how the electoral process drives the discharge of public duties. Specifically, the inquiry on officeholding asks whether the electoral system leads the political class to offer private gain from public action to distinct, tightly organized constituencies, who in turn may be mobilized to keep compliant public officials in office.

The outputs account of corruption is concerned with the subversion of the classic account of the role of government as a provider of public goods, such as security, environmental protection, foreign relations—matters from which private initiative cannot realize gains and that in turn require public coordination. It is precisely this benevolent use of public authority to overcome the collective action barriers to the production of public goods that is increasingly subject to challenge. The public choice accounts of recent political economy claim instead that the existence of public power is an occasion for motivated special interests to seek to capture the power of government not to create public goods, but to realize private gains through subversion of state authority.

This strategy—identified in the political science literature as *clientelism*—defies easy categorization as corruption under current campaign finance law precisely because the concern is what happens in office, rather than during the election campaign.[29] At its simplest, clientelism is a patron-client relationship in which political support (votes, attendance at rallies, money) is exchanged for privileged access to public goods.[30] The concept differs in emphasis from quid pro quo corruption. The traditional account of corruption assumes that the harm is the private benefit obtained by the politician. While the concept of quid pro quo corruption is ample enough to include almost any benefit obtained, the focus of clientelism is not the enrichment of an individual politician, but continued office-holding on the condition that "party politicians distribute public jobs or special favors in exchange for electoral support."[31] For all democracies, there are aspects of clientelism in any responsiveness to constituent interests.[32] A pathology ensues when political decisions are made to allow important sectional supporters "to gain privileged access to public resources" for profit.[33] Weak political parties and candidates with difficulty holding a programmatic electoral base begin to rely on patron-client networks to retain their positions.[34] "As it becomes increasingly costly to connect with groups of voters, candidates prefer to organize smaller subsets of the electorate and target them with larger transfers."[35]

The pathology of clientelism then rewards incumbent politicians for an expansion of the public sector in a way that facilitates sectional rewards to constituent groups.[36] Private gain may abound in large-scale government enterprise that is non-transparent to the public and that resists either monitoring or accountability. The extreme form is the earmark, which does not even require formal identification of its existence.[37]

Implications of Clientelism for Reform

Unfortunately, any attempt to act on the danger of clientelism runs into the inescapable problem that government is a blur of the high-minded and the petty, and that it is often difficult to distinguish between rewards to constituents and matters of policy and principle. The American recognition of the risk of legislation in the private interest dates at least to *The Federalist No. 10,* in which Madison identified as a central problem of republican governance the ability to resist "a number of citizens . . . who are united and actuated by some common impulse of passion, or of interest, adverse to the rights of other citizens, or to the permanent and aggregate interests of the community."[38] The Framers appear to have conceptualized corruption as a derogation of the public trust more than as the narrow opportunity for surreptitious gain.[39] But the distinction between public and private regarding legislation is difficult, and efforts to try to review legislation on the basis of its public-regarding character have largely failed.[40] The debate over whether political initiative is dominated by public or private purposes proves to be too great an invitation to reargue the politics of legislation that any particular group finds objectionable.[41]

Despite the difficulty in drawing clear substantive lines, there are concerns that our political process introduces pathways for private motivations to capture the use of governmental processes—and that these may not be pathways but rather avenues, boulevards, perhaps express lanes. Clientelist pressures erode public institutions with incentives to increase the size, complexity, and non-transparency of governmental decisionmaking, with the corresponding impetus simply to increase the relative size of the public sector, often beyond the limits of what the national economy can tolerate. Political accountability through a robust and competitive political system may check some pressures toward the excessive rewarding of private constituencies through public authority.[42] But, if unchecked, clientelism breeds the perception of "systemic corruption, which cripples institutional trust and public confidence in the political system"[43]—a parallel to the Court's concern in *Buckley* over the detrimental effects of the appearance of quid pro quo corruption.

No doubt money is at the root of the problem, but the problem is not limited to the wealthy or the corporations or even the institutional actors such as public sector unions or Indian tribes. Like the overbroad prohibition on corporate independent expenditures that proved problematic in *Citizens United,*[44] simply trying to root out money in undifferentiated fashion miscasts the problem of the compromise of public authority. More closely hewn, the issue is not money as such but the potential private capture of the powers of the state. The Supreme Court acknowledged this concern a year prior in *Caperton v. A. T. Massey Coal Co.*,[45] in which the Court ruled unconstitutional a state judge sitting in judgment on a case involving a major campaign supporter. *Caperton* suggests a concern for the ability to use privileged positions in the democratic process to gain control over the exercise of governmental authority. Under this view, the problem is not the ability to deploy exceptional resources in election campaigns, but the incentives operating on governmental officials to bend their official functions to accommodate discrete constituencies.

The risk of private-regarding legislation is heightened when groups are able to bypass the normal process[46] of interest group bargaining in favor of securing benefits for groups with special holds on government. Ordinary democratic politics may be a messy and imprecise construct, but the contrast is to groups that have dual mechanisms of influence over political outcomes—that is, claims both within and outside of the political process.[47] For example, several decades ago Professors Harry H. Wellington and Ralph K. Winter found public sector unions to possess such double claims of interest, thus exercising "a disproportionate share of effective power in the process of decision."[48]

If we look beyond campaign finance, there has been some recognition of clientelist-style double claims on the political process, particularly with regard to government contractors. Beginning with a 1940 amendment to the Hatch Act, all federal government contractors were prohibited from "mak[ing] any contribution, to any political party, committee, or candidate for public office or to any person for any political purpose or use," during the period of contract negotiation or performance.[49] That prohibition does not turn on the form of organization as a corporation, a partnership, or an individual contractor—indeed, the Tillman Act has prohibited corporate contributions to candidates for federal office since 1907[50]—but rather on the same idea that contractors engage the decisionmaking processes of elected officials in dual fashion.[51] While this provision has never been in the Supreme Court, parallel provisions of the Hatch Act have been twice upheld against constitutional challenge.[52]

The prohibition on contractor contributions in federal elections continues in force and was basically integrated into the 1974 election reforms of the Federal Election Campaign Act (FECA), though somewhat weakened by expressly allowing contractors to make contributions to political activities through political action committees.[53] In its current form, federal election law not only prohibits federal contractors from making contributions for any purpose related to a federal election,[54] but also makes it illegal for anyone to "knowingly solicit" such contributions.[55] Whatever their limitations, the restrictions on contractor contributions attempt to insulate politics from the demands of those who would use public power for private aims. As with the arguments advanced by Wellington and Winter in the context of public employee strikes, the basic intuition is that claims on the decisions of political officeholders should be played out in the political process, and that legal means must be sought to shut down the mechanisms that induce politicians to contort the outputs of the political process for the gain of the few at the expense of the many.

A Clientelist Approach to Pay-to-Play Regulation

In light of *Citizens United,* the question arises whether parties in contractual relations with public bodies may be prohibited not only from contributing to the campaigns of elected officials, but also from directing independent expenditures to elections for the same officials. There is significant constitutional risk in crossing the divide from contributions to expenditures, and the overwhelming body of doctrine reveals a high barrier to any congressional efforts along this line,[56] with only the now-aging Hatch Act cases offering a safe harbor. Nonetheless, a prohibition on contractor expenditures in connection with the election of public officials with whom they contract would be premised on the risk of improper conduct (that is, the state's interest in preventing corruption or the appearance of corruption) rather than on the disfavored status of corporations as such.

While *Citizens United* gave new vitality to the fundamental *Buckley* divide between contributions and expenditures, it did not exhaust the possible range of concerns occasioned by how money is utilized. When abstracted from the broader rhetoric on the role of corporations, the majority opinion in *Citizens United* is actually less sweeping than might appear. The Court is concerned only with the inputs to the electoral process, not the outputs of the ensuing legislative process. Thus, in overturning *Austin*, Justice Kennedy concluded that *Buckley* categorically prohibited regulations aimed at "equalizing the relative ability of individuals and groups to influence the *outcome* of elections."[57] Similarly, Justice Kennedy distinguishes *Caperton*[58] as distinctly about post-election conduct, not campaign speech: "*Caperton's* holding was limited to the rule that the judge must be recused, not that the litigant's political speech could be banned."[59]

A tightly drawn prohibition that is premised on the effects of "pay-to-play" on public policy could survive as a constitutional first step, and might even be welcomed by the subjects of the regulation as a protection against being shaken down for campaign expenditures by public officials, in much the same way that the prohibition on federal employee contributions was designed to avoid coerced solicitations of money. Likewise, the protections offered by the Hatch Act amendments may be broadened by prohibiting contractors from engaging in expenditures through political action committees (PACs), political groups operating under Section 527 of the tax code, or bundling efforts without running afoul of the underlying rationale in *Citizens United*. Admittedly, these are partial steps. Such measures would be only a partial inroad into the accompanying world of lobbying and the sector of the economy that does not face incumbent state officials as contracting parties but as subjects of regulation.[60] Nonetheless, such approaches do offer alternative insights into the problem of money, not so much in terms of election outcomes but in terms of public policy. Whether an incumbent Congress would welcome such legislation is another matter.

Does Money Necessarily Corrupt?

The most striking and perhaps the oddest feature of *Citizens United* is no doubt the extravagant endowment of rights upon corporate actors, a result that appeared to reach beyond what was necessary to strike down an overbroad restriction on contributions. But that fact alone does not signal that the Court was doing the bidding of corporate interests eager to further engage the electoral arena. For most corporations, elections are noisy events that may prove a poor forum for advancing their interests. Most publicly traded corporations do not want to be associated with controversial positions on social issues that define many election campaigns, such as abortion or capital punishment. At their core, corporations are business rivals, and there are substantial collective action problems preventing them from coordinating in the political arena, except through trade associations such as the Chamber of Commerce. That is why corporations have difficulty overcoming the concentrated pull of public employee unions, even on matters of concern to the business community.[61] PACs funded from individually pooled funds provide a way to signal support for candidates without opening the corporate treasury to ever-ravenous politicians.[62]

To pursue the direct interests of a particular corporation, moreover, lobbying is a more effective means of securing desired ends, and the amounts that appear to be spent on lobbying rather than campaign activities (even in states that permit contributions) reflect corporate understanding that the work of securing compliant government is best carried out in the legislative rather than electoral arena.[63] The likeliest source of interest of corporations in the legislative arena is gaining a competitive advantage on rivals or other sources of economic challenge, something that further stands in the way of concerted activity in politics generally.[64] The corporations that do wish regularly to engage in speech turn out to be either the ideological organizations that have plagued the campaign finance case law (for example, Massachusetts Citizens for Life,[65] Wisconsin Right to Life[66]) or closely held companies, including publicly traded corporations still dominated by a founding family (for example, Walmart). There are exceptions, of course, in local elections, especially judicial elections, but for most corporations, elections are a precarious and indirect means for advancing their interests.

The facts of *Citizens United* are significant in terms of potential subsequent reforms. At issue before the Court were the BCRA prohibitions on corporate and union contributions to independent expenditure groups during the run-up to federal elections; hence the critical finding of there being no risk of quid pro quo corruption. The Court left untouched not only limitations on contributions,[67] but the broad disclosure requirements currently in force.[68] The Court also did not address the longstanding prohibition on direct contributions by corporations and unions, something that dates back more than a century for corporations and more than half a century for unions. However, in treating corporations to all the prerogatives of natural persons in terms of independent expenditures, the logic of the Court's holding could signal a willingness to open the door to allowing corporations the right to donate directly to candidates and parties. As shocking as that is to century-old settled practice, it is unclear how big a difference even that step would actually make. Would the world look all that much different if corporations could contribute $2,400 to a candidate, the current federal contribution limit on individual donations? Perhaps, but probably not.

For all the attention devoted to campaign finance reform, the challenge remains straightforward: "the need for funding sufficient to enable candidates to mount competitive races without rendering them unduly dependent on large donors."[69] It is here that the reform impulse to constrict money is most problematic. For example, the first effort to offer candidates for office public funding—the post-Watergate presidential election subsidies—set the amount of the public contribution at two-thirds of what George McGovern had spent in his disastrous presidential run of 1972.[70] Once the cap on expenditures was removed in *Buckley*, the race was on to collect money to satisfy the mounting costs of campaigns, but with the constraints imposed by low contribution limits.[71]

Whatever the failings as a matter of regulatory policy, the Court has weighed in most readily on the side of protecting expenditures. The first prohibition of BCRA to fail was the so-called Millionaire's Amendment that permitted increased hard money fund-raising for incumbents challenged by self-financed campaigns, which was struck down in *Davis v. Federal Election Commission*.[72] This particular provision appeared to carry none of the anti-corruption logic of the *Buckley* exception and carried the redolent whiff of self-dealing by politicians. Instead, the Court held that BCRA "imposes an unprecedented penalty on any candidate who robustly exercises that First Amendment right [to expend lawfully obtained funds. The Act] requires a candidate to choose between the First Amendment right to engage in unfettered political speech and subjection to discriminatory fund-raising limitations."[73]

Similar logic carried over into the Court's order upholding an injunction against a longstanding Arizona policy of matching small contributions with state financial support of grassroots-based candidacies. The practice was known as "clean money" financing because of the small-donor constituency.[74] At issue, specifically, was Arizona's further policy of giving an additional clean-money subsidy to gubernatorial candidates under challenge from self-funded candidates.[75] Presumably, the same concern would apply to burdening expenditures by individuals who would, in effect, be putting one dollar in their opponents' coffers for every dollar they themselves spent. The result would be a "drag on First Amendment rights," as Justice Samuel Alito described the concern in *Davis*.[76] A careful reading of *Davis*, however, reveals that the concern is not contribution limits or even clean money matching systems, but the implicit efforts to rein in expenditures of individuals who self-finance, and whose expenditures do not readily fall into any theory of corruption—save the now-rejected equality concerns from *Austin*.

The logic of *Davis* poses a dilemma for the reform impulse as the Court invites a segregation of the seed money approach of clean money from the reformers' lurking desire to use the public money carrot as a stick to limit expenditures. There is no constitutional issue raised by the use of matching funds to reward candidates for mobilizing many small donors. For example, there are a number of clean money programs that offer the quid pro quo recognized in *Buckley*, by which candidates accept public money and contractually agree to a limit on their own expenditures.[77] These programs are all premised on the idea that candidates should be rewarded for engaging the voting public and should get public moneys to the extent that they expand the network of citizens who participate through small donations. Indeed, such programs have generally survived constitutional challenge when they release publicly funded candidates from the expenditure limitation if their opponents threatened to spend in excess of the public limitations.[78]

Davis would call these programs into question to the extent that they couple the inducement to expand the base of popular participation with a heavy-handed effort to dampen expenditures by the opponent. Almost invariably, these clean money programs seek to limit contributions to participating candidates, even below the generally established contribution limits for the office in question. In other words, rather than simply match a low figure (for example, five-to-one public matching for the first $100 contributed by any donor), these programs seek to limit the size of contributions participating candidates may receive, even below the threshold deemed not to risk candidate corruption.[79] Moreover, most of these programs have been tried in local elections or states without a history of heavy media expenditures. To the extent that public financing is likely to be successful, it has to provide enough money to candidates to control the agenda of the election campaign, lest they be at the mercy of tertiary organizations (PACs, 527 groups, and the panoply of denizens of the "Swift Boat" or "MoveOn.org" side of politics).[80]

The 2008 election invites a revisiting of the reform premise that money is unrelated to participation and that less money is inherently a good thing. Paradoxically, creating an incentive for candidates to raise more money *from more people* may actually reduce the risk of the clientelist pressures to capture political outputs. One of the keys to fund-raising in 2008 was the significant increase in the amount of hard money available to candidates and parties.[81] The greater ability to raise money from individuals combined with the eased ability to reach small donors through the Internet. As a result, the 2008 Obama campaign was not only able to raise money prodigiously, but able to engage millions of citizens at the same time. In the process, President Obama raised $745 million and spent $730 million—figures that surpassed the fund-raising and expenditure marks of all prior candidates.[82] Those contributions came from more than 4 million unique individual donors, again more than any candidate in American history.[83] And while the vast majority of money raised was from donors outside of the small donor category[84]—with contributions of less than $200[85] making up one-quarter of all the Obama fund-raising—the diffusion of the fund-raising base and the sheer quantity of donations defies any easy story of corruption of democratic politics. Problems arise when there are only a few large donors, not when there are many donors who may be substantial but not critical. Thus, reforms that create incentives for campaigns to solicit money from more sources may actually be more effective at diminishing the distortive effects of money on public policy than those that seek to limit the amount of money in the system.

Conclusion

The aim of using campaign finance law to limit the amount and influence of money on elections has run into two barriers, one constitutional and the other practical. Viewed in retrospect, the Supreme Court's unsatisfying jurisprudence in this area has actually settled on an organizing logic that grants constitutional protection to the ability to spend money in furtherance of electoral speech. That logic may not appeal to reformers, but its failure is not one of incoherence, no matter how difficult the *Buckley* divide proves to be on the implementation side. Modern technology has, if anything, reinforced this constitutional stand because the diffusion of information outlets places a premium on organization and control over content, lest candidates and parties be swamped by well-heeled tertiary organizations and the hysterical poles of the media.

Paradoxically, the most significant reform in *lessening* the role of special interest money in elections may be the one recent reform that actually facilitated the ability of candidates to raise money. The combination of BCRA's raising of contribution levels and the emergence of Internet fund-raising did two things: it allowed for unprecedented amounts of money to be raised in the 2008 election cycle *and* it incentivized candidates to raise funds from an unprecedented number of citizens. The combination enabled both greater engagement in the election of 2008 and a strengthened ability of the candidate-driven political message to dominate the electoral debate.

On this view of the aims of the electoral process, *Citizens United* is a distraction of limited consequence. Putting aside the elusive leveling aspiration of equality of all individuals in privately funded campaigns, the question is how to use campaign finance regulation to enhance a competitive electoral system and to guard against the corrosive distortion of political decisionmaking as a means toward incumbent entrenchment. This in turn requires rethinking the incentives toward candidate engagement of the electorate as they compete for office, including in the process of fund-raising, and a more nuanced understanding of the corrupting influence of incumbent reelection on the outputs of the political process.

9

The Unenforceable Corrupt Contract: Corruption and Nineteenth-Century Contract Law

*Zephyr Teachout**

In the nineteenth century, courts frequently refused to enforce contracts that undermined the integrity of the political process. While admittedly ad hoc, there were a non-trivial number of cases in which courts used contract law to discourage the self-serving use of public offices. For example, the U.S. Supreme Court refused to enforce a contract between a quartermaster and his partners when the contract encouraged the quartermaster to use his public office for private gain. The Court also refused to enforce a contract for paid lobbying of Congress. And, in a typical state court case, the Indiana Supreme Court refused to enforce an otherwise legal contract to use personal influence to persuade the government to place a post office in a particular location. In each of these cases, the reason for refusing to enforce the contract was not an underlying statute that made the behavior illegal, but concern that the contract was corrupt.

This chapter is the first examination of this now-defunct practice, which has been overlooked in the scholarship around corruption and only mentioned in passing in contract law scholarship. These cases suggest a new way to think about dealing with money and politics in light of *Citizens United v. Federal Election Commission*.[1] It is not

---

* This chapter also appears in NYU's *Review of Law and Social Change* 35, no. 3 (2011). Reproduced by permission.

intended as a comprehensive review, but as a provocative introduction to a different way of thinking about courts and corruption.

Accordingly, the primary goal of this chapter is descriptive. The nineteenth-century practice of refusing to enforce contracts to sell public obligations provides an intriguing possibility for exploration. It challenges Justice Anthony Kennedy's view that *Austin v. Michigan Chamber of Commerce*[2] was an outlier, instead of consistent with generations of cases that had recognized the public danger of money having too much influence in politics. It illustrates that, even prior to modern statutory campaign finance law, courts would use their power to refuse to enforce contracts as a method to limit the power of money in the political sphere. This description augments Justice John Paul Stevens' dissenting argument in *Citizens United* that courts should give great weight to anti-corruption concerns.

The second goal of the chapter is exploratory. In *Citizens United,* Justice Kennedy heavily emphasized the criminal nature of the sanctions against corporate political speech. If we take Kennedy's repeated reference to criminal liability seriously, we might fruitfully explore ways to revive using judicial non-enforcement of contracts to discourage the corruption of our electoral system. Outside of criminal law, there may be different tools that could be used to discourage private companies trying to use their wealth to influence public bodies for private advantage. Indeed, the different way in which nineteenth-century courts dealt with political corruption is so striking that it might open the imaginations of scholars and politicians struggling with ways to limit government capture. What if, for example, Congress did not criminalize independent corporate expenditures, but enabled courts not to enforce contracts related to independent expenditures? Similarly, what if Congress did not try to limit certain kinds of lobbying through criminal law, but simply refused to enforce contracts to lobby?[3] There are real difficulties with these ideas—complicated interactions with the law of jurisdiction stripping, for example—that I do not explore in this chapter. Instead, I simply raise the question about whether this form of non-criminal law might dissuade behavior that distorts democratic self-governance. The goal is to spark discussion and open the range of options available to Congress, and to continue in a larger project of exploring the relationship between courts and public corruption.

CITIZENS UNITED V. FEDERAL ELECTIONS COMMISSION

In *Citizens United,* the Supreme Court held that the Constitution forbids Congress from banning independent corporate efforts to influence the outcome of elections.[4] The decision rested on two connected determinations. First, that the First Amendment protects political speech regardless of the identity of the speaker.[5] Second, that there is no sufficiently important countervailing governmental or constitutional goal that is served by limits on corporate political advertising.[6] Independent expenditure limits do not cause corruption or its appearance, according to the majority.[7] Since corruption is the only possible countervailing interest recognized by the majority, the conclusion that the limits do not dissuade corruption decides the question.[8] And, Justice Kennedy defined corruption as only meaning "quid pro quo corruption," explicitly overturning prior precedent.[9] Other articles more fully interrogate other aspects of the case, but for our purposes, two features are salient: Kennedy's definition of corruption and the focus on the criminal law liability that burdens the First Amendment free speech rights.

A description of the constitutionally important meaning of "corruption" was a critical piece of Kennedy's opinion,[10] albeit less definitive than he claimed. Kennedy framed the case as a decision between two inconsistent precedents: *First National Bank of Boston v. Bellotti,*[11] which held that a state could not limit a corporation from speaking about politics, and *Austin*, which held that because of the disproportionate aggregated wealth of corporations, the state could limit their political activity. As framed by Kennedy, *Buckley v. Valeo*[12] and almost all its progeny concluded that corruption is only quid pro quo corruption, and *Austin* was an outlier.[13] Moreover, excessive influence or access did not constitute "corruption." Instead, Kennedy argued, a preference for a contributor's policy preferences because of the contribution is unavoidable human nature. He endorsed as "well understood" and "legitimate" that contributors make contributions in order to impact policy. He hinted that the desire to use money to influence policy was arguably "the only reason . . . to make a contribution to . . . one candidate over another."[14]

While undoubtedly narrow ("crabbed" in Justice Stevens's view),[15] Kennedy's definition is also not precise. He does not lay out the elements of quid pro quo corruption. In fact, the description Kennedy gives of a campaign contribution in exchange for a policy arguably falls within a quid pro quo definition. Kennedy's conceptual looseness around quid pro quo corruption means that it might bear more study. Regardless of the critical focus, the opinion severely curtailed the options available to Congress in responding to widespread concerns about corruption. It forces us to look creatively at other ways to strengthen latent concepts and mechanisms for dealing with political money. One of the best sources of inspiration is the past.

In parsing the arguments, Kennedy also repeatedly emphasized the criminal liability imposed by the campaign finance laws. He described the law as creating an "outright ban, backed by criminal sanctions,"[16] and repeatedly referred to the "criminal liability" and "criminal penalties" created by the law.[17] He emphasized that the law subjected speakers to "criminal sanctions" and discussed the chilling effects of costly defensive litigation.[18] The law could lead to "fining or jailing."[19] The most emphatic discussion of criminal liability arises when Kennedy writes about the First Amendment: "When government seeks to use its full power, including the criminal law, to command where a person may get his or her information . . . it uses censorship. . . . This is unlawful."[20] While Kennedy did not say that non-criminal sanctions might survive, the repeated emphasis on the criminal law at issue at least raises the question of how important the jail time and criminal liability might be to the existing majority.

The Corrupt Quartermaster, the Lobbyist, and the Postmaster

Contract law has undergone many changes in the last two-hundred years. In the earlier part of the nineteenth century, judges in contract cases were less focused on precedent, and freely referenced public policy and political concerns in their decisions. While they cited cases, they felt less bound by precedent than later judges. In the latter part of the nineteenth century, this changed. Judges became more formal in their reasoning. They grounded their decisions in precedent, which they saw as binding, and inasmuch as they referenced public policy directly in deciding individual cases, it was much more constrained.

But in the modern era, courts retain some latitude through the doctrine that allows them to refuse to enforce contracts as against public policy. This is a blend of discretion and doctrine; the discretion is loosely constrained by precedent. The practice is often divided into three parts: courts can refuse to enforce contracts that are against public policy, unconscionable, or illegal. In modern case law, the two latter parts of the doctrine are alive and well: courts refuse to enforce contracts for illegal activity (like a contract for gambling that is against the law in the jurisdiction), and in certain circumstances, they refuse to enforce contracts that are unconscionable. But, today's courts almost never invoke the public policy exception unless the conduct in question is patently illegal.[21]

The against-public-policy exception was not always so thin. In between the freewheeling early nineteenth century and the mid-twentieth century, when the public policy exception effectively vanished except for unconscionable and illegal contracts, courts developed a body of cases that used the public policy exception as a freestanding reason not to enforce contracts. These cases governed contracts that were "legal but unenforceable."[22] "The parties did not violate any criminal law by entering the contract," but "neither party [could] call on the power of the state to enforce the contract against the will of the other."[23] The nineteenth-century courts were "frequently willing to subordinate freedom of contract, or at least some types of freedom of contract, to other social concerns."[24] While modern courts still may closely scrutinize the fairness of the particular contract as between the two parties and each other, nineteenth-century courts were more willing to scrutinize the impact of the contract more broadly, and the possible effect of the contract on the relationship between the society and citizens.[25]

One type of legal but unenforceable contract was that which was fundamentally corruptive of representative government. If one does a search for "corruption" in nineteenth-century state and local cases, a substantial proportion of the results will be found in contract cases.[26]

In this category of cases, the courts refused to enforce contracts that they understood to be subverting the public good for private gain in public affairs. As an Indiana court explained, "a wholesome rule of law is that parties should not be permitted to make contracts which are likely to set private interests in opposition to public duty or to the public welfare."[27] One of the jobs of courts was to protect against private interests corrupting public offices.

It is beyond the scope of this chapter to canvass all of nineteenth-century contract law related to corruption. Instead, this chapter introduces three cases, notable because of their prominence at the time, and because of how they differ from the modern understanding of the judicial relationship to private contracts around public matters. In each case, a court refused to enforce an otherwise legal contract because it concluded that the underlying contract was corrupt and the social implications of enforcing the contract would be too great. Enforcement would encourage people to try to manipulate government services for private benefit, leading to a culture in which people saw government as a place to go to for special treatment and favors.

The Corrupt Quartermaster: Law Will Not Degrade Itself

In 1830, in *Bartle v. Nutt,*[28] the U.S. Supreme Court confronted a dispute over a government contract went awry. One of the men, Marsteller, was the deputy quartermaster of the United States. One of his jobs was to manage supplies for the military; it was a position of public trust, because he was responsible for attempting to get the best prices for these supplies. Marsteller and two others entered into an agreement regarding a contract with the government to rebuild Fort Washington. Marsteller was to provide funds and materials; another man, Bartle, was to oversee the contract; and all three would share in the profits.[29]

During the rebuilding, the threesome sent intentionally inflated reports of the cost of the building to the government, which were noticed by officers of the U.S. Treasury. The correction of these false reports meant that the contractors ultimately completed the job at a net loss. Bartle sued the quartermaster for the costs he incurred, arguing that they had a contract to share profits and losses, and the losses must be shared.[30] The quartermaster counter-sued for costs he incurred.[31]

The Supreme Court held that the contract was unenforceable, and seemed to consider its decision inevitable, noting that "to describe such a case is to decide it." The Court opined that "public morals, public justice, and the well established principles of all judicial tribunals, alike forbid the interposition of courts of justice to lend their aid to purposes like this."[32] The Court explained that "to enforce a contract which began with the corruption of a public officer, and progressed in the practice of known and wil[l]ful deception in its execution, can never be consummated or sanctioned by any court."[33] The political corruption described is understood in a broader sense than that imagined by Justice Kennedy. There was no explicit quid pro quo or bribery; instead, a public officer was using his public position for private gain.

While the reported decision lacks some detail, it does not appear that it was illegal for a quartermaster to be involved in securing a public contract that he might benefit from. Indeed, no particular crime was charged in the case. This is important—modern invocations of unenforceable-by-reason-of-public-policy contracts invariably cite criminalizing legislation as the reason for non-enforcement.

The *Bartle* Court concluded that it would not "degrade itself"[34] by aiding these corrupt characters by enforcing the private contract, but would leave them as they found them. This language too is important, because it puts law—private law—in a different relationship to itself than is typically assumed in modern law. The modern tendency is to imagine the courts as infrastructure, and providing a necessary public service in enforcing private contracts. The *Bartle* Court clearly regards itself as actively supporting or discouraging publicly desirable activities. The case illustrates an understanding of the judiciary as a *subsidy* to business and to private arrangements. It was not so much that the Court withdrew its support, but that it declined to offer it in the first place.

A Nineteenth-Century View of Lobbying as Contrary to Public Policy

The most interesting example of the unenforceable corrupt contracts cases comes from the United States Supreme Court in 1874. *Bartle v. Nutt* is a curiosity, but it can be reconciled with modern law in other ways—contemporary courts might refuse to enforce the same contract because they would find statutes forbidding such contracting, and refuse to enforce it because of the underlying illegal nature of the enterprise. However, the 1874 case, *Trist v. Child,*[35] is unimaginable today, and directly conflicts with modern First Amendment doctrine and the modern law of contracts.

Trist has its roots in the Mexican-American war. Trist performed services relating to the peace treaty that ended the war. Two decades later, he had still not been compensated. However, he was too old and sick to travel to Washington himself to make his demands. Instead, he hired Linus Child, a Boston lawyer, and his son to represent him. Trist agreed to pay Child a contingency fee—25 percent of whatever he secured—and nothing else.[36] Child and his son were successful, and Congress gave Trist the right to withdraw $14,559. After Child and his son performed the contract, however, Trist simply refused to pay. The junior Child successfully petitioned the Treasury to suspend payment, and then filed a suit to enjoin the Treasury from releasing the money unless $5,000 was given to Child. Trist responded by arguing that the agreement was an unenforceable and corrupt contract. The Court considered the case in terms of the contract law elements raised by it.

Child reasoned that this was like any attorney/client relationship and that, unlike prior cases in which secret collusion was used to secure government funding, all was above board.

The lawyer for Child argued that this was simply a matter of a normal contingency fee, and was insistent that the payment was not for "corrupt" "lobbying." "We are not here asking the court to open the door to corrupt influences upon Congress, or give aid to that which is popularly known as 'lobbying,' and is properly denounced as dishonorable."[37] His core argument depended on Trist's right to personally petition Congress—if Trist had the right, he should have a right to hire an agent to do it on his behalf.[38]

The Court rejected these arguments, holding that, while an individual can petition on his or her own behalf, a paid second party petitioner is corrupt. It held that the entire contract was against public policy and that the letters written to Congress members by Child—straightforward letters asking for help—were "if not corrupt, . . . illegitimate, and considered in connection with the pecuniary interest of the agent at stake, contrary to the plainest principles of public policy."[39]

It rested no part of its conclusion upon contingent fees but entirely based its arguments upon the illegitimacy of paid political petitioning.

The Court grounded its opinion in two features of corruption that do not appear in *Citizens United:* that anyone could be corrupted, and that moral failure—not bribery, which was not at issue in the case—threatened society. Corruption in this view is different than crime.[40] The Court never explicitly explained what it meant by corruption or the threat of corruption, but it suggested that a Congress member selling influence would be corrupt, and moreover, that a widespread practice of paying for influence would undermine the integrity of the entire political system.

In particular, the Court suggests that, while an individual instance of lobbying may seem benign, if it is allowed for an individual, it will be allowed for everyone, and if it is allowed for everyone, it would be allowed for corporations:

> If any of the great corporations of the country were to hire adventurers who make market of themselves in this way, to procure the passage of a general law with a view to the promotion of their private interests, the moral sense of every right-minded man would instinctively denounce the employer and employed as steeped in corruption, and the employment as infamous.[41]

The Court is not precise about the particular harm imagined. Is it that money would have too great an impact? Is it inequality? The concern seems to be that widespread lobbying will erode confidence in the legitimacy of representative government. This sentiment is an early precursor to the *Buckley* doctrine that allows that not only corruption, but the appearance of corruption, causes significant democratic erosion.[42] The Court described a slippery slope: "If the instances were numerous, open, and tolerated, they would be regarded as measuring the decay of the public morals and the degeneracy of the times."[43] The private act was thus measured not by its impact on the parties in the case, or on future parties in similar cases, but by its impact on society and democratic culture.

Finally, the Court argued that there is no clear way to distinguish between private pleas to Congress and demands for more broad-sweeping legislation. It assumed, without argument, that paid persuasion around general legislation must be condemned. So it focused instead on the problems of small, private bills. Because they are not open to the public, and the discussions around the bills are often "whispered," such legislation created huge opportunities for making decisions for the wrong reasons and, again, for bribery. "Those whose duty it is to investigate"[44] hear unsupported facts by self-interested parties—and then vote to pass it, because there is no public awareness or check on the facts communicated by the self-interested parties. "If the agent is truthful and conceals nothing, all is well. If he uses nefarious means with success, the springhead and the stream of legislation are polluted."[45]

Today, courts and many academics not only tolerate, but celebrate, paid lobbying. They see it as a fundamental First Amendment right, and a necessary part of the legislative process.[46] But *Trist* shows that this was not always the general view.

The logic of *Trist* and that in *Citizens United* are opposite, but the questions underlying each are similar. Laws that once restricted lobbying are similar to laws that once restricted independent corporate expenditure. They are designed to limit how much money can be spent to distort democratic desires. They both implicate speech rights. Both are designed to limit inappropriate dependencies in government. Both paid lobbying and campaign donations allow companies or individuals with amassed wealth to have disproportionate political power in a society.

Between *Trist* and *Citizens United*, there is no question that the Supreme Court narrowed its view of corruption substantially; it also narrowed its understanding of its own duty to protect democratic integrity. In *Trist*, an essential job of any court is limiting corruption and its perception; in *Citizens United*, this job is seen as more secondary and technical. Moreover, the case represents the mainstream nature of the practice of using contract law (and its limits) instead of criminal law for limiting corruption.

The Post Office and the Public Good

The two prior cases were Supreme Court cases, but the practice of deeming contracts void by virtue of corruption was much more widespread in state court. This case from Indiana is fairly typical of the cases of the time. In the late 1800s, postmasters were frequently paid by the federal government, and had to use part of their salary to pay for the building where they would accept and pass out mail for the town.[47] Because post offices were the center of public traffic at the time, the location of a post office would have a huge impact on the success of nearby offices. In Elkhardt County, Indiana, a room used as a post office was getting a little run down, so the government started looking for a new place to put a post office.[48] The proposed contract was for ten years.[49] Two different groups of businessmen wanted the post office near their businesses.

A brick building, under construction, seemed ideal for the post office, and certainly ideal for one business group. The businessmen went to the owner of the building, who was also a personal friend of the postmaster, and proposed that he offer a room in the building for nominal rent to the government, and suggest to the postmaster that the building was a good location.[50] In essence, one private party paid another private party to use his powers of personal persuasion to convince a federal official to select a particular location for a building.

After a dispute, the building owner did not want to pay. The owner argued that the "consideration" given in exchange for the promised money was illegal, and that the contract was void for being against public policy. The court agreed, holding that the public good is harmed when public decisions are made because of private interests, instead of because of public interests: "The case . . . falls fully within the principle that contracts which tend to improperly influence those engaged in the public service, or which tend to subordinate the public welfare to individual gain, are not enforceable in any court of justice."[51]

The court's reasoning depends upon an idea of the public good. If there is no idea of public good, but only of competing private interests, then subordination becomes an unintelligible idea. Because there is a public good, it is the responsibility of law to protect it, and to shape law not to harm it. In this passage there is a theory, or ideology of public good, and a theory, or ideology of the purpose of law, both. In the courts' view, public good exists, and law exists in order to serve it.

"Personal influence . . . is not a vendible," the court held.[52] In this area, the court appears to be veering into property law, where the bounds of alienability are created. Questions of what is and is not alienable, in close cases, always come down to a public policy discussion—policy creates the nature of property. The policy, in this case, is the policy expressed above—that the arrangement would harm the public good—but there is an implicit strain in this discussion that the recognition of political belief as a transferrable, sellable thing, would itself diminish the person who holds political beliefs.

In effect, the court concluded that "personal influence" is a good, just like a bodily organ, or sexual services—something that any individual can use on their own, but not something that one can sell. This is a fascinating analogy, of course, because it makes "personal influence" in the conduct of public affairs something very much like the vote, like sexual affection, or bodily organs—a good that one can, and should, vigorously use, but fundamentally unalienable in the eyes of the law. Some of these prohibitions exist in statutory law, but some are common law that has developed in response to particular public policy arguments. Courts now consistently refuse to enforce contracts for prostitution, for example, or contracts for marriage that allow for no chance of divorce.

A Constitutional Law of Corruption?

At the same time as the private law of corruption was being quietly enshrined, the Supreme Court also recognized something related, but slightly different, in *Ex Parte Yarbough*.[53] *Yarbough* is best known as a landmark civil rights case, but it also suggests a constitutional law of corruption. Several members of the Ku Klux Klan threatened and beat a black man in order to intimidate him out of voting. After conviction for conspiracy to violate federal laws, they brought a writ of habeas corpus against the warden in the prison where they were held, claiming that the laws they were punished under were invalid and unconstitutional. The defendants argued that the federal government had no authority to prosecute them, as there was no constitutional text giving the federal government the power to regulate this kind of crime.

The Court's response was impassioned. The temptation to subvert elections "by violence and by corruption is a constant source of danger. Such has been the history of all republics."[54] The Court refused to entertain the argument that combatting corruption would exceed the state's constitutional grant of power, rejecting this possibility as "so startling as to arrest attention and demand the gravest consideration."[55] The very fact of government, it concludes, implies the capacity to enact and prosecute laws protecting the integrity of that government. Without such ability, the government is at great risk:

> If the government of the United States has within its constitutional domain no authority to provide against these evils,—if the very sources of power may be poisoned by corruption or controlled by violence and outrage, without legal restraint,—then, indeed, is the country in danger, and its best powers, its highest purposes, the hopes which it inspires, and the love which enshrines it, are at the mercy of the combinations of those who respect no right but brute force, on the one hand, and unprincipled corruptionists on the other.[56]

The Court further argues that republican, elected governments have a uniquely strong implied right to combat corruption. "If it has not this power it is left helpless before the two great natural and historical enemies of all republics, open violence and insidious corruption."[57] Congress has a power to limit corruption based solely on its power to protect itself—the government is fundamentally fragile, and great vigilance is needed.

If corruption is only bribery and its ilk, then the discussion of the inherent power to limit corruption is dicta. If corruption includes other forms of perverting governmental authority and elections, the corruption holding is a holding. Staying within the four walls of the opinion, it appears that the court takes a broad view of corruption, and considers the intimidation of voters a form of corruption. This is interesting, because it suggests that the court considered the dissuasion of a citizen from performing his civic duties akin to the dissuasion of, say, a judge from performing his civic duties. Much as one might say that a person who threatens a judge corrupts the system, a person who threatens a citizen—in his citizenship activities—threatens the system.

While not a contract case, *Yarbough* expresses the same view seen throughout the other cases—that corruption is a broad problem, and that courts have a special responsibility to respond to it and protect against it.

Why Nineteenth-Century Contract Law Matters in Light of *Citizens United*

These historical authorities are important to highlight on their own for a richer understanding of the history of both contract law and corruption law. However, they have special resonance in light of Kennedy's opinion in *Citizens United*. First, they further undermine the simple notion that courts have always had a narrow view of corruption. Second, they suggest that contract law might provide an intriguing avenue for experimentation.

Corruption Redefined

A key feature of Kennedy's decision was that *Austin* was an outlier case in the law defining the scope of corruption. He describes the cases as pre-*Austin* and post-*Austin*, and emphasizes the singularity of the opinion. He describes *Austin* as uniquely giving weight to the governmental interest in prohibiting aggregated wealth from unduly influencing politics.[58] I have argued elsewhere that corruption is a fundamental constitutional concern that is given far too little deference by the modern Supreme Court.[59] Corruption was the founders' paramount concern when drafting the Constitution. By the terms of the debate in Philadelphia, and by the terms the founders used to describe the purpose in creating the constitution, limiting corruption was the most important goal of the convention.[60] Corruption is not only a serious concern, it is a constitutional concern. The Constitution was drafted with the purpose of limiting corruption in the new republic; it was the paramount concern that drove hundreds of drafting decisions in the summer the Constitution was written. It was, according to various accounts by Founders as diverse as James Madison, Alexander Hamilton, George Washington, and Benjamin Franklin, the driving motivation behind the Constitution's final form. Moreover, their understanding of corruption was not cash-for-votes, but conduct that used public channels for private gain. I argued that the judicial branch ought to recognize an "anti-corruption" principle, akin to federalism or the separation of powers, that would guide constitutional decision-making. My previous argument ended when the constitutional convention ended. However, if one extends the historical inquiry to the nineteenth century, at least some courts understood corruption far more broadly than Justice Kennedy. Corruption, under this line of cases, referred to personal failures that posed structural threats to democracy, often caused by inappropriate dependencies.

There are hundreds of examples of courts throughout the nineteenth century assuming a broader definition of corruption, one that encompasses undue influence. High contingent fees were described as "bribes," because "the use of such means and such agents will have the effect to subject the State governments to the combined capital of wealthy corporations, and produce universal corruption, commencing with the representative and ending with the elector."[61] Courts refused to enforce contracts that would "tend[] to corrupt or contaminate, by improper influences, the integrity of our social or political institutions. . . . Legislators should act from high considerations of public duty."[62] "The law in its wisdom we think has a tendency to close the door of temptation by refusing to recognize contracts which in any way hamper the faithful discharge of the trust which the railroad company owes to the people in the location of public conveniences."[63]

Justice Kennedy concluded that improper influence is not corruption, and that the appearance of influence would not lead to perceptions of corruption;[64] this view is in direct conflict with decades of nineteenth-century precedent, as well as *Austin*. In refusing to enforce a contract in 1920, the Nevada Supreme Court explicitly held that a contract need not be illegal, and the actors involved need not have a corrupt motive, if the overall effect of similar contracts would be to allow people to "assum[e] a position where selfish motives may impel them to sacrifice the public good to private benefit."[65] Kennedy concludes that only direct "quid pro quo" is corrupt, whereas these courts routinely concluded that quid pro quo was not required in each instance, but the court recognized the "corrupting tendencies of such contracts."[66] They recognized that the definition was not pat or simple, but that the lack of simplicity did not relieve courts of the responsibility of trying to define it.

Courts thus had little difficulty in talking about corruption in a way that included almost any effort to use money to put private interests before public interests in what they perceived to be fundamentally public-facing decisions.[67]

If one peels back history and looks at cases from the nineteenth century, *Austin* feels more mainstream, and *Buckley*'s quid pro quo reference (along with *Citizens United*), looks more like an outlier. At the very least, it seems that courts have long struggled with the difficulty of defining corruption in tractable terms, but that there is no long-standing consensus that corruption is limited to quid pro quo exchanges. Kennedy's characterization of *Austin* as an unruly outlier that needs to be tamed is weak, even if one looks only at the modern jurisprudence.[68]

A Modern Law of Contract Enforcement?

A second reason the nineteenth-century laws might matter is that they provide a precedent for the use—or withholding—of the state's power to enforce contracts to dissuade corporate powers from exploiting weaknesses and dependencies in the electoral machinery for private ends. After all, the courts' doctrine of refusing to enforce contracts on political corruption grounds never died, exactly—it was just slowly whittled away as American courts become much more skeptical of the public policy exception.[69] Thus, as of 2011, there still exists the doctrine of not enforcing contracts on public policy grounds. The current *Restatement of Contracts*, for instance, states that "[a] promise or other term of an agreement is unenforceable on grounds of public policy if legislation provides that it is unenforceable or the interest in its enforcement is clearly outweighed in the circumstances by a public policy against the enforcement of such terms."[70]

More importantly, the Supreme Court, while very stern on criminal sanctions, has been less stern when it comes to Congress using non-criminal powers to have the impact of dissuading certain kinds of political speech. It has held that Congress may withhold otherwise available subsidies to avoid facilitating lobbying. Congress can "reasonably refuse to subsidize the lobbying activities of tax-exempt charitable organizations by prohibiting such organizations from using tax-deductible contributions to support their lobbying efforts."[71] In conditioning tax-exempt status on a commitment not to lobby, "Congress has not infringed any First Amendment rights or regulated any First Amendment activity. Congress has simply chosen not to pay for [appellee's] lobbying."[72] "Otherwise, public funds might be spent on an activity Congress chose not to subsidize."[73]

By an extension of that same logic, a common-law or even statutory rule refusing to enforce contracts to lobby might be slightly more likely to survive a First Amendment challenge. A commitment to enforcing contracts is not free—it is meaningful, costly, material support for those who use it. So Congress would not be criminalizing electioneering—it would be refusing to subsidize it, a distinction with potential constitutional significance.

As mentioned previously, Justice Kennedy's opinion in *Citizens United* relied very heavily on the criminality, and the criminal sanctions in the act. Kennedy refers to a series of burdens on First Amendment activities, but none are the non-subsidy of refusing to enforce a contract.[74] Of these, he gives special attention to criminal laws, noting that "the law before us is an outright ban, backed by criminal sanctions,"[75] and "when Government seeks to use its full power, including the criminal law, to command where a person may get his or her information or what distrusted source he or she may not hear, it uses censorship to control thought,"[76] and finally "if the First Amendment has any force, it prohibits Congress from fining or jailing citizens, or associations of citizens, for simply engaging in political speech."[77]

By turning to contract law, instead of criminal law, the state might soften these direct attacks of prior efforts to limit corruption using criminal sanctions. But more importantly, it would send a strong signal that the courts are fundamentally public spaces, publicly funded, and they should not be used to enforce contracts that do, in fact, undermine the fundamental public-ness of our democracy.

Conclusion

The majority opinion in *Citizens United* purported to close the debate about corruption in campaign finance law. However, it left open a few opportunities for greater exploration. The ad hoc nineteenth-century practice of refusing to enforce contracts to sell public obligations provides an intriguing possibility for exploration. In the nineteenth century, courts used contract law to discourage public corruption. They would sometimes refuse to enforce contracts that they deemed corrupt; just as they would refuse to enforce contracts for prostitution, they would refuse to enforce contracts between public servants and private entities that undermined the integrity of representative government. In the most striking instance of this practice, the United States Supreme Court refused to enforce a contract to lobby Congress, holding that it was a corrupt practice and against the public policy of the United States.

These cases challenge Kennedy's view that *Austin* was an outlier. They show that there are generations of cases that had recognized that undue influence could constitute corruption and create the appearance of corruption. They also open the imagination; in the modern framework, contract law is rarely considered as a possible tool to discourage political dependencies on concentrated financial power. The nineteenth century contract law of corruption suggests that we might fruitfully explore the structure of contract enforcement, and reminds us that courts can never be neutral in their relationship to corruption. The stability and certainty declared by Justice Kennedy is fundamentally elusive; we must always engage in a more searching, difficult, textured understanding of the way the legal system discourages and encourages relationships between institutions, people, money, and power.

10

Citizens United and Equality Forgotten

Mark C. Alexander[*]

Starting with the landmark 1976 *Buckley v. Valeo*[1] decision, the U.S. Supreme Court has analyzed efforts to regulate money in politics under a First Amendment framework. Spending has been equated with speech in the political world, and the individual right to speak—and to spend money to do so—has enjoyed the utmost constitutional protection. That tradition has carried over the past thirty-plus years, including and through last term's *Citizens United v. Federal Election Commission* decision, in which the Court struck down restrictions on corporate political spending.[2] While the Court is right to exalt First Amendment values—central to our nation's governmental and political systems—its analysis has paid scant attention to broader, collective concerns about equality.

As this chapter explores in full, there is a serious democratic tension when one constitutional value (speech) gets promoted over another (equality). In our modern fund-raising machinery, as candidates and elected officials raise money from a small set of elite donors, they are disproportionately responsive to the few, not to the many, and not to their constituents. When this occurs, elected officials cannot do their jobs as well, the few have concentrated power, the many have diluted power, and political equality is trampled. In this context, individual free speech interests effectively trump equality interests. And, as equality is forgotten, the American people and our political and governmental systems suffer.

---

* For Owen Fiss my teacher, mentor, and friend. This chapter also appears in the *Review of Law and Social Change* 35, no. 3 (2011). Reproduced by permission.

I start this chapter by generally discussing the importance of First Amendment speech rights and the legal analysis that has been applied to efforts to regulate money in politics. Having laid out the relevant First Amendment considerations, I then address a central question: What else matters? I explore competing values that should also inform the constitutional analysis of campaign reform measures. Specifically, I am concerned with three equality-based arguments. First, I argue that protecting the time of candidates and elected officials from the grind of fund-raising is a compelling governmental interest that needs to be properly recognized as such.[3] Next, I posit that the current state of campaign finance that puts a disproportionate amount of power in the hands of the few—those with wealth and with wealthy friends—is a modern equivalent of vote dilution.[4] Third, I point out the grave consequence that flows from those and other concerns: our republican form of government, promised by the Guarantee Clause, is threatened.[5] In the end, I suggest that these other values, firmly rooted in principles of equality in our government and politics, have been forgotten in the modern analysis of campaign finance reform generally, and *Citizens United*, specifically.

The heart of the majority's argument is that money and political spending can be equated with speech, corporations can be considered as persons with speech rights, and the restrictions that the Bipartisan Campaign Reform Act (BCRA) placed on corporate spending improperly violates the First Amendment. Justice Anthony Kennedy wrote: "if the First Amendment has any force, it prohibits Congress from fining or jailing citizens, or associations of citizens, for simply engaging in political speech." While the Court appropriately celebrates the First Amendment, it does not adequately address the importance of equality concerns in our democracy.

Speech in Democracy

The *Citizens United* opinion may be described as a triumph of the First Amendment over government attempts to regulate core protected political speech. As Justice Kennedy framed the majority opinion, the Court's concern was our nation's commitment to vigorous unrestrained debate on all matters pertaining to our politics and government.[6] There can be no doubt that the Constitution places a premium on free expression and the First Amendment.[7] But while amplifying the importance of individual speech, the majority analysis fails to properly consider values of collective equality. While this is hardly a tiny flaw, my broader criticism of *Citizens United* in no way is meant to diminish those speech values. In fact, those values merit elevation here, before the discussion of that which was left out of the Court's analysis.

As Justice William Brennan explained in *Texas v. Johnson*, "if there is a bedrock principle underlying the scope of the First Amendment, it is that the government may not prohibit the expression of an idea simply because society finds the idea itself offensive or disagreeable."[8] The First Amendment can protect the uninhibited marketplace of ideas in which the truth rises to the top and the falsities fall to the bottom. Further, the people's rights and liberties are protected by the government and against the government through an open exchange of debate and ideas.

Speech is at the core of our democratic process, an essential part of "a profound national commitment to the principle that debate on public issues should be uninhibited, robust, and wide-open."[9] By allowing each of us our own freedom to speak individually, and all of us to shop in the marketplace of ideas, we ultimately decide how we want to govern.[10] In that sense, the First Amendment is the guarantor of a participatory democracy, in which the people are essential to the project of governance. This conception of speech also echoes the Declaration of Independence: government derives "their just powers from the consent of the governed."[11] Likewise, Justice Louis Brandeis articulated this core understanding of the First Amendment in his concurring opinion in *Whitney v. California*: "Those who won our independence believed . . . that public discussion is a political duty; and that this should be a fundamental principle of the American government."[12]

The First Amendment fosters a process of open discussion,[13] and the people are allowed to speak freely so that they can safely vent their ideas, frustrations, and anger. In doing so without government interference, the broader debate is enriched, and ideas are tested.[14] The First Amendment removes "governmental restraints from the arena of public discussion, putting the decision as to what views shall be voiced largely into the hands of each of us, in the hope that use of such freedom will ultimately produce a more capable citizenry and more perfect policy."[15] Free speech ultimately allows for a nonviolent means of venting one's anger and frustration at government.[16] "There is no greater safety valve for discontent and cynicism about the affairs of Government than freedom of expression in any form."[17] The remedy for alienation and discontent is not less, "but more free expression of ideas," and in this way, the First Amendment "acts as a safety valve and tends to decrease the resort to violence by frustrated citizens."[18] Unrestrained expression allows ideas to be put out there, and also for the proponents to let their own emotion show, much like a steam valve allows for the escape of pressure so as to prevent a buildup that causes an explosion.[19] But also, some voices are louder than others, and some have greater ability to dominate the political marketplace of ideas due in large part to money. Large sums of money can buy a louder megaphone, proverbially speaking, thus drowning out smaller voices, distorting political debate in the market of ideas.

Political Speech as the Highest Priority

The previous discussion briefly sketched out broad conceptions of the importance of speech in the context of government and politics. More to the specific point, there is a body of case law and literature on the application of First Amendment values in the regulation of campaigns. Free speech is an indispensible part of our system of government, and under the First Amendment political speech is the highest priority. Political speech enables all to contribute to the marketplace of ideas to allow the strong ideas to rise and the rest to fall away in shaping our ever-changing country. Accordingly, "Supreme Court precedent . . . leaves no doubt that the constitutional protection of political speech is essential to the very framework on which our political system is built."[20] In *Buckley v. Valeo*, the Court affirmed that core political speech is essential to the free flow of ideas within a democracy, and should be given the highest protected place within the First Amendment.[21] The First Amendment is anchored in the belief that it is the right of the people to bring forth ideas and discussion to create a never-ending cycle of political and social change, which they desire.[22] As part of the process of a participatory democracy, both candidates and the electorate enjoy the highest First Amendment protection to engage each other to find out what the candidate truly stands for and the people truly desire.

Protection of Campaign Activities

The machinery of elections also occupies a particularly protected space within First Amendment jurisprudence. The guarantee of the First Amendment "has its fullest and most urgent application precisely to the conduct of campaigns for political office."[23] Such high protection is given to elections because of the robust debate they foster and campaigns' connection to directly electing a candidate of the people.

In the context of campaign finance reform, the line of cases that came before *Citizens United* further frames judicial analysis of campaign activities. *Buckley* is the seminal modern-era campaign reform decision, and the Court squarely placed campaign finance under a First Amendment umbrella of protection. The *Buckley* framework equated speech with money and thus placed the strictest standard on future review of campaign finance reform laws. In doing so, the Court preferred speech over equality and took a very long first step down the road to *Citizens United*.

In 1974, Congress amended the Federal Election Campaign Act of 1971 (FECA) so that it had four major components, two of which are of interest here: contribution limits[24] and expenditure limits.[25] In 1976, the Supreme Court decided a challenge to FECA in *Buckley*.[26] The *Buckley* Court's guiding principle was stated as follows:

> The Act's contribution and expenditure limitations operate in an area of the most fundamental First Amendment activities. Discussion of public issues and debate on the qualifications of candidates are integral to the operation of the system of government established by our Constitution. The First Amendment affords the broadest protection to such political expression in order "to assure (the) unfettered exchange of ideas for the bringing about of political and social changes desired by the people."[27]

The Court thus not only reinforced the preeminence of political *speaking* as a fundamental First Amendment activity, it elevated political *spending* to this level of importance as well.[28] Because money can be spent to help communicate political messages, the Court equated political speech with money in politics, finding that campaign expenditures are central to the communication of political ideas.[29] As with other laws that restrict core First Amendment activity, these regulations would have to meet strict scrutiny, requiring narrow tailoring to meet a compelling governmental interest.[30]

Consequently, spending limitations were found to offend the First Amendment because—in the Court's view—restricting the amount of money spent on political communication inevitably decreases political speech.[31] Under the framework of strict scrutiny, it would be nearly impossible for an asserted governmental interest to justify such a First Amendment infringement. Contribution limits, by contrast, were upheld, justified by the high probability that direct donations to political candidates could cause either actual corruption or the appearance thereof.

Notably, the *Buckley* Court disregarded the way that large sums of money can effectively drown out smaller voices, and thus effectively remove the people from their politics and government. While First Amendment values were appropriately elevated, the Court unfortunately relegated notions of equality to the constitutional trash heap. The Supreme Court has extended *Buckley* over the past several decades in a wide variety of campaign finance regulations, each time reinforcing the money-as-speech paradigm and further ignoring increasing inequalities. The Court has consistently focused on the anti-corruption rationale as the sole justification for regulating money in politics. In so doing, the Court has ignored the way in which large amounts of campaign cash can drown out smaller voices, turning a blind eye to principles of equality.[32] It has also ignored the common search for ideas and good governance at the heart of First Amendment values.[33]

There is little doubt that free speech is essential to the proper function of American politics and government and thus deserves the exalted position it occupies in our legal system. But exalting individual speech rights over the participation rights of the collective is short-sighted; it ignores the way in which a few loud voices—in campaigns, those with access to large amounts of campaign cash—

can drown out the voices of the many, ultimately *distorting* speech values. Ironically, completely uncontrolled speech can have the effect of complete cacophony, or allowing the few with power and money to shout down the many. It further conflicts with important values of equality, as will be explored below. This values-clash most recently came to a head in *Citizens United*.

What Else Matters? Competing Values

Under the *Buckley* framework, the key question is whether there is a compelling government interest to justify a campaign finance regulation. Thus, courts and litigators look for compelling governmental interests that may justify reform, constitutionally speaking. The *Buckley* analysis treats campaigns as if they are pure debating exercises, in an almost theoretical market of ideas. It ignores the real world context of politics, soft money, and the election of actual individuals to serve as representatives in government.[34] In order for further reform of campaign finance laws to withstand constitutional challenge, the Supreme Court must be presented with, and recognize, additional compelling interests that justify restrictions on the "money-equals-speech" rationale.

The road to *Citizens United* started with *Buckley*, and the Court has followed one narrow path. Thus, the *Citizens United* majority makes an apparently logical argument and draws an apparently logical conclusion, starting as it does from *Buckley*. But, of course, if you start from a flawed premise, then you get a flawed result. We should challenge the flawed starting point and elevate the missing element of equality in this whole debate. Bringing equality into the picture helps address concerns about the ways in which elected officials spend more time chasing money than doing their jobs; the way in which power concentrated in the hands of a relative few fund-raisers dilutes the power of the many; and basic problems with how our republican form of government is trampled in the stampede for campaign cash.

Our political process heavily emphasizes the importance of individual participation. The line running from *Buckley* through

Citizens United refuses to give full force to the importance of equality of the collective people in the political process. The arguments that follow can be seen on the one hand as compelling government interests in the *Buckley* framework, and on the other as independent interests that have been simply overlooked in the conversation. However viewed, they highlight the fundamental shortcomings of *Buckley* and the cases that have followed it, culminating in *Citizens United*.

In the following pages, I will first look at the way elected officials and candidates lose time to the fund-raising race and how that detracts from their ability to do their jobs. Next, I will explore the concentration of power in the hands of an elite group of fund-raisers. Analogizing to case law that established the one-person, one-vote rule, I argue that it is an unconstitutional dilution of the power of the many. And finally, I will point out how these and other concerns in the area of campaign reform speak to the central issue of how our government works. That opens up an argument that there is a constitutional issue presented via the Guarantee Clause. All these ideas speak to central notions of equality of participation in the political process, an idea that is forgotten when individual First Amendment liberty is the focus of the debate, as in *Citizens United*.

Time Protection

The *Citizens United* Court fails to give adequate weight to the compelling interest of protecting the time of elected officials.[35] Candidates are locked in an escalating cycle of fund-raising for campaigns that consumes their time. They spend more money each election, therefore they must start fund-raising earlier and do so more often in order to raise more for the next election.[36] These candidates are often incumbents; consequently they spend less time doing the job they were elected to perform and more time campaigning for their reelection. This presents several issues: First, candidates do not engage with their constituents on the campaign trail. Additionally, elected officials must become full-time fund-raisers, which inevitably leads them to devote less time to their official duties. As time is lost, attention to constituents and the broader good is lost, and elite interests get a disproportionate voice; ultimately, egalitarian principles of democracy are threatened.

The costs of campaigns continually increase at a rate greater than inflation. The amount of money that an individual can give is capped and the amount of Americans who actually contribute has remained static.[37] Therefore, members of Congress must engage in a money chase in which they are constantly making fund-raising phone calls, travelling to and attending fund-raising events, and speaking to wealthy contributors.

In order to meet the ever-growing demand for campaign cash, candidates must reach beyond friends, voters, and their own constituents, and travel to the wealthy, contributor-rich areas of the country.[38] By engaging in this type of fund-raising with the elite donors, elected officials from all over the country lend their ear to the same moneyed individuals over and over—rather than their own respective constituents. This in turn conflicts with their job performance, creating "'a very real distraction from the real business of legislating.'"[39] This time should otherwise be used for interacting with voters and, in the case of candidates who are already officeholders, this is time stolen from the people's business. Public officials focused on fund-raising are not doing the people's work.

Protecting the time of candidates and elected officials helps ensure greater equality of participation in our democracy. As I have argued elsewhere, time protection enhances the political process by allowing candidates to be educated by their constituents, empowering the people, thereby enhancing representative democracy.[40] In a functional way, campaigns should be viewed as the job interview by which we choose our elected leaders.[41] We the people have the power to choose who will represent us in our local, state, and national governments, and campaigns should help us in the decision-making process. In that sense campaigns serve a basic function of representative democracy, and in the ideal they are conversations between the people and the candidates, empowering the people.[42]

But there's more. Interaction between candidates and the citizenry is central to creating the kind of debate that is at the heart of American democracy. "In a republic where the people are sovereign, the ability of the citizenry to make informed choices among candidates for office is essential, for the identities of those who are elected will inevitably shape the course we follow as a nation."[43] Political discourse reflects the Framers' values and maintains the ultimate purpose of a representative democracy by empowering the people. Speeches at rallies, debates, meetings in living rooms, and so on make the American people direct participants in democratic dialogue. Elected officials themselves recognize that the campaign fund-raising pressures force them to neglect their responsibilities as lawmakers.[44] Candidates neglecting their duties diminish the representation provided by an individual elected official and the overall capacity of the body to function to its fullest.

There is one other notable aspect to the time protection concern. Elected officials face great pressure to pursue and woo the wealthy few who fund political campaigns, and they spend less time on the daily business of governing, and less time with constituents.[45] In addition to the lack of representation faced by the people when their elected officials are on the fund-raising circuit, that representation is further undermined by the undue influence placed in the hands of the wealthy few who support the campaign machine.[46] Meaningful campaign finance reform protects the time of elected officials by attempting to limit overall campaign expenditures, so that candidates spend less time fund-raising and more time serving the compelling interests outlined above.[47]

In *Randall v. Sorrell* the Supreme Court was urged to accept the protection of elected officials' time as a compelling interest. Justice John Paul Stevens articulated the issue clearly:

> Without expenditure limits, fundraising devours the time and attention of political leaders, leaving them too busy to handle their public responsibilities effectively. That fact was well recognized by backers of the legislation reviewed in *Buckley*, by the Court of Appeals judges who voted to uphold the expenditure limitations in that statute, and by Justice White—who not incidentally had personal experience as an active participant in a Presidential campaign. The validity of their judgment has surely been confirmed by the mountains of evidence that has been accumulated in recent years concerning the time that elected officials spend raising money for future campaigns and the adverse effect of fundraising on the performance of their official duties.[48]

Further, Justice David Souter, joined by Justices Ruth Bader Ginsburg and Stevens, criticized the plurality for treating *Buckley*'s brief mention of time protection as if it were a thorough review of a governmental interest.[49] Justice Souter rightly noted that the decision in *Buckley* is centered on the corruption argument and "the Court did not squarely address a time-protection interest as support for the expenditure limits, much less one buttressed by as thorough a record as we have here."[50] Ultimately, and unfortunately, a majority of the Court failed to reach a consensus on the issue.[51]

This decision highlights the way in which the Court ignores the reality of time constraints on candidates due to fund-raising pressures in pursuit of a narrow First Amendment analysis. Campaign finance reform, and specifically expenditure limits, directly responds to this failure in our democracy by freeing up time spent fund-raising so that elected officials can get back to work.[52] The time protection rationale promotes and protects representative equality, in addition to the speech concerns that the Court so heavily relies upon. A narrow focus on individual speech rights obscures the big picture of a distorted political process.

Vote Dilution

A narrow focus on individual speech rights also ignores the broad problem of disproportionate power resting in the hands of the few. Equality in political participation and popular sovereignty are the roots of the American republic, going back to the nation's inception. For example, in *The Federalist No. 39*, James Madison wrote:

> We may define a republic to be, or at least may bestow that name on, a government which derives all its powers directly or indirectly from the great body of the people, and is administered by persons holding their offices during pleasure, for a limited period, or during good behavior. It is essential to such a government that it be derived from the great body of the society, not from an inconsiderable proportion or favored class of it. . . . It is *sufficient* for such a government that the persons administering it be appointed, either directly or indirectly, by the people.[53]

The Framers thus established a representative government that was largely designed to give power to the many. "The command of Art. I, §2, that Representatives be chosen 'by the People of the several States', means that as nearly as is practicable one man's vote in a congressional election is to be worth as much as another's."[54] And since the early days of the republic, the nation has become more and more inclusive—an increasing commitment to the constitutional promise of equality.[55]

There is little doubt that equality of participation is central to our modern democracy. From the founding principles of representational government, to the post–Civil War Amendments, to Women's Suffrage and the Warren Court of the 1960s, we have witnessed a common theme of expansion of equality and a strong belief that the power in a representative democracy should rest with the people, not with the wealthy few. The Supreme Court rejected vote dilution based on racially motivated voting patterns and voting districts in the early 1960s and established precedent that the Equal Protection Clause of the Fourteenth Amendment required equality of representation *and* participation.[56] The same Equal Protection principles prohibiting vote dilution should apply equally to modern day politics and the concentration of power and access in the wealthy.

Unequal participation offends Supreme Court precedent and the nation's representative principles. As the few elite fund-raisers coalesce more power, the many lose power. Campaign finance reform regularly enhances equality of political participation, but that benefit has been overlooked by the case law running from *Buckley* to *Citizens United*. As fund-raising relies heavily on the wealthiest donors, it concentrates power.[57] Because they have the money to support many candidates, this effectively gives the wealthy greater representation.[58] The modern concentration of power dilutes the power of the average voter who is denied equal participation in the process. After *Citizens United*, the flow of money from corporations and unions compounds the political influence of the wealthy elite.[59] The few can increase their contributions and their power more than ever before.[60]

As noted, the Supreme Court has repeatedly embraced the importance of equality of representation and participation in the political process. First, the Court interpreted the Equal Protection Clause to reject vote dilution and the concentration of power that came with malapportionment.[61] In a series of cases, the Court found that the Fourteenth Amendment Equal Protection Clause specifically demanded equality of participation in the political process and established the one-person, one-vote principle.[62] By looking at the Fifteenth and Nineteenth Amendments' requirement of voting equality in cases such as *Gray v. Sanders*, the Court also built on Fourteenth Amendment equality concerns.[63]

In *Reynolds v. Sims*, the Court spoke expansively, positing that voting is emblematic of the equality that defines a representative democracy:

> Representative government is in essence self-government through the medium of elected representatives of the people, and each and every citizen has an inalienable right to full and effective participation in the political processes of his State's legislative bodies. Most citizens can achieve this participation only as qualified voters through the election of legislators to represent them. Full and effective participation by all citizens in state government requires, therefore, that each citizen have an equally effective voice in the election of members of his state legislature. Modern and viable state government needs, and the Constitution demands, no less.[64]

With phrases like "inalienable right to full and effective participation," the Court broadened the notion of equality in America's representative government.[65]

The foundation of popular sovereignty honors equality of participation from the electorate. Vote dilution and its corollary, concentration of political power, run directly contrary to this ideal.[66] Power derives from all the people; it should be distributed evenly and not rest disproportionately in the hands of the few. But vote dilution concentrates power in the hands of the few, and thus runs counter to the principles announced in the Supreme Court decisions on voting, the Constitution and its amendments, and the fundamental spirit of American representative democracy. That was the challenge of a generation past.

Today power is concentrated in the hands of the few, and the wealthy possess inordinate influence and access in politics and government. *Citizens United* overturned prior decisions as it removed restrictions on corporate and union spending in campaigns. Now, multi-billion dollar corporations can spend unlimited amounts to influence elections in this country. Power can accrete in the hands of the wealthy, even more than before. The voices of individual citizens and candidates can easily be drowned out by the avalanche of unchecked corporate spending, negating the promise of equality that allows for all to be heard.

The Guarantee Clause and the Republican Form of Government

The time protection and vote dilution concerns directly lead to one final issue of equality of participation in our political process. A larger structural issue sheds light on the limited nature of the constitutional analysis in *Citizens United*. The heart of the American republic is popular sovereignty—the people are supreme, and their political will is done in the central government by duly elected representatives.[67] As Thomas Jefferson put it: "A government is republican in proportion as every member composing it has his equal voice in the direction of its concerns (not indeed in person, which would be impracticable beyond the limits of a city, or small township, but) by representatives chosen by himself."[68] In the republic, the people must have control of their choices—not simply by being able to vote, but having the government act in their best interest.[69] The Guarantee Clause mandates that the federal government protect the republican form of government.[70] Today, the increased influence of the few is diminishing the responsiveness of the representative to the many.[71] The republican form of government is thus in jeopardy, now more than ever, following the *Citizens United* decision.

Article IV, Section 4 carries a command that, coupled with the republic created in the previous three articles, the entire nation—federal and state governments—always would be republican.[72] The Guarantee Clause ensures that the states maintain the same basic form of government as the Constitution created for the national government: "The United States shall guarantee to every State in this Union a Republican Form of Government. . . ."[73] Properly understood, campaign finance reform protects the republican form of government upon which the nation was founded.

In the republic created by the Framers the people could reign supreme without surrendering their daily lives, and the government could function without the gridlock of every citizen's individual participation. As the new system defied easy labeling, the Framers sought common understandings, consistently emphasizing the power of the people. Again, we look to *The Federalist No. 39*:

> We may define a republic to be, or at least may bestow that name on, a government which derives all its powers directly or indirectly from the great body of the people; and is administered by persons holding their offices during pleasure for a limited period, or during good behaviour. It is *essential* to such a government that it be derived from the great body of the society, not from an inconsiderable proportion or a favored class of it. . . . It is *sufficient* for such a government that the persons administering it be appointed, either directly or indirectly, by the people.[74]

While the people cede power to their representatives, they retain the leverage of holding their representatives accountable at the ballot box.[75] Speaking to this point, Alexander Hamilton believed that "the people remained 'sovereign' only through the carefully guarded and complex machinery of election."[76]

The unchecked presence of money in politics presents a threat to the republican form of government. Currently, wealthy individuals maintain a disproportionate influence at the expense of the many, resulting in the potential for elected officials to betray their responsibility of representation. As the few maintain a disproportionate sway over elected representatives, the representative is more likely to exercise judgment on behalf of the few than on behalf of the many.[77] Former U.S. Senator Bill Bradley offered the following assessment:

> Nothing breaks down trust in democracy as powerfully and surely as money. The truest model of how our republic is supposed to work is citizens speaking to their representatives and representatives responding to their constituents' voices and concerns. Big money gets in the way of that. It's like a great stone wall separating us from our representatives in Congress and making it almost

> impossible for them to respond to our commonsense request that they address the profound issues that affect all of us.[78]

The influence of the few deprives the people of their representation and diminishes the republic.[79] In order for the republic to be truly representative, the people must have control of their choices—not simply being able to vote, but having their representatives reflect their interests, not those whose financial support enabled their election.[80] Properly understood against this backdrop, regulating money in politics is essential to ensuring a republican government that is responsive to the people.

The unequal influence of monied interests such as corporations imperils the republic, as the people cannot match resources with them and therefore have less sway over Congress. Without even acknowledging it, the *Citizens United* decision further cements this inequality, and accordingly increases the threat that this inequality poses to the republic. Without regulation, the unelected few will continue to tighten their grasp on the process, their influence will corrupt the representative system of government, and inequality will increase.[81] The *Citizens United* analysis fails to consider this reality, overlooking the Guarantee Clause and forgetting broad structural principles of equality.

With popular sovereignty at the heart of the republican form of government, the people reign supreme, and representatives in the central government act in the best interest of all the people—the many, not the few. The Guarantee Clause provides an affirmative obligation for the United States to protect the republican form in the states.[82]

Conclusion

Buckley set in motion a long line of cases that logically culminated in *Citizens United*. Beginning with *Buckley*, you start with a premise that money equals speech. From there, things degenerate rapidly, so that unlimited spending by corporations and unions seems only logical. The case law has been so ill-considered for so long, as it grew from such a myopic opinion. The problem has only gotten worse, so that now we look at *Citizens United* as only the most recent step. The constitutional promise of equality has always carried us forward in our nation's struggle to form a more perfect union. But ironically, in the area of campaign finance reform, equality has been forgotten. We should not be surprised at the result in *Citizens United*, but as much as the Court celebrates speech values, we also need to elevate the promise of equality.

Money drives the political process, and campaign finance regulation appropriately tries to curb that influence. In part, because of the role that money plays in American politics, the few have great power, and candidates spend inordinate amounts of time chasing funds from the elite. Because they are so caught up spending time in the money chase, candidates and elected officials lose time that could be spent on behalf of constituents. In addition, the time spent with the elite few concentrates power in the hands of the few, further robbing the many of full representation. Ultimately, this undercuts the nature of the American republic, which was founded on egalitarian notions of collective participation.

The prevailing paradigm in campaign finance reform cases, however, focuses on individual free speech rights. In doing so, it ignores the broader principles of First Amendment theory and the importance of the robust public debate. Further, elevation of speech rights with a more libertarian focus ironically allows for the few to drown out the many. *Citizens United* elevates the individual right and extends it to corporations and unions, at the expense of the broad egalitarian conception of the American republic. Speech rights, vital as they are, inappropriately trump essential egalitarian concerns. There is much dissatisfaction with the Court's approach to campaign reform, along the lines of *Buckley* and *Citizens United*, but there is little consensus as to a better approach. I urge judges, lawmakers, and litigators alike to resurrect equality principles in their approach to this thorny issue.

Part IV

A Judge-Made Democracy

The Constitutionalization of Political Spending

11

On Dejudicializing American Campaign Finance Law

Richard Briffault[*]

The U.S. Supreme Court dominates American campaign finance law. *Citizens United v. Federal Election Commission*[1] dramatically illustrates this basic truth, but *Citizens United* is nothing new. The Court has been the preeminent force in shaping and constraining our campaign finance laws since *Buckley v. Valeo*[2] in 1976, and the Court's role as arbiter of what rules may or may not be enforced only continues to grow. The president of the United States can wag his finger at the Court during the State of the Union Address and denounce its *Citizens United* ruling to the justices' faces on national television, but even he does not propose to overturn any element of their decision. Instead, the president calls only for new laws in those areas where the Court indicated some regulation is permissible. According to public opinion polls, as much as 80 percent of the population opposes the Court's holding that corporations and unions have an unlimited right to spend money in elections.[3] But the public is, in practice, powerless to have the law changed.

The central features of American campaign finance law—its rules, its goals, and its scope—are the product of the Court's actions and opinions. To be sure, our campaign finance laws have been adopted by our elected representatives in Congress or state and local

---

* An unabridged version of this article will appear in the *Georgia State University Law Review*. Richard Briffault, *On Dejudicializing American Campaign Finance Law*, 27 Ga. St. U. L. Rev. (forthcoming May 2011).

legislatures, or by the people acting through state or local voter initiatives. But the Court consistently—and, particularly during the time of the Roberts Court, aggressively—has had the last word in deciding which laws may be allowed to take effect.

Court determination of campaign finance law might not be a bad thing if the Court's campaign finance jurisprudence were (i) stable and coherent, (ii) clearly determined by the text and values of the Constitution, or (iii) functionally necessary to protect democratic self-government. Unfortunately, our Court-determined campaign finance law is none of these things. The Court's campaign finance jurisprudence is a mess, marked by doctrinal zigzags, anomalous distinctions, unworkable rules, and illogical results. The law governing corporate spending may be the poster child for the instability of campaign finance law—and the complexity such instability has bred—but it is far from unique. The Court has careened back and forth on the definition of the scope of campaign-related speech, and on the nature of the "corruption" necessary to justify campaign finance regulation. Moreover, the centerpiece of the Court's approach to campaign finance law—the contribution/expenditure distinction—has been difficult to apply and has given rise to some of the worst features of our current campaign finance system. From an internal perspective, after almost thirty-five years, the Court has failed to develop a consistent and workable body of doctrine.

Nor is the Court's jurisprudence clearly required by the text, values, or structure of the Constitution. The Constitution does not speak to campaign financing, or at least it does not speak clearly or univocally. The Constitution brings multiple concerns to bear in addressing campaign financing—including the right to vote, freedom of speech and association, equality, and self-government. These values can come into conflict—and typically they do—in the making of campaign finance policy. The Constitution provides no standard for resolving those conflicts. The Court has no greater legitimacy than the other branches of government in weighing and balancing the political values that go into campaign finance law. Moreover, it surely has much less expertise than the other branches of government in understanding how campaign finance works in practice and how legal rules can shape, or distort, the flow of money in elections.

Finally, there is no good functional argument for the judicialization of campaign finance regulation. In theory, there is some danger that elected officials will misuse campaign finance law to entrench themselves in office. But there is actually little evidence that campaign finance regulation has been used to favor incumbents—or that it favors incumbents more than an absence of regulation. Judicialization of campaign finance law is no more functionally necessary than it is constitutionally required.

Campaign finance law ought to be, to a considerable degree, dejudicialized—not deconstitutionalized, but dejudicialized. Campaign finance law inevitably is shaped by and reflective of constitutional values, and like election law more generally it is constitutive of our polity. But the Court has failed to develop a coherent and workable doctrine, fully reflective of the relevant constitutional norms, that justifies the aggressive and constraining role it has assumed. The Court should step back and be more deferential to the decisions of elected representatives or of the people themselves. This does not mean judicial abandonment of the field. The Court still needs to police against laws that would discriminate against minorities and political outsiders or that would entrench incumbent officeholders or parties. That is the path taken by the courts in Canada,[4] and by the European Court of Human Rights,[5] of marking the outer limits of legislative regulation but not imposing tight prescriptions on political choices. But short of these extreme cases, the Court should let the democratic process play the leading role in determining how democratic elections ought to be financed.

This chapter will review some of the internal problems with the Court's campaign finance doctrine, consider how the Court has rejected or ignored many of the legitimate political concerns underlying campaign finance law, and rebut the argument that aggressive judicial policing of campaign finance law is justified by a concern about incumbent self-entrenchment. I will conclude by suggesting, with reference to some of the Court's other election law doctrines, how a more dejudicialized campaign finance law—with a Court more deferential to the decisions of elected representatives and to the electorate—might work.

The Court's Doctrinal Difficulties

Among the key goals of legal doctrine are temporal stability, internal consistency, and practical workability. By that measure, the Court's campaign finance doctrine has long been a failure. This can be seen in the Court's shifting approach to laws regulating corporations, and in the Court's efforts to maintain the distinction between contributions and expenditures first drawn in *Buckley*.

Corporations

In 1978, in *First National Bank of Boston v. Bellotti*,[6] the Court struck down a Massachusetts law forbidding corporations from spending to influence the vote in ballot proposition elections. After *Bellotti*, however, the Court shifted gears and repeatedly upheld federal and state laws that subjected corporations to special campaign regulations. In a succession of cases—*Federal Election Commission v. National Right to Work Committee* (1982),[7] *Federal Election Commission v. Massachusetts Citizens for Life, Inc.* (1986),[8] *Austin v. Michigan Chamber of Commerce* (1990),[9] *Federal Election Commission v. Beaumont* (2003),[10] and *McConnell v. Federal Election Commission* (2003)[11]—the Court determined that the longstanding governmental interest in "ensur[ing] that substantial aggregations of wealth amassed by the special advantages which go with the corporate form of organization should not be converted into political 'war chests'" justified the specially restrictive treatment of corporations.[12]

The Court began its about-face on corporations following Justice Sandra Day O'Connor's retirement and her replacement by Justice Samuel Alito. In 2007, in *FEC v. Wisconsin Right to Life, Inc.*,[13] the Court sharply cut back on the limits on corporate spending it had just approved in *McConnell*. And in *Citizens United*, the Court fully invalidated the limits previously sustained in *McConnell*. *Citizens United* determined that the corporate form is irrelevant to the constitutionality of limits on corporate spending.

Yet even after three decades of doctrinal zigzag the question of whether corporations present special problems justifying campaign finance restrictions is still not fully laid to rest. Although *Citizens United* overruled *Austin* and the relevant portion of *McConnell,* it left alone the cases that upheld the longstanding laws prohibiting corporate contributions to candidates. Given that contributions enjoy some constitutional protections—albeit less protection than expenditures receive—it is uncertain if a complete ban on corporate donations can be sustained without some judicial endorsement of the view emphatically disavowed in *Citizens United* that corporate campaign participation presents no special dangers of corruption.[14] It is not clear if the absolute federal and state bans on corporate campaign contributions ultimately will survive *Citizens United.* The fundamental uncertainty in the Court's treatment of campaign finance restrictions on corporations for the last third of a century remains.

The Contribution/Expenditure Distinction

The contribution/expenditure distinction has been at the heart of American campaign finance jurisprudence since *Buckley v. Valeo*. The term *contribution* refers to money or other things of value provided by one campaign participant to another, such as a donation by an individual to a candidate, political party, or political action committee (PAC) or a donation by a PAC to a candidate or political party. The term *expenditure* refers to the money spent by a campaign actor—such as a candidate, political party, or PAC—on communications or other efforts to affect voters' decisions. For all but self-financing candidates, campaign contributions supply the funds that campaign actors use to pay for campaign expenditures. *Buckley* treated expenditures as the highest form of campaign speech; consequently, restrictions on expenditures were subject to strict judicial scrutiny. Contributions, by contrast, were treated as a lower order of speech. The Court asserted that, unlike an expenditure, a contribution does not entail an expression of political views. As a result, contribution restrictions were subject to less strict review, and would be upheld if "closely drawn" to advance "sufficiently important" government interests. The prevention of corruption and the appearance of corruption were held to be interests important enough to justify contribution limits.

For more than three decades, *Buckley*'s contribution/expenditure distinction has shaped the Court's campaign finance doctrines. However, the sharp separation of the two categories of campaign money has created serious problems. By permitting candidates to spend unlimited funds but requiring them to collect campaign funds in only limited sums, the *Buckley* regime pushes candidates to devote enormous amounts of time and effort to fund-raising. Indeed, fund-raising ability itself has become a prerequisite to candidacy. So, too, the contribution/expenditure distinction has provided an enormous opening to political intermediaries such as political action committees (PACs) and bundlers that can enable candidates to address the fund-raising problem inherent in the system created by the Court of unlimited spending financed by limited donations. When candidates need to spend large sums of money but can raise contributions only in small amounts, the assistance provided by PACs and bundlers can be vital, and a great source of influence with the candidates they aid.

The most vexing application of the contribution/expenditure distinction has involved independent expenditures. The Court has recognized that expenditures that are coordinated with a candidate's campaign present the same dangers of corruption and the appearance of corruption as contributions and, accordingly, has held that they may be regulated like contributions.[15] However, the Court has rejected the idea that independent expenditures can be limited—even though such expenditures aid a candidate and may be likely to cause a candidate to feel just as obligated to the spender as to the donor of a comparable amount of money to the candidate's campaign. This has led to some bizarre results. In *Colorado Republican Federal Campaign Committee v. Federal Election Commission*,[16] the Court held that spending by a political party in support of its own Senate candidate must be treated as independent—and thus not subject to restriction—as long as the spending was not actually coordinated with the candidate. The lack of any formal coordination with that candidate was treated as of greater constitutional significance than the ongoing institutional relationship between a party's candidates and the party.

In *Caperton v. A.T. Massey Coal Co., Inc.*,[17] the Court actually recognized that independent spending could be the functional equivalent of a contribution and just as corrupting as a contribution of comparable size. *Caperton* held that a judge elected after an election campaign in which he had been the beneficiary of millions of dollars of independent expenditures was required, as a matter of due process, to recuse himself from a case involving the independent spender. The Court determined that the enormous amount of campaign assistance had created "a serious risk of actual bias—based on objective and reasonable perceptions—" in favor of the independent spender.[18] Stunningly, *Caperton* completely blurred the contribution/expenditure distinction that the Court had spent thirty-three years developing and sustaining when it repeatedly referred to the large independent expenditures in the case as "contributions,"[19] not independent expenditures. In *Caperton*, functional reality finally overwhelmed the legal categories.

But in *Citizens United*, barely six months after *Caperton*, the Court not only returned to the contribution/expenditure distinction, but also made it absolute, shutting the door to any recognition of the potentially corrupting effects in practice of at least some independent expenditures. The Court acknowledged that elected officials might "succumb to improper influences from independent expenditures."[20] Nonetheless, *Citizens United* declared limits on independent spending unconstitutional under all circumstances and regardless of the empirical evidence of the effects of such spending on the elected officials who benefit from them.

The Court has also experienced difficulty in determining when contributions have sufficient corruptive potential to be subject to limitation. In *Buckley*, the Court stressed that corruption is not limited to the kinds of quid pro quo deals already addressed by bribery laws. Bribes, the Court observed, are only "the most blatant and specific attempts of those with money to influence government action."[21] Subsequently, the Court reemphasized that the corruption concern is "not confined to bribery of public officials, but extend[s] to the broader threat from politicians too compliant with the wishes of large contributors."[22] In other cases, however, the Court has stated that "[t]he hallmark of corruption is the financial *quid pro quo*: dollars for political favors."[23]

The issue came to a head in *McConnell*, when the Court addressed Congress's restrictions on soft money contributions, that is, donations by wealthy individuals, corporations, and unions that were dramatically greater than the dollar caps on individual donations or that flatly violated the ban on corporate and union donations to federal candidates and parties. Technically, soft money donations did not go to specific candidates or to parties for direct support of specific candidates, but were given to the parties to finance party activities generally or to pay for party activities that aid candidates across the board, like voter registration and get-out-the-vote drives and generic party advertising, not specific candidates. Citing the absence of a direct relationship between the donor and a specific candidate, defenders of soft money contended that the practice did not raise an issue of corruption that would justify restriction. A closely divided Court, however, found there was substantial evidence that federal officeholders and candidates avidly sought soft money and that major donors provided it "for the express purpose of securing influence over federal officials."[24] The Court concluded that Congress could decide that the preferential access special interest donors obtained from large soft money donations was corruption.[25]

But, in *Citizens United,* the Court rejected its own prior broad reading of corruption. Justice Anthony Kennedy cited and quoted extensively from his *McConnell* dissent—which he cited as an "opinion" and not a "dissenting opinion." He emphasized that "[t]he fact that speakers may have influence over or access to elected officials does not mean that these officials are corrupt,"[26] and that concern about undue influence cannot be a basis for limiting campaign money. Although a consistent theme in *Citizens United* is that expenditures are categorically different from contributions, the Court cited and quoted language that would lead to a much more restrictive approach to contribution limitations as well. Indeed, after *Citizens United,* it is far from clear whether the soft money restrictions upheld in *McConnell* will survive.

The contribution/expenditure distinction is, thus, both fundamental to campaign finance jurisprudence and riddled with line-drawing issues and inconsistencies. Many of the justices have realized this, and in recent cases a majority of the justices have hinted they no longer agree with *Buckley*'s central holding. In 2006, in *Randall v. Sorrell,*[27] Justices Clarence Thomas and Antonin Scalia indicated they would subject contribution restrictions to strict judicial scrutiny, just like expenditure limits.[28] Justice Kennedy also voiced his "skepticism regarding that system and its operation."[29] On the other hand, Justices John Paul Stevens,[30] David Souter,[31] and Ruth Bader Ginsburg[32] in *Randall* indicated they were willing to reconsider *Buckley*'s ban on expenditure limits. Justice Stephen Breyer, joined by Justice Ginsburg, previously had written to suggest that "it might prove possible to reinterpret aspects of *Buckley* in light of the post-*Buckley* experience . . . making less absolute the contribution/expenditure line, particularly in respect to independently wealthy candidates."[33] In *Citizens United*, Justice Stevens, joined by Justices Ginsburg, Breyer, and Sonia Sotomayor, contended that "even technically independent expenditures can be corrupting in much the same way as direct contributions."[34]

The contribution/expenditure distinction still stands, not because it is logically persuasive or operationally successful, but because so far there has not been an alternative approach that commands majority support. At present, as *Citizens United* suggests, it is likely that any change by the Roberts Court would involve greater restrictions on public power to limit contributions rather than a relaxation of the ban against expenditure restrictions. Doctrinal inconsistency and incoherence are serious problems, but they may be the price that has to be paid for a continuing measure of regulatory flexibility.

The Permissible Purposes of Campaign Finance Regulation

The Court's difficulties in framing a stable, coherent, and workable doctrine are not entirely surprising. Campaign finance law implicates multiple constitutional concerns, including freedom of speech and association, voter information, political equality, the integrity of the electoral process, and the consequences of the campaign finance system for the effectiveness and integrity of government. These constitutional concerns often come into conflict, but the Constitution does not indicate how they are to be weighed and balanced against each other. The conflicts are often deeply normative, and include the trade-offs between equality and free speech raised by the imposition of limits on campaign money; between political participation and government integrity posed by contribution restrictions; and between political participation and voter information posed by disclosure rules. These conflicts also often turn on the resolution of empirical questions, such as whether independent spending has the same potential to influence government officials as direct contributions, or whether spending limits affect fair electoral competition by helping or hindering incumbents.

The Court has, to a considerable degree, assumed the authority to resolve these questions. But it has done so largely by dismissing outright certain values (such as equality) or by narrowly defining the role played by other considerations (such as competitive elections and the impact of campaign finance on governance). In so doing, the Court has rejected the judgments of elected officials, and of voters approving ballot propositions, that those values matter and ought to be taken into account in the rules that govern campaign contributions and spending. And, it has done so without a clear constitutional mandate to privilege the Court's values over the political judgments endorsed by elected officials and voters.

Equality

The most important constitutional value the Court has rejected is, of course, voter equality, which is a central premise of our democratic system. Over the course of our history, the electorate has been expanded from a relatively narrow set of white male property owners or taxpayers to virtually all adult citizens. Modern constitutional developments such as the one person, one vote doctrine[35] and the anti-vote-dilution doctrine[36] have sought to ensure not simply that every adult citizen enjoys the right to vote, but that each voter has an equally weighted vote and an equal opportunity to influence the outcome of an election. Moreover, modern constitutional law emphatically denies a special place for wealth in voting and elections. Most states long ago scrapped wealth or tax-payment requirements for voting, and the Court made the elimination of such wealth or tax-payment tests constitutionally mandatory. Wealth may not be a criterion for the right to cast a ballot,[37] or to be a candidate,[38] nor may the wealth of a voter be a factor in deciding how much weight a particular vote may be given.[39]

The role of voter equality in our electoral system has implications beyond the actual casting and counting of ballots. For the election to serve as a mechanism of democratic decision-making there must be a considerable amount of election-related activity before balloting can occur. Candidates, parties, interest groups, and interested individuals need to be able to attempt to persuade voters as to how to cast their ballots. The election campaign is an integral part of the process of structured choice and democratic deliberation that constitutes an election. The political equality norm that governs the right to vote, the aggregation of votes into election districts, and the right to be a candidate is similarly relevant to the right to present choices to the general electorate and to attempt to persuade the electorate to support certain candidates or a particular position on a ballot proposition. Political equality is undermined when some individuals or interest groups with greater private wealth than others can draw on those resources and make more frequent, more extensive, and more sophisticated appeals to the electorate, and undertake greater efforts to reach out to and mobilize supporters and get them to the polls.

Buckley famously and emphatically rejected the idea that the advancement of political equality can justify spending limits, declaring that "the concept that government may restrict the speech of some elements of our society in order to enhance the relative voice of others is wholly foreign to the First Amendment."[40] But the Court provided absolutely no support for this stark proposition other than by citing cases attesting generally to the value of political speech.[41] The Court observed that "the First Amendment's protection against abridgment of free expression cannot properly be made to depend on a person's financial ability to engage in public discussion"[42]—which seems at best orthogonal to the political equality goal of limiting the possibility that a "person's financial ability" will enable him to dominate "public discussion."

As Justice Breyer has pointed out, *Buckley*'s flat rejection of limits on spending as a means of ensuring that all may be heard "cannot be taken literally."[43] As he explained, "[t]he Constitution often permits restrictions on the speech of some in order to prevent a few from drowning out the many—in Congress, for example, where constitutionally protected debate . . . is limited to provide every Member an equal opportunity to express his or her views. Or in elections, where the Constitution tolerates numerous restrictions on ballot access, limiting the political rights of some so as to make effective the political rights of the entire electorate."[44] Indeed, prior to *Buckley*, spending limits were a long-established part of American campaign finance law.[45]

Although *Citizens United* has drawn the most public attention, the case that best illustrates the Roberts Court's hostility to equality as a justification for campaign finance regulation is *Davis v. Federal Election Commission*.[46] The so-called Millionaires' Amendment invalidated in *Davis* did not limit the amount of money wealthy candidates could spend. All it did was make it easier for the non-wealthy opponent to raise money by lifting contribution ceilings, and only up to the point where she achieved resource parity with the self-funding candidate. The amendment was proposed and defended as a mechanism for partially leveling the playing field to make it easier for non-wealthy candidates to run against wealthy opponents and, more generally, to reduce the need for personal wealth in pursuing electoral office. For the Supreme Court majority, however, "level[ing] electoral opportunities" was a constitutional vice, not a virtue.[47] *Buckley* had said that the "governmental interest in equalizing the relative ability of individuals and groups to influence the outcome of elections" could not justify limits on spending.[48] *Davis* went much further in rejecting equality as a regulatory justification entirely.

Ameliorating the Burdens of Fund-raising

In a world without spending limits, elected officials are forced to devote enormous amounts of time to fund-raising, thereby cutting into their ability to devote the necessary time and attention to their public duties—"to information gathering, political and policy analysis, debating and compromising with their fellow representatives, and the public dissemination of views."[49] According to Columbia law professor Vincent Blasi, concern about the quality of the representation impaired by endless fund-raising is a matter of constitutional magnitude, derived from the norms of popular election and governance by elected representatives embodied in Article I, the Seventeenth Amendment, and the Republican Form of Government Clause.[50] In a sense, this time-protection concern is akin to the anti-corruption concern the Court endorsed in upholding contribution limits. Both reflect a well-founded recognition that a campaign finance process that entails the raising of large sums of money in private contributions can have adverse consequences for governance, either by skewing it in the direction of major donors or by denying elected officials the time they need to analyze, understand, debate, and resolve critical public issues.

A number of lower-court judges embraced this office-holder time-protection concern as a justification for limits on total candidate spending.[51] The Supreme Court, however, in *Randall v. Sorrell*, summarily dismissed this concern. The plurality opinion did not actually address the merits of the argument that the constitutional interest in representative government could support spending limits in order to protect representatives' time. Instead the opinion simply found the argument had been implicitly rejected in *Buckley* and was thus precluded by *stare decisis*.[52] However, the only discussion of the burdens of fund-raising in *Buckley* occurred in the context of the Court's affirmation of the presidential public funding program, which ameliorated those burdens. *Buckley* never discussed the time burdens of fund-raising or the constitutional value of officeholder time protection in its analysis of spending limits. In *Randall*, the Court took the argument off the table without ever having fully discussed it.

Fair and Competitive Elections

Elections are about giving voters choices. If one candidate has significantly more resources than his or her opponents, that candidate can have an advantage in campaigning and in getting his or her message to the voters. This can affect campaign outcomes. Moreover, if the election campaign is seen as financially unfair, it can undermine the legitimacy of the election in the eyes of the voters. Indeed, it is commonplace to say that a candidate who greatly outspends the opposition is attempting to "buy" the election, even if there is no evidence of literal vote-buying.

The concern about fair competition is particularly focused on the willingness of political newcomers to enter the fray, or the ability of challengers to take on incumbents effectively, and on the capacity of non-wealthy candidates to compete against wealthy candidates who self-fund their campaigns. In each of these situations, both the appearance and the reality of fair electoral competition are advanced when the difference in resources available to different candidates is moderated. This is particularly important in contests between challengers and incumbents. An incumbent typically enjoys many built-in electoral advantages, ranging from the free media attention he or she gets while in office, to the opportunity to use the office to provide constituency service, to the superior ability to raise campaign money, particularly from individuals, organizations, and interest groups that have a material stake in government action. One goal of campaign finance regulation is to promote fair elections by controlling the financial advantages that some candidates, particularly incumbents, enjoy.

The Court has given some attention to the concern about competitive elections in the context of campaign contributions. In upholding contribution limits, the Court has cautioned that the limits may not be so low that they prevent challengers from raising enough money to challenge incumbents effectively.[53] However, the Court has never considered the implications of this "constitutional concern for electoral accountability" for unlimited spending that may enable incumbents to radically outspend their challengers. Indeed, in *Davis,* the Court rejected improving competitiveness as a justification altogether. Rather than recognize that the Millionaires' Amendment could promote competitive elections without limiting the right to spend, the Court invalidated the law because it aimed to level electoral opportunities.

Strikingly, the Court has, in one way or another, recognized the power of each of the campaign finance norms that it has also rejected or dismissed. *Austin* was rooted in a concern to protect the political equality of voters from corporate war chests. *Buckley* cited the value of “free[ing] candidates from the rigors of fund-raising”[54] when it upheld the constitutionality of the presidential public funding system. The *Randall* plurality opinion relied heavily on a concern about the impact of campaign finance law on electoral competitiveness. *McConnell* embraced a broad definition of corruption. *Caperton* is premised on a concern about the corrupting effects of independent expenditures. These norms are sufficiently central to thinking about the financing of elections in a democratic society that the Court can repress them but cannot entirely deny them. Nonetheless, for the most part the Court has narrowed the field of constitutionally permissible bases for campaign finance regulation, and it has done so without either a clear constitutional directive or a fully reasoned analysis of why free speech concerns ought to dominate the field so utterly and displace all other values.

In so doing, the Court has been making political judgments about which values ought to count in framing campaign finance law. These are political judgments in the highest sense in that they involve a determination of how competing concerns for free speech, political equality, fair and competitive elections, and honest and effective government ought to be balanced. But they are also political in the sense that they are value judgments, not driven by the Constitution. These may be reasonable judgments, but it is not clear why these are the Court’s judgments to make. The Court has no greater constitutional authority and no greater political legitimacy than Congress or state or local legislatures in weighing and balancing the respective roles of free speech, political participation, voter information, competitive elections, voter equality, government integrity, and elected official time-protection in determining campaign finance law.

Moreover, the Court certainly lacks the deep understanding of how campaign finance operates in practice—how money affects elections and how the raising and spending of campaign money affect the behavior of government and its ability to represent and respond to the interest of the entire electorate—that is hard-wired into the consciousness of elected officials. Today, we have a Court in which not a single justice ever ran for or held elective office. It is perhaps not surprising that some of the justices most deferential to campaign finance laws were either justices who had once held elective office themselves, like Justice O’Connor—the coauthor of the *McConnell* decision upholding the key elements of the Bipartisan Campaign Reform Act (BCRA, also known as the McCain-Feingold Act)—or who had been involved in managing an election campaign, like Justice Byron White, the only dissenter in *Buckley*. Campaign finance jurisprudence entails practical empirical judgments, which elected officials are clearly better equipped to make than justices who have never subjected themselves to the rigors of an election campaign.

The Limits of the Functional Argument for Aggressive Judicial Review

It could be argued that aggressive judicial policing of campaign finance law is appropriate because of the danger that elected officials will adopt laws that are self-serving, incumbent-protective, and ruling-party entrenching. Even if it is true that only politicians can understand campaign finance well enough in practice to produce workable campaign finance laws, it also can be argued that campaign finance is too political to be left to the politicians. Much as the Court's intervention into the political thicket of legislative apportionment was justified by the ongoing unwillingness of elected officials to change the rules under which they had been elected,[55] the Court's extensive intervention into campaign finance law can be justified by a well-founded fear that incumbents will manipulate campaign finance laws in their own interest.

There are four problems with this argument. First, historically, campaign finance regulation has not reflected an effort by the party in power to entrench itself. Typically, campaign finance laws are enacted by cross-party coalitions, often consisting of a minority faction of the party in power acting in alliance with the party out of power.[56] Thus, the first federal campaign finance laws enacted in the period between 1907 and 1925—an era of clear Republican dominance—were pushed through by the Progressive minority within the Republican Party working with the Democratic minority in Congress. These reforms were intended to weaken, not strengthen, the leading party.[57] Similarly, the campaign laws adopted in the period between 1939 and

1947—a period of Democratic dominance—were pushed through by a combination of the conservative wing of the Democratic Party in alliance with Republicans, and were aimed in large part at weakening the financial role of key groups in the Democratic Party—public employees and unions.[58]

More recently, BCRA's soft money limits were adopted as a result of the efforts of a minority of ideological activists in the Democratic Party, notwithstanding the Democrats' greater dependence on soft money, joined by a reform remnant in the Republican Party clearly out of sync with the majority of the GOP.[59] BCRA was not an effort by a dominant party to entrench itself as there was no truly dominant party in Congress when BCRA was enacted in 2001–02. Democrats held the narrowest possible majority in the Senate, while Republicans controlled the House and the presidency. Only the Federal Election Campaign Act of 1971 (FECA) and the FECA amendments of 1974 can be seen as the product of a clear one-party (Democratic) Congressional majority. But, even those measures addressed the concerns of a Republican president,[60] and both received considerable Republican support.[61]

Second, it is not at all clear that the effect of campaign finance laws is to entrench parties in power. Other countries that have enacted spending limits have witnessed major swings in political control. Canada, for example, limits party campaign spending, independent spending, and spending on broadcast advertising in elections for its federal parliament. Yet, Canadian spending limits have not prevented major shifts in partisan alignments over the past two decades; spending limits did not lock the Progressive Conservatives into power in 1993, when they lost their parliamentary majority to the Liberals in a landslide, nor did it prevent them from regaining control from the Liberals in 2006. More strikingly, a Canadian Liberal Party government first limited, in 2003, and then barred in 2006, corporate contributions even though the Liberal Party was the prime beneficiary of corporate donations.[62] So, too, Great Britain voted its Labor government out of power in 2010, just a few years after a Parliament controlled by Labor adopted significant new campaign finance laws.

Third, it is far from clear that campaign finance laws are more advantageous to incumbents than no laws at all. Incumbents have built-in advantages in raising money. In the absence of contribution and expenditure limits, incumbents most likely would raise more money and spend more money than their challengers. Financially, incumbents as a group almost surely would be better off with less rather than more regulation.

Finally, concern about incumbency protection does not explain the Court's campaign finance decisions. The Court has never provided different constitutional treatment to laws adopted by voter initiative as opposed to those enacted by legislatures, yet surely the former measures are less likely to be intended to entrench incumbents. The campaign finance regime the Court has produced seems particularly likely to benefit incumbents, since they are best positioned to utilize the PACs, bundlers, and other political intermediaries necessary to collect the large number of dollar-limited contributions needed to finance the unlimited spending that the Court permits. Indeed, PACs consistently have favored incumbents, as well as the party in power or the party thought likely to win the election, in their campaign donations.[63]

Incumbency entrenchment is a plausible justification for aggressive judicial review of campaign finance law in theory, but it does not hold up that well in practice. Moreover, concern about incumbency protection does not require the rigid, categorical approach that the Court has taken to certain campaign finance laws, such as absolutely forbidding spending limits for candidates or independent committees or rejecting special attention to the needs of the opponents of wealthy self-funded candidates. Challenger interests can be vindicated by a close review of the details of particular laws in the relevant political context, rather than by per se rules.

Dejudicialized Campaign Finance Law

Campaign finance law ought to be dejudicialized. By that I do not mean that it ought to be deconstitutionalized. Campaign finance law has broad implications for a host of constitutional concerns—freedom of expression and association, the right to vote, fair electoral competition, honest government—so that constitutional review is entirely appropriate, indeed, necessary. But it ought to be dejudicialized so that courts play a lesser role in determining both the permissible goals of campaign finance law and the proper regulatory techniques. The determination of the values that ought to go into the financing of democratic elections; the weighing and balancing of competing concerns; and the fitting of campaign finance rules to particular political needs, settings, and practices are primarily political decisions that ought to be left to the politically accountable branches of government. The courts should continue to review specific laws in context to see if they are intended to, or are likely to, advantage incumbent officeholders or parties, and they also should strike down laws that are aimed at or unduly burden particular political viewpoints, especially those of minorities, the politically marginal, or adherents to unpopular causes or groups. Courts should, in effect, police the outer bounds of regulation—but they should stick to the outer bounds.

There are other instances of this approach in our election law jurisprudence. A good example is the Court's treatment of the state rules that limit the ability of third parties and independents to win places on the ballot. In *Williams v. Rhodes*,[64] the Court held that such laws burden two different, but overlapping, constitutional rights—"the right of individuals to associate for the advancement of political beliefs, and the right of qualified voters, regardless of their political persuasion, to cast their votes effectively." The Court then invalidated laws that raised such high hurdles to ballot access that new parties and independents were effectively barred from competing and the two major parties were given a "permanent monopoly on the right to have people vote for or against them."[65] However, in subsequent decades, the Court has upheld a host of restrictive ballot access rules, including significant signature requirements,[66] anti-sore-loser rules precluding primary election losers from running as independents in a general election,[67] laws barring the counting of write-in ballots,[68] and anti-fusion laws that have the effect of barring minor parties from nominating the candidates of a major party.[69] In so doing, the Court emphasized the positive value of state laws that regulate elections and limit electoral choices: "Common sense, as well as constitutional law, compels the conclusion that government must play an active role in structuring elections; as a practical matter, there must be a substantial regulation of elections if they are to be fair and honest and if some sort of order, rather than chaos, is to accompany the democratic process."[70] The Court's rules prevent total entrenchment of the two major parties but otherwise let the state political processes work out varying combinations of openness and stability, which inevitably reflect political judgments. The Court has limited its own role largely to policing only against "unreasonably exclusionary restrictions,"[71] not exclusionary restrictions per se.

A second instance of the Court letting states balance competing political considerations in the framing of election laws, subject to a judicially enforceable outer bound, may be partisan gerrymandering. In *Davis v. Bandemer*,[72] the Supreme Court held that partisan gerrymandering presents a justiciable constitutional question. The *Bandemer* majority, however, fragmented over how to determine what constitutes unconstitutional partisan gerrymandering, with the plurality opinion setting a very high bar for proving that a particular apportionment scheme is unconstitutional. Indeed, in the two decades after the decision, all assertions that particular districting plans imposed unconstitutional partisan gerrymanders were rejected.[73] In *Vieth v. Jubelirer*, the Court came close to disavowing the justiciability of claims of unconstitutional gerrymandering, but Justice Kennedy provided the fifth vote to keep the possibility of judicial oversight of partisan districting schemes alive. *Vieth*, like *Bandemer* before it, leaves the role of partisan concerns in legislative districting largely to the political process, but with a hint of a constitutional big stick in reserve in case of extreme partisan abuse.

To a considerable extent, the Court's treatment of contribution restrictions and disclosure requirements already follows this model of giving political decision-makers discretion to determine regulatory goals and techniques in general, while reviewing specific claims that, under certain circumstances, ordinarily acceptable rules have unduly burdensome consequences for challengers or political minorities. Contribution limits are generally acceptable, but the Court reviews them to see if they unduly burden the rights of donors or, especially, of candidates who need contributions to fund their campaigns. Although most limits on donations to candidates and parties have been upheld, excessively restrictive limits or prohibitions have been struck down. So, too, while the Court has held that disclosure requirements promote voter information and are constitutionally justified, the Court has invalidated some laws and created as-applied exceptions from others when the costs from the loss of political privacy exceed the value of the information provided.

This model should be expanded to deal with campaign finance regulation as a whole by expanding the permissible goals of campaign finance law to include promoting political equality and fair and competitive elections, addressing the burdens of fund-raising, and reducing the impact of campaign money on governance more broadly. Furthermore, it should recognize that regulatory techniques such as spending limits, differential contribution limits to address radically uneven campaign resources, and fair fight or matching funds in public funding programs ought not to be categorically ruled out. This is not to say that any of these ideas are necessarily ideal policies, but rather that they are plausible mechanisms for advancing the legitimate goals of campaign finance law, and do not inherently place an undue burden on fundamental rights, discriminate against minorities, or entrench incumbents. If the electorate passes a ballot initiative or a legislature enacts one of these regulatory techniques, it would be better to examine the context in which it was adopted and to see how it works in practice instead of ruling it out categorically.

The Supreme Court should step back from the dominant role it has undertaken in overseeing American campaign finance law. There is no one, clear constitutional norm driving campaign finance regulation. Rather, the law in this area involves the reconciliation of multiple, and sometimes conflicting, constitutional values. There is no reason to believe that the Court is any better at weighing and balancing these values than politically accountable decision-makers. Moreover, the record over the past thirty-five years demonstrates the Court's failure to develop a consistent, coherent, and workable jurisprudence that respects all the political values at stake. There are no obvious right answers in campaign finance—no one clearly correct way of combining freedom of speech and association, voter information, political equality, competitive elections, government integrity and effectiveness, and political administrability. Dejudicializing campaign finance law would, at the very least, facilitate variation according to state and local preferences and circumstances, and experimentation at the local and state levels that could enhance our understanding of how campaign finance law works in practice. So, too, a more modest judicial role would respect the inevitably political nature of campaign finance decision-making while still providing an outer bound of protection of constitutional rights.

12

Felix Frankfurter's Revenge: An Accidental Democracy Built by Judges

*Burt Neuborne**

The first decade of the twenty-first century opened and closed with two bitterly contested U.S. Supreme Court decisions impacting American democracy. In *Bush v. Gore*,[1] five members of the Court prevented Florida from completing a recount of the potentially deciding votes in the 2000 presidential election, judicially awarding the election to George Bush. In *Citizens United v. Federal Election Commission*,[2] a five-vote majority overturned two recent precedents and a century of practice in ruling that for-profit business corporations enjoy a First Amendment right to spend unlimited sums to influence elections.

Many have noted the artificially rigid nature of the electoral equality analysis in the *Bush v. Gore* majority opinion,[3] and the majority's departure from federalism principles in depriving Florida of the final decision about whether to continue the recount.[4] *Citizens United* is also vulnerable to doctrinal critique. Crucially, Justice Anthony Kennedy's majority opinion never persuasively confronts the threshold issue of whether for-profit business corporations are comparable to individuals for the purposes of First Amendment analysis.

While it is tempting to continue to pound on the two cases' doctrinal shortcomings (I will do more pounding on *Citizens United*, *infra*), doctrinal criticism, while important, almost never demonstrates definitively that a hard democracy case was wrongly decided. In both *Bush v. Gore* and *Citizens United*, plausible

*This chapter also appears in NYU's *Review of Law and Social Change* 35, no. 3 (2011). Reproduced by permission.

readings of constitutional doctrine point in two directions. In *Bush v. Gore*, seven justices, including Justices David Souter and Stephen Breyer, were persuaded that unconstitutionally unequal criteria were being applied in different Florida counties to measure the validity of contested presidential ballots. Justices Souter and Breyer disagreed only with the five-justice majority's decision to prevent Florida from seeking to correct the equality violation.[5] Even the five-justice decision to end the Florida recount, while deeply problematic as a matter of federalism, was based on a fear that unless the Court acted immediately, expiration of the congressional safe-harbor period designed to insulate state presidential electoral results from congressional challenge might result in disenfranchising the entire state, or worse.[6] While I believe that Florida should have had the final say on whether to take such a risk, and while the Court's refusal to trust Congress to act responsibly in dealing with a contested Electoral College issue bordered on contempt for the democratic process, I concede that treating the issue as one for Supreme Court resolution was defensible in the special context of a presidential election with immense national and international repercussions.[7] Similarly, in *Citizens United*, First Amendment stalwarts like Floyd Abrams and the American Civil Liberties Union have applauded Justice Kennedy's opinion as a great victory for free speech.[8] Viewed solely from a doctrinal perspective, therefore, while I believe that both cases got the law wrong, I cannot deny that reasonable people might differ as a matter of pure doctrine.

There is, however, a second level of critique potentially applicable, not only to both *Bush v. Gore* and *Citizens United*, but to the full range of judicial decisions that have shaped the contours of American democracy for the past half-century—the critique of democracy. Under existing constitutional ground rules, American judges, confronted by a hard constitutional case with implications for democracy, are not required—indeed, they may not even be permitted—to ask whether the outcome is good or bad for democracy. Rather, at least since *Baker v. Carr*[9]—a 1962 decision holding that federal courts could rule on voting district reapportionment issues—they are expected to resolve the case by shoehorning it into one or another doctrinal category, such as equal protection, freedom of association, or free speech, without ever asking what kind of democracy they are building. The result has been the emergence of a dysfunctional, accidental democracy built by judges operating with doctrinal tunnel vision.

It is long past time to bring concern over the quality of American democracy back into the judicial equation. The Constitution rests on three non-textual structural ideas—democracy, separation of powers, and federalism. Despite the absence of explicit textual guidance, the Supreme Court has forged effective constitutional doctrine protecting both federalism and the separation of powers.[10] There is no reason why a body of substantive doctrine could not be forged, as well, protecting democracy. I recognize, of course, that "democracy," like "the freedom of speech," or "Our Federalism," or "the separation of powers" is not a self-defining idea. But, like most of the luminous but abstract ideas in the Constitution, American democracy has an understandable core—robust self-government by citizens exercising equal political power—that can guide judges in deciding hard constitutional cases with implications for the working of the democratic process.

At a minimum, when constitutional doctrine is narrowly balanced and one outcome clearly impedes robust egalitarian self-government, while the other enhances it, preserving robust democracy should be an important factor in judicial decision-making.

When *Bush v. Gore* and *Citizens United* are viewed through a democracy-sensitive lens, they emerge as judicially imposed democratic disasters. Cutting off the Florida recount prevented the democratic resolution of a presidential election, resulting in a judicially imposed president. From a democracy standpoint, it does not get any worse.[11] Similarly, unleashing unlimited partisan spending by for-profit corporations on the eve of an election may be good for corporations, but it threatens to increase exponentially the already excessive role played by money in our political process. I do not believe for a minute that a rational Founder would have knowingly designed a democracy where judges pick the president and for-profit corporations dominate political discourse.

I hope to explain how we got to a place where judges ignore the quality of the democracy they are building, and to demonstrate that judges, operating solely at the level of doctrine, have accidently developed a profoundly dysfunctional law of democracy. I will argue that it is not too late to undo the damage. We can and should recognize that the judicially enunciated constitutional law of democracy is more than the interplay of unrelated formal constitutional doctrines, however correct the doctrinal analyses may be on their own terms. Rather, deciding democracy cases should be viewed as a free-standing process designed to advance, enhance, and protect the ability of "We the People" to govern ourselves as equal and effective participants in the democratic process.

How Did We Get Here?

A half-century ago in *Baker v. Carr* and its progeny, three iconic Supreme Court justices—Felix Frankfurter, William Brennan, Jr., and John Marshall Harlan—disagreed over the role of American judges in protecting democracy. Dissenting in *Baker*, Justice Frankfurter warned that we would rue the day that judges were given substantial power to set the constitutional ground rules for American democracy. Where, Frankfurter asked, would unelected judges, functioning as armchair political scientists, find the "judicially manageable standards" to guide their democracy decisions?[12] Frankfurter spoke for much of the old left in mistrusting the ability of an unelected federal judiciary to shape a fair democracy.[13] After a brilliant career as an academic reformer in the heyday of substantive economic due process, and as the faithful political agent of Justice Louis Brandeis, Felix Frankfurter believed that government by judges is bound to be a class-ridden exercise in preserving the economic and social status quo.[14] His mentor Justice Brandeis' twin parting shots in *Erie v. Tompkins* [15] and *Ashwander,*[16] were designed to eliminate the unelected federal judiciary's power to shape the common law, and to cabin the federal judiciary's use of the Constitution to interfere with the workings of democracy. Frankfurter, continuing where Brandeis left off, would probably take one look at *Bush v. Gore* and *Citizens United* and ruefully tell himself that Brandeis had been right as usual.

Justice Brennan, unburdened by Frankfurter's lifelong mistrust of the unelected federal judiciary, saw federal judges (most of whom had been appointed by Franklin Delano Roosevelt and Harry

Truman) as potential agents of change, capable of extricating the nation from locally embedded political majorities deeply committed to racial discrimination, and hostile to speech corrosive of the social and political *status quo*.[17] Brennan could have confronted Frankfurter directly in *Baker*, challenging the view that federal judges could not be trusted to shape American democracy. He could have argued that the "Republican form of government" clause[18] or the First Amendment provided textual support for a constitutional right to participate in the democratic process.[19] Alternatively, he could have argued that, having successfully forged constitutional protections for federalism and the separation of powers, no basis existed for the Court to ignore democracy. But any one of those approaches would have required a monumental undertaking without any assurance of success. Instead, ever the canny strategist, Brennan took the surest way to a majority in *Baker*, choosing not to confront Frankfurter directly. Instead, in the intellectual equivalent of a demurrer, Brennan insisted that, even if Frankfurter were correct about the inability of judges to forge non-textual protections of democracy, the Equal Protection Clause could act as both a classic doctrinal source of judicial power and a textual check on judicial overreaching.[20]

Seeking to avoid a head-on confrontation with Justice Frankfurter, a majority of the Warren Court used the Equal Protection Clause to develop the doctrinal underpinnings of a law of democracy based almost exclusively on the proposition that, if one person could vote or run for office or be represented in the legislature, everyone else is entitled to an equal opportunity to participate in the democratic process in the absence of a very powerful reason why not. The Court eventually called it "fundamental rights" strict scrutiny.[21]

Since, in *Baker* and its immediate progeny, the Equal Protection Clause seemed to get the job done effectively and with a minimum of fuss,[22] Justice Brennan and his allies made no effort to rescue the "Republican form of government clause" from the political question dustbin, to ground the emerging law of democracy in the First Amendment, or to forge a freestanding non-textual constitutional law of democracy similar to the non-textual judicial protections of federalism and the separation of powers. It was a fateful strategic decision that tied the emerging constitutional law of democracy to the vagaries of Equal Protection jurisprudence.

Justice Harlan weighed in a year or two later, observing that relying on strict equality as a one-size-fits-all judicial formula for deciding democracy cases risks blinding judges to larger concerns about the proper functioning of democracy itself.[23] Harlan warned that things could be both absolutely equal and appallingly undemocratic. *Bush v. Gore* proves his point.

Almost fifty years have elapsed since Frankfurter's dire prophecy, Brennan's confident rejoinder, and Harlan's cautionary warning—time enough to assess the wisdom of each. Most importantly, after a half-century of judicial decision-making that has shaped American democracy, we are now in a position to assess the success or failure of Justice Brennan's strategic concession to Justice Frankfurter that courts could shape a fair and effective democracy as a matter of pure Equal Protection doctrine without asking hard questions about the quality of the resulting democracy—a process that I call "doctrine without democracy."

Campaign Finance Law: A Judge-Made Dysfunctional Democracy

Any effort to assess our judge-made democracy must address at least five sets of issues that, taken together, determine the quality of any democracy: (1) cases defining the eligible electorate; (2) cases limiting the power to curtail participation by otherwise eligible voters; (3) cases shaping the electoral and representative processes; (4) cases preserving the ability of voters to challenge entrenched political power centers; and (5) cases determining the role of money in politics. While Justice Brennan's idea of an equality-driven law of democracy has been largely (if not wholly) successful from a democracy standpoint in broadly defining the eligible electorate, I fear that reliance on doctrine without democracy in the other four settings has resulted in the accidental emergence of a dysfunctional democracy that no rational Founder would have designed. In the longer version of this piece,[24] I canvass and critique the Court's democracy-shaping decisions in all five areas from a democracy-centered perspective. Here, I focus on money in politics, where the Supreme Court's jurisprudence has reached a dysfunctional nadir.

In 1974, in the wake of ugly financial scandals during the Nixon administration, political momentum built for an effort to enact comprehensive legislation regulating the role of money in American political campaigns. Instead of a genuine reform bill, though, Congress delivered a blueprint for purging money from elections that just happened to coincide with the best interests of incumbents. Election spending by presidential candidates was capped at two-thirds of the amount spent by George McGovern in the worst presidential loss of the twentieth century.[25] Campaign contributions were limited to $1,000, and independent election spending was capped at less than the cost of a quarter-page ad in the *New York Times*.[26] In short, under Congress's "reform" agenda, it would be illegal to spend enough money to oust an incumbent. The bill also had a public funding scheme for presidential elections that tilted strongly toward the two major parties.[27]

In *Buckley v. Valeo*, a team of ACLU lawyers challenged the so-called reform statute, focusing on its absurdly low spending and contribution ceilings, and on the unfairness of using discriminatory public subsidies to cement the hegemony of the two major parties.[28] While the challenge to discriminatory public subsidies failed, the Supreme Court struck down much of the rest of the statute, except for the $1,000 limit on contributions and the disclosure rules.[29] The *Buckley* opinion rests on four fiercely contested holdings—each of which is doctrinally wrong. Taken together they are a democratic disaster.

First, the *Buckley* Court held that spending an unlimited amount of money during an election campaign is "pure speech," requiring a showing by the government that the spending regulation is the least drastic way to advance a compelling governmental interest.[30] The Court rejected the lower court's ruling that spending money to influence an election is a mixture of speech and conduct entitled to lesser First Amendment protection.[31] Earlier Supreme Court cases, like *United States v. O'Brien*,[32] involving the prosecution of draft card burners, had held that, when speech and conduct are closely linked, government may regulate the conduct as long as the regulation is no broader than necessary and is not intended to suppress the speech. The *Buckley* Court insisted, however, that spending unlimited amounts of money on a political campaign involves no conduct whatever; just pure speech.[33]

Second, the *Buckley* Court held that avoiding undue concentration of electoral power is not a sufficiently compelling governmental interest to justify limits on campaign spending viewed as "pure speech." The government could only subsidize weak voices, ruled the Court, not limit strong ones.[34] Once again, the *Buckley* Court appeared to ignore precedent, for example, applying antitrust principles to newspapers and the movie industry to prevent the emergence of communications monopolies.[35]

Third, the Court ruled that an "independent expenditure" (spending campaign money independent of any candidate's campaign) is virtually immune from government regulation under the First Amendment, while a "contribution" (giving money to a candidate, or coordinating spending with the candidate) may be restricted as to size and source.[36] The Court reasoned that an independent expenditure was a direct exercise of free speech, while a contribution merely enables a third person to speak. Such a razor-thin distinction overlooks the fact that a campaign contribution is the quintessential act of political association, fully protected by the First Amendment.

Finally, the Court ruled that preventing corruption is a compelling governmental interest that would justify limiting the size and source of a campaign contribution, but would not justify limiting independent expenditures in support of a candidate.[37] Reasoning that independent expenditures occur without the prior communication needed to agree on a quid pro quo, the Court simply ignored the sense of obligation and fear generated by huge independent political expenditures, to say nothing of the hope that they will be repeated in future elections.

In the end, the *Buckley* Court upheld congressionally imposed limits on the size of campaign contributions, upheld the discriminatory presidential public financing scheme, and upheld broad disclosure rules, but struck down Congress's effort to place ceilings on electoral spending by candidates, campaigns, and independent players supporting or opposing the candidate, leaving us with a campaign finance system that no legislator had supported, and that no rational Founder would have established. In the campaign finance world that *Buckley* built, no ceiling can be placed on the demand for campaign cash, but limits can be imposed on the supply. Without a ceiling on expenditures, though, candidates are trapped in a classic arms control spiral, unable to stop raising campaign money because they fear being outspent by an opponent, but forced to raise the needed money in small amounts from a limited circle of contributors who are subject to a statutory maximum. The net result is a world of unlimited demand and limited supply—a classic invitation to lawlessness. In *Buckley*'s world, ideological outriders (and very rich candidates) exercise disproportionate political power because they are constitutionally guaranteed the right to spend as much as they wish, as long as they do it independently from the candidate. What's worse, the ideological spending can now be channeled through organizations falling outside the *Buckley* disclosure rules, making it impossible to track its source. And, into this already deeply dysfunctional world, *Citizens United* has now parachuted the vast trove of corporate wealth, vesting for-profit corporations with First Amendment rights to pour unlimited amounts into a campaign on the eve of an election without public disclosure.

Justice Kennedy's undoubtedly well-meaning opinion in *Citizens United* is an exercise in question-begging, and an unprincipled mixture of reverence for precedent when it suits him and willingness to jettison precedent when it gets in his way. As noted above, Justice Kennedy begins his majority opinion in *Citizens United* by putting the First Amendment rabbit into the hat when he claims that the case involves the constitutionality of treating two categories of speakers—corporate and non-corporate—differently.[38] Classic First Amendment doctrine, Justice Kennedy observes, requires a very powerful justification before allowing the government to treat similarly situated speakers differently. He's right. First Amendment doctrine is deeply mistrustful of government regulations that pick and choose among similarly situated speakers—and rightly so—recognizing that discriminating between or among comparable speakers is often driven by hostility to a speaker's message or status.[39] But, the central legal issue in *Citizens United* was whether for-profit business corporations and human beings are similarly situated First Amendment speakers in the first place. The status of the for-profit business corporation as an artificial, state-created legal entity vested with unlimited life, blessed with highly favorable techniques of acquiring, accumulating, and retaining vast wealth through economic transactions having nothing to do with politics, and animated by one purpose—making money—raises important philosophical questions about whether corporate and human speakers are even in the same First Amendment ballpark. Justice Kennedy's opinion begs that question by assuming away that central legal issue. He ignores the fact that, one hundred years ago, confronted by the same philosophical question, the Court ruled that for-profit business corporations are sufficiently different from human beings to fall outside the protection of the Fifth Amendment's self-incrimination clause.[40] That is still the law.[41] In his dissent in *Braswell*, Justice Kennedy explicitly notes,

> Our long course of decisions concerning artificial entities and the Fifth Amendment served us well. It illuminated two of the critical foundations for the constitutional guarantee against self-incrimination: *first, that it is an explicit right of a natural person, protecting the realm of human thought and expression*; second, that it is confined to governmental compulsion.[42]

The *Citizens United* majority never persuasively confronts the issue of why the First Amendment's free speech clause should not also be deemed a "right of a natural person, protecting the realm of human thought and expression." In fairness, Justice Kennedy argues in *Citizens United* that hearers would be benefited by granting First Amendment protection to for-profit corporations.[43] But, if *Citizens United* rests primarily, or even solely, on the alleged benefits to "human thought and expression" of unlimited corporate electioneering immediately before an election, surely the majority was obliged to confront the argument that unlimited corporate electioneering threatens to overwhelm opposing messages to the detriment of a fully informed electorate.

It is no answer to point to the decision to treat corporations as "persons" for the purposes of Section 1 of the Fourteenth Amendment in connection with efforts to deprive them of property or otherwise interfere with their economic operations.[44] Since the very purpose of inventing the for-profit business corporation was to unleash its economic potential, it makes sense to vest corporations with constitutional protection against improper economic regulation. It is, however, a huge—and unsupported—jump to vest corporations with non-economic constitutional protections that flow from our respect for human dignity. Robots have no souls. Neither do for-profit business corporations. Vesting robots or corporations with constitutional rights premised on human dignity is legal fiction run amuck.

Nor is it persuasive to argue that, since certain for-profit corporations, such as newspapers, engaged in the business of speech, enjoy First Amendment protection for their speech activities, all other for-profit corporations, such as oil companies, must also be vested with First Amendment protection to speak as well. The constitutional protection afforded to the business of speech—whether it involves publishing a newspaper, producing a movie or a television program, or running an Internet outlet—derives from the special textual protection afforded the "press" by the First Amendment. The business of the press is the only business explicitly protected by the Constitution. It is, therefore, impossible to leverage the clearly functional protection of "the press" into a general protection of corporate speech.

Finally, the fact that the Court has recognized a First Amendment right to commercial speech (which is often disseminated by corporations) not only fails to support a general right of corporate free speech, it cuts strongly against it. Commercial free speech is avowedly designed to maximize the economic efficiency of the market.[45] As such, it is closely linked with the other constitutional protections afforded corporations in order to permit them to fulfill their economic mandate. Precisely because the corporation lacks the dignitary status of human beings, however, commercial speech may be regulated in ways that would never be permitted in the first-class speech compartment—most importantly on grounds of its falsity or misleading nature, or to prevent harm to hearers.[46] If the same criteria were imposed on corporate political advertising, very little would survive.

Having begged the central legal question of whether a for-profit business corporation is a First Amendment speaker, Justice Kennedy then relies on respect for precedent to reject the two major justifications for treating for-profit business corporations and human beings differently for First Amendment purposes. Confronted by an argument that the vast, artificially generated economic resources of for-profit corporations risk overwhelming the capacity of most flesh-and-blood opponents to contest elections, Justice Kennedy, instead of confronting the argument on its merits, cites to precedent holding that a First Amendment resource imbalance (between human speakers) may never be corrected by silencing the overly strong speaker, but must always seek to strengthen the weak voice.[47] No one who has ever argued in court, addressed a legislature, or participated in a serious academic discussion can take such an absolute assertion seriously. The rules of courtroom procedure, Robert's Rules of Order, and the guidelines of the academy are all designed to assure that a strong speaker does not overwhelm a weak one to the detriment of an institution dependent on the flow of ideas. Justice Kennedy is correct, though, in asserting that, as a general principle, the First Amendment requires that, whenever possible, weak speakers should be strengthened before strong speakers are silenced. Kennedy argues that the *Buckley* Court had applied this general principle to electoral resource differentials between and among human beings, and reasserts *Buckley*'s statement that "the concept that government may restrict the speech of some elements of our society in order to enhance the relative voice of others is wholly foreign to the First Amendment."[48]

But the argument from *stare decisis* cannot justify Kennedy's absolutist application of this principle, since in *Austin v. Michigan Chamber of Commerce*,[49] as well as in *McConnell v. Federal Election Commission*,[50] the Court declined to apply this general principle to the massive potential electoral resource imbalance that separates individuals from for-profit business corporations immediately before an election. *Austin*, a 1990 precedent, had upheld a state ban on pre-election spending by for-profit corporations, and *McConnell*, a 2003 decision, had addressed the same issue as *Citizens United* and had upheld the federal restrictions on corporate electoral spending. Justice Kennedy's invocation of *Buckley* as precedent is, therefore, hardly a conclusive basis to reject massive resource imbalance out of hand as a justification for treating corporations differently from human beings in the period immediately before an election. If anything, precedent in *Austin* and *McConnell* tilted the other way. At a minimum, except for *Austin* and *McConnell*, the issue had never been confronted in the context of electoral speech by massive for-profit corporations. Indeed, the record was devoid of factual material on the question.

Justice Kennedy then goes on to reject the argument that fear of electoral corruption would justify treating corporate political speakers with massive resources and a mandate to maximize short-term profits differently from human beings. Once again, he invokes precedent, observing that *Buckley* had held that independent expenditures do not create a substantial risk of corruption because the donor does not confer with the candidate in advance.[51] But, in the only context the current Justices really know anything about—judging—the Court (including Justice Kennedy) rejected the wafer-thin distinction between contributions and independent expenditures as a potential source of corruption. In *Caperton v. A.T. Massey Coal Co.*,[52] the Court required a justice of the West Virginia Supreme Court to step aside in a case where one of the litigants had independently spent $3 million to get the judge elected. Justice Kennedy recognized in *Caperton* that a judge's gratitude for past favors and hope for future ones created an unacceptably high risk of judicial bias. Why elected judges are vulnerable to such "corruption" but elected legislative and executive officials are immune is a mystery known only to the Court's majority.

Thus, while the *Buckley* precedent weighed against the corruption argument, the precedent had been eroded in *Caperton*, and had never even been considered in the economically charged atmosphere of huge for-profit corporations.

Having relied heavily on the precedential value of *Buckley*, a 1976 precedent arguably weakened by later cases such as *Austin* and *Caperton*, Justice Kennedy then dramatically switches *stare decisis* gears and overrules both *Austin* and *McConnell*.[53] It is a master class on how precedent can be binding and non-binding at the same time.

The doctrinal critique of the Kennedy opinion does not stop with its question-begging First Amendment analysis and its arbitrary and inconsistent approach to precedent. Ignoring canons of judicial restraint dating from Justice Brandeis,[54] the *Citizens United* ruling unleashing unlimited corporate electioneering is far broader than necessary to decide the actual case or controversy before the Court, and considerably broader than any remedy the litigants sought. The case involved a one-hour video hatchet job on Hillary Clinton entitled *Hillary: The Movie*, a purported documentary produced by Citizens United, a right-wing, nonprofit group that had received trace amounts (less than 1 percent) of funding from for-profit corporations.

According to the sparse record, no for-profit corporation had played a role in the video's genesis or production. Citizens United distributed the video by making it available on cable television free of charge, but only if a prospective viewer took affirmative steps to download it. When the Federal Election Commission (FEC) made no effort to regulate the video's distribution, Citizens United, anxious to provoke a test case, waived a red flag in front of the government bull, demanding a promise that no action would be taken against the distribution and downloading of the video. The government foolishly took the bait. Advised, no doubt, by General Custer, the FEC refused to concede that the video could not be regulated, and the game was on.

It is hard to list the many reasons why the FEC was wrong in seeking to regulate the video, and the numerous narrower grounds for decision that were available to the Supreme Court. Most importantly, it was necessary for a prospective viewer to take the affirmative step of downloading the video in order to view it, the functional equivalent of taking a book off a library shelf. Congress's power to regulate electioneering communications is limited to messages (such as broadcast commercials) delivered without the active collaboration of the viewer/reader/listener. Once a willing hearer actively collaborates in receiving a message from a willing speaker, the government's regulatory power is at its lowest ebb. Whether approached as a matter of the definition of the term "electioneering communication" in the governing statute, or as a freestanding First Amendment defense, the necessity of active collaboration by a hearer/viewer in the dissemination of *Hillary: The Movie* should have ended the *Citizens United* case without any need to consider the general free speech rights of for-profit corporations.

But wait, there is much more. Two dispositive statutory issues were simply ignored. Pursuant to the federal statute, the ban on disseminating electioneering communications funded by for-profit corporations is applicable in the thirty days preceding a covered primary election—in this case a state Democratic presidential primary—but only if 50,000 eligible voters in that election are likely to view or hear it on an electronic media. How likely was it that more than 50,000 persons eligible to vote in a state Democratic presidential primary would have affirmatively elected to download a one-hour hatchet job on Hillary Clinton during the thirty days before the primary? Moreover, since the trace corporate funding involved (less than 1 percent) was *de minimis*, federal appellate precedent had already recognized an implied statutory exemption for electioneering communications bearing merely trace corporate funding.[55] Finally, even if, despite the canon on constitutional avoidance, the statute was deemed applicable, the Supreme Court had already carved out a First Amendment safe harbor (deemed the "MCFL exemption") for electoral communications by grassroots nonprofit groups such as Citizen United with *de minimis* for-profit corporate funding.[56]

As Justice John Paul Stevens caustically pointed out, Justice Kennedy simply leapfrogged the numerous narrower grounds for decision in order to overrule two precedents and decide the case in the broadest possible way. Given its self-propelled, gratuitous nature, much if not all of *Citizens United* is *dicta*, good law as long as five votes support it, but not worthy of the *stare decisis* respect accorded to a case's holding.

Most recently, the Court has even poured cold water on some efforts to develop a viable system for subsidizing campaign spending.[57] The *Buckley* Court had upheld government subsidies as a legitimate means of advancing electoral equality, but had insisted that the subsidy program be voluntary.[58] In return for voluntary subsidies, the Court recognized that candidates could be required to limit total campaign spending. That places many candidates in a dilemma. If both sides opt for public financing, the system works fine. But if only one candidate accepts the spending limits that usually go with public subsidies, that candidate risks being badly outspent by an opponent using privately raised funds. Several states, including Arizona, tried to use "triggers," funneling additional campaign subsidies to a publicly funded candidate to keep up with the spending of privately funded opponents if the spending differential got too big.[59] The Court is now considering the question of whether Arizona's decision to increase subsidies to match an opponent's private fund-raising success unconstitutionally "penalizes" the privately funded candidate for fund-raising success. If matching funds are deemed unconstitutional, the public funding system may be doomed to irrelevance.[60] Why it is an unconstitutional "penalty" for a wealthy candidate to be allowed to spend unlimited sums, but to be forced to campaign on a level playing field is known only to the challengers of the Arizona program.

Tell the truth: If you had tried, could you have developed a worse way to finance democracy? If the answer is "yes," you may be a candidate for the next Supreme Court vacancy.

Can Anything Be Done?

It does not have to be this way. The Supreme Court is fully capable of committing to the model of robust, egalitarian self-government latent in the Constitution. That is exactly what it has done with the free speech aspects of the First Amendment. In *New York Times v. Sullivan*,[61] decided scarcely two years after *Baker*, Justice Brennan infused the First Amendment with a theoretical model—the notion of a free market in ideas. Although many have observed that the text of the First Amendment is ambiguous and that numerous alternative theories of the First Amendment are plausible, once the justices settled on a theory—even a contestable theory—the Court was able to embark on a half-century of remarkably effective judicial protection of free speech. It is no more difficult to develop a judicially principled theory of robust democracy than it was to adopt a principled approach to free speech, but Frankfurter bluffed Brennan away from the table.

The path not taken in the Court's democracy cases has led us to Felix Frankfurter's revenge: an accidental democracy built by judges who connect the doctrinal dots without ever asking themselves what kind of democracy they are painting. It is not a pretty picture. The justices could start repainting it by recognizing that the First Amendment's text was intended by the Founders to be democracy's best friend. Indeed, its text is a blueprint for a functioning democracy.[62] The six luminous ideas in the First Amendment—no establishment of religion; free exercise of religion; freedom of speech; freedom of the press; freedom of assembly; and freedom to petition for redress of grievances—are carefully organized by the Founders on an "inside/out" axis, beginning with Establishment and Free Exercise in the interior precincts of the human conscience, proceeding in concentric circles of increasingly public interaction through the speech, press, and assembly clauses, and culminating in the petition clause with formal interaction with the state. The careful inside/out order of the ideas may have been random, but I doubt it. The First Amendment sets out the Founders' vision of the half-life of a democratic idea, beginning in the recesses of the human (not corporate) mind, proceeding through increasingly public stages of communication and interaction with fellow citizens through speech, press, and assembly, culminating in an effort in the petition clause to turn the idea into law.

It borders on the tragic that the First Amendment, designed by the Founders to be democracy's best friend, has been turned by the Court into its enemy in so many settings. Sometimes, as in *Bush v. Gore*, courts approach a democracy case as an exercise in equality. Sometimes, as in *Citizens United*, they approach a democracy case as an exercise in autonomy. But they never view a case as an exercise in democracy. Under such a doctrinally dominated decisional process, American judges may well get the formal legal doctrine right, but we wind up with an accidental, dysfunctional democracy that no one would have designed.

A half-century after *Baker*, voter turnout in presidential elections still hovers at 60 percent or less, at 40 percent in mid-term elections, and much lower in most state and local elections; voting is still disproportionately skewed to the wealthy and better educated;[63] most election districts are gerrymandered to assure that the incumbent wins; both major parties routinely manipulate the districting process for partisan gain; the two major parties often run a duopoly in which political bosses select the candidates; minor parties cannot effectively challenge the major parties' hegemony; and the rich, including for-profit business corporations, own the democratic process lock, stock, and barrel. Surely, our judges can do better. If they cannot, or will not, maybe Felix Frankfurter was right in arguing that We the People should take the job away from them.

Notes

Preface

1. Eric Lichtblau, *Long Battle by Foes of Campaign Finance Rules Shifts Landscape,* N.Y. Times, October 16, 2010, http://www.nytimes.com/2010/10/16/us/politics/16donate.html.

1

1. 424 U.S. 1 (1976).
2. *FEC v. Wis. Right to Life, Inc.,* 551 U.S. 449, 478 (2007).
3. *See* Eliza Newlin Carney, *Campaign Finance Rules May Take a Beating*, Nat'l J. (May 18, 2009) (quoting Richard Hasen), http://www.nationaljournal.com/columns/rules-of-the-game/campaign-finance-rules-may-take-a-beating-20090518; *Money In Politics 2009—Panel Two*, Brennan Ctr. for Justice (May 8, 2009), http://www.brennancenter.org/content/pages/money_in_politics_2009_videos_panel_two.
4. *Citizens United v. FEC,* 130 S. Ct. 876, 890 (2010) (internal quotation marks and citation omitted).
5. *See* David D. Kirkpatrick, *A Quest to End Spending Rules for Campaigns*, N.Y. Times, January 24, 2010, at A11, http://www.nytimes.com/2010/01/25/us/politics/25bopp.html; Philip Rucker, *Citizens United Used* 'Hillary: The Movie' *To Take on McCain-Feingold*, Wash. Post, January 22, 2010, http://www.washingtonpost.com/wp-dyn/content/article/2010/01/21/AR2010012103582.html.
6. *Citizens United*, 130 S. Ct. at 887.
7. *Id.*
8. *FEC v. Mass. Citizens for Life, Inc.,* 479 U.S. 238 (1986).
9. *McConnell v. FEC,* 540 U.S. 93 (2003). Note that the Taft-Hartley law was passed in 1947, although there is evidence that Roosevelt meant for the Tillman Act (passed in 1907) to ban corporate independent expenditures as well.
10. *Id.* at 203. The *McConnell* Court also cited the "unanimous view" of the Supreme Court in *National Right to Work,* that the electioneering communications restriction "permits some participation of unions and corporations in the federal electoral process by allowing them to establish and pay the administrative expenses of 'separate segregated fund[s],' which

may be 'utilized for political purposes.'" *Id.* at 203 n.86 (quoting *FEC v. Nat'l Right to Work,* 459 U.S. 197, 201–02 (1982) (citation omitted)).

11. 494 U.S. 652 (1990).

12. *See* Supplemental Brief of Former Officials of the ACLU as Amici Curiae on Behalf of Neither Party, *Citizens United v. FEC,* 130 S. Ct. 876 (2010) (No. 08-205), 2009 WL 2365208.

2

1. *See, e.g.,* Frances R. Hill, *Corporate Political Speech and the Balance of Powers: A New Framework for Campaign Finance Jurisprudence* in Wisconsin Right to Life, 27 St. Louis U. Pub. L. Rev. 267, 290–92 (2008); J. Skelly Wright, *Politics and the Constitution: Is Money Speech?* 85 Yale L.J. 1001 (1976).

2. *See* Frederick Schauer, *The Boundaries of the First Amendment: A Preliminary Exploration of Constitutional Salience,* 117 Harv. L. Rev. 1765, 1769 (2004).

3. *See* Thomas I. Emerson, *Toward a General Theory of the First Amendment,* 72 Yale L. Rev. 877 (1963).

4. 418 U.S. 405 (1974).

5. *Id.* at 410–11.

6. *Id.* at 412–15.

7. *See, e.g.,* Geoffrey R. Stone, *Free Speech in the Twenty-First Century: Ten Lessons from the Twentieth Century,* 36 Pepp. L. Rev. 273, 297-98 (explaining that speeding in one's car to protest the speed limit is not covered by the First Amendment).

8. *See Abrams v. U.S.* 250 U.S. 616, 630 (1919) (Holmes, J., dissenting) ("[T]he best test of truth is the power of the thought to get itself accepted in the competition of the market."); Vincent Blasi, *Holmes and the Marketplace of Ideas,* 2004 Sup. Ct. Rev. 1 (2004).

9. *See* Robert Post, *The Structure of Academic Freedom,* in *Academic Freedom After September 11,* at 61 (Beshara Doumani ed., Zone Books 2006).

10. As the Court recently reiterated in *Snyder v. Phelps,* 562 U.S. --- , --- (2011):

"Speech on 'matters of public concern' . . . is 'at the heart of the First Amendment's protection.' "). The First Amendment reflects "a profound national commitment to the principle that debate on public issues should be uninhibited, robust, and wide-open." That is because "speech concerning public affairs is more than self-expression; it is the essence of self-government." Accordingly, "speech on public issues occupies the highest rung of the hierarchy of First Amendment values, and is entitled to special protection."

11. *See* Robert Post, *Between Governance and Management: The History and Theory of the Public Forum,* 34 UCLA Law Review 1713 (1987).

12. For a nice recent illustration of the importance of the institutional character of elections, *see Doe v. Reed,* 130 S. Ct. 2811, 2833–34 (2010) (Scalia, J., concurring).

13. *Burson v. Freeman,* 504 U.S. 191 (1992).

14. *See* Robert Post, *Regulating Election Speech under the First Amendment,* 77 Tex. L. Rev. 1837 (1999).

3

1. 523 U.S. 666 (1998).

2. *See id.* at 678–82 (holding that the debate in Arkansas Educational Television Commission was a non-public forum rather than a designated public forum).

3. *Forbes,* 523 U.S. at 675–76.

4. 424 U.S. 1 (1976). Among other things, *Buckley* held that campaign contributions and expenditures were both a form of political speech for First Amendment purposes. *See id.* at 14–23. However, no governmental interest was deemed sufficient to justify state-imposed caps on expenditures, though the state interest in preventing "corruption and the appearance of corruption" was sufficient to justify contribution limitations. *Id.* at 33, 45. *See* C. Edwin Baker, *Campaign Expenditures and Free Speech,* 33 Harv. C.R.-C.L. L. Rev. 1, 2 (1998) (asserting that *Buckley v. Valeo* was "wrong both in a normative or theoretical sense and . . . wrong given the Court's own precedents"); Richard Briffault, *Issue Advocacy: Redrawing the Elections/Politics Line,* 77 Tex. L. Rev. 1751 (1999); Ronald Dworkin, *Campaign Finance Reform: The Jurisprudential Background* (March 19, 1998) (unpublished manuscript) (on file with author).

5. *See generally* Alvin I. Goldman and James C. Cox, *Speech, Truth, and the Free Market for Ideas,* 2 Legal Theory 1 (1996) (criticizing the "market for speech approach" to the First Amendment for failing to account for certain inadequacies in the regulatory power of markets).

6. For an account of counteracting the tendency toward governmental self-preservation as an argument for freedom of speech, *see* Frederick Schauer, *Free Speech: A Philosophical Enquiry,* 73–86 (1982). For an explanation of the general tendency of political insiders to manipulate the ground rules of electoral politics for self-interested reasons, *see* Samuel Issacharoff and Richard H. Pildes, *Politics as Markets: Partisan Lockups of the Democratic Process,* 50 Stan. L. Rev. 643, 651 (1998) (explaining the second form of political locking as incumbents using state authority to control challengers).

7. For example, the Supreme Court held in *Brown v. Hartlage,* 456 U.S. 45 (1982), that regulation of campaign promises and statements must meet the stringent standards of *New York Times Co. v. Sullivan,* 376 U.S. 254 (1964). But it is not inconceivable that the Court could have said that campaign promises and statements are never regulable (except by the voters in casting their ballots), even if the same statements made with the same intentions would have been regulable outside of the electoral process so long as the standards of *New York Times v. Sullivan* had been met.

8. 395 U.S. 444 (1969).

9. 403 U.S. 713 (1971).

10. 403 U.S. 15 (1971).

11. 491 U.S. 397 (1989).

12. *See generally* Frederick Schauer, *Exceptions,* 58 U. Chi. L. Rev. 871, 880–86 (1991) (characterizing "exceptions" proposed in the free speech context as debates over the definition or scope of the relevant speech protections).

13. *See Buckley v. Valeo,* 424 U.S. 1, 48–49 (1976); Lillian R. BeVier, *Money and Politics: A Perspective on the First Amendment and Campaign Finance Reform,* 73 Cal. L. Rev. 1045, 1089 (1985) (concluding that "strict means scrutiny" is the better test for political speech cases); Daniel Polsby, *Buckley v. Valeo: The Special Nature of Political Speech,* 1976 Sup. Ct. Rev. 1, 16 (stating that the Court applies strict scrutiny in First Amendment cases).

14. *See* Richard H. Fallon, Jr., Foreward, *Implementing the Constitution,* 111 Harv. L. Rev. 56, 79 (1997) (recognizing as "commonplace" the idea that strict scrutiny tests are fatal to government regulation); but *see Adarand Constructors, Inc. v. Pena,* 515 U.S. 200, 237 (1995) ("We wish to dispel the notion that strict scrutiny is 'strict in theory, but fatal in fact.'"). For an

older version of this argument in the equal protection context, *see* Gerald Gunther, Foreword, *In Search of Evolving Doctrine on a Changing Court: A Model for a Newer Equal Protection,* 86 Harv. L. Rev. 1, 8 (1972) (coining the phrase "strict in theory, fatal in fact").

15. Ronald Dworkin, *Taking Rights Seriously* 184–205 (1977).

16. *Id.* at 193.

17. *Id.* at 269.

18. *See* Richard H. Pildes, *Why Rights Are Not Trumps: Social Meanings, Expressive Harms and Constitutionalism,* 27 J. Legal Stud. 725, 727–29 (1998).

19. For a fuller elaboration of these views, *see* Richard H. Pildes, *Two Conceptions of Rights in Cases Involving Political "Rights,"* 34 Hous. L. Rev. 323 (1997); Richard H. Pildes, *Avoiding Balancing: The Role of Exclusionary Reasons in Constitutional Law,* 45 Hastings L.J. 711 (1994); Frederick Schauer, *A Comment on the Structure of Rights,* 27 Ga. L. Rev. 415 (1993); *see also* Matthew D. Adler, *Rights Against Rules: The Moral Structure of American Constitutional Law,* 97 Mich. L. Rev. 1, 3 (1998) ("A constitutional right protects the rights-holder from a particular rule (a rule with the wrong predicate or history); it does not protect a particular action of hers from all the rules under which the action falls."). In the First Amendment context itself, this view of rights has been developed in detail by Robert Post. *See generally* Robert C. Post, *Constitutional Domains: Democracy, Community, Management (1995)* (reconceptualizing First Amendment protections as reflections of different forms of social orders).

20. *See, e.g., Board of Educ. v. Pico,* 457 U.S. 853, 870 (1982) (holding that public officials cannot remove books from the school library based on the purpose of expressing disapproval of the ideas those books present).

21. *See, e.g., Capitol Square Review and Advisory Bd. v. Pinette,* 515 U.S. 753, 760–61 (1995) (analogizing the protection of free speech without including religious speech to "Hamlet without the Prince," but at the same time explaining that not all speech is guaranteed a forum on all state property); *Lee v. Weisman,* 505 U.S. 577, 587 (1992) (espousing the principle that the government's accommodation of the free exercise of religion does not supersede the fundamental limitation imposed by the establishment clause); *Wallace v. Jaffree,* 472 U.S. 38, 53 (1985) (explaining that the individual freedom of conscience protected by the First Amendment embraces the right to select any religious faith or none at all).

22. *See, e.g., Rutan v. Republican Party,* 497 U.S. 62, 75 (1990) (holding that "promotions, transfers and recalls after layoffs based on political affiliation or support are an impermissible infringement on First Amendment rights of public employees"); *Branti v. Finkel,* 445 U.S. 507, 520 (1980) (holding that a public employee can obtain an injunction against his termination if the termination was based on purely political grounds); *Elrod v. Burns,* 427 U.S. 347, 357 (1976) (arguing that patronage dismissals are "at war with the deeper traditions of democracy embodied in the First Amendment").

23. *Compare Harper v. Virginia State Bd. of Elections,* 383 U.S. 663, 688 (1966) (rejecting the idea that voting may be conditioned on payment of poll taxes), *with Lassiter v. Northampton County Bd. of Elections,* 360 U.S. 45, 53 (1959) (permitting voting to be conditioned on establishing literacy).

24. For an example of this interpretation of the original purposes of the First Amendment, *see* Vincent Blasi, *The Pathological Perspective and the First Amendment,* 85 Colum. L. Rev. 449, 463 (1985).

25. For this view of the original purposes of the Bill of Rights as a whole, which argues that they were designed to protect structures of self-governance, rather than atomistic rights of individuals, *see* Akhil Reed Amar, *The Bill of Rights: Creation and Reconstruction* at xiii (1998) (arguing that the central concern in the minds of those who framed the Bill of Rights was to protect the ability of local governments to monitor and deter federal government officials who might try to rule in their own self-interest).

26. *Id.* at 21–25.

27. For the emphasis on the language and concept of "public liberty" in the constitutional period, *see* Gordon S. Wood, *The Creation of the American Republic: 1776–1787,* at 536–67 (1969) (articulating the antifederalist view that experience throughout time confirmed that rulers were always eager to enlarge their powers and infringe upon the essential rights of the people).

28. *Id.* at 537 (quoting Whig politician and antifederalist Robert Yates who argued that the eagerness of rulers to abridge public liberty "'has induced the people . . . to fix barriers against the encroachments of their rulers'").

29. For pragmatic accounts of justification along these lines, *see, e.g.,* Elizabeth Anderson, *Value in Ethics and Economics,* 91–116 (1993); Don Herzog, *Without Foundations,* 218–44 (1985).

30. *See* Robert Post, *Recuperating First Amendment Doctrine,* 47 Stan. L. Rev. 1249, 1271 (1995) ("There is in fact no general free speech principle . . . ").

31. *See generally,* Schauer, *supra* note 6.

32. *See Burdick v. Takushi,* 504 U.S. 428 (1992).

33. *See Buckley v. Valeo,* 424 U.S. 1, 64–74 (1976) (upholding financial disclosure obligations for election-related "speech" while distinguishing constitutional protections against mandatory identity disclosure in other domains of political speech).

34. *See Burson v. Freeman,* 504 U.S. 191 (1992).

35. *See Austin v. Michigan State Chamber of Commerce,* 494 U.S. 652 (1990).

36. For general accounts of the structural features of elections as a distinct domain already recognized in constitutional law, *see* Baker, *supra* note 4, at 24–33; Briffault, *supra* note 6, at 1753–55.

37. This claim is famously challenged in J. Skelly Wright, *Politics and the Constitution: Is Money Speech?* 85 Yale L.J. 1001, 1018–19 (1976), but defended in Kathleen M. Sullivan, *Political Money and Freedom of Speech,* 30 University of California, Davis Law Review 663–90 (1997). For a related inquiry, see J. Skelly Wright, *Money and the Pollution of Politics: Is the First Amendment an Obstacle to Political Equality?* 82 Colum. L. Rev. 609 (1982) (insisting that the Court's decision to protect money in election campaigns restricts our political system's most powerful defenses against electoral inequalities).

38. *See* Frederick Schauer, *Categories and the First Amendment: A Play in Three Acts,* 34 Vand. L. Rev. 265, 270 (1981) (explaining that although several areas of the law are affected by the First Amendment, courts have had no trouble finding, in some cases, that speech in those contexts is not protected).

39. *See* Schauer, *supra* note 12, at 880 (insisting that however useful it may be to consider specific exceptions in particular doctrinal realms, ideas about exceptions are not very useful in analyzing the First Amendment).

40. *See* Geoffrey R. Stone, *Content Regulation and the First Amendment,* 25 Wm. & Mary L. Rev. 189, 198, 197–200 (1983) (arguing that "excising a specific message from public debate" results in a distortion of that debate); *see also* Marjorie Heins, *Viewpoint Discrimination,* 24 Hastings Const. L.Q. 99, 103 (1996) (criticizing as viewpoint-based the obscenity exception to the First Amendment, which allows prohibition of some sexually explicit speech).

41. *See* Frederick Schauer, *Principles, Institutions, and the First Amendment,* 112 Harv. L. Rev. 84, 84–85 (1998) (noting that institutions

such as the press and universities have failed to gain special status under the First Amendment).

42. *See McIntyre v. Ohio Elections Comm'n,* 514 U.S. 334, 346 (1995) (describing advocacy of a politically controversial viewpoint as "the essence of First Amendment expression").

43. *See City of Ladue v. Gilleo,* 512 U.S. 43, 48-49 (1994) (striking down a yard sign ban as a nearly complete repression of a "venerable means of communication"); *New York Times Co. v. Sullivan,* 376 U.S. 254, 265–66 (1964) (rejecting the characterization of a paid editorial as "commercial" and holding that statements do not lose protection simply because they were paid for); William J. Brennan, *The Supreme Court and the Meiklejohn Interpretation of the First Amendment,* 79 Harv. L. Rev. 1, 5–6 (1965) (mentioning that one view is that only speech that has "redeeming social importance" is fully protected); Daniel A. Farber, *Free Speech without Romance: Public Choice and the First Amendment,* 105 Harv. L. Rev. 554, 555 (1991) (utilizing public choice theory to characterize speech as an undervalued public good).

44. *See Members of City Council of L.A. v. Taxpayers for Vincent,* 466 U.S. 789, 792–93 (1984) (involving political signs on public property).

45. *See Red Lion Broad. Co. v. FCC,* 395 U.S. 367, 370–71 (1969) (concerning the application of the fairness doctrine in broadcasting).

46. *See Tinker v. Des Moines Indep. Community Sch. Dist.,* 393 U.S. 503, 504 (1969) (regarding a school district's prohibition of wearing arm bands to protest the Vietnam War).

47. *See Rutan v. Republican Party of Ill.,* 497 U.S. 62, 75 (1990) (finding that denials of "promotions, transfers, and recalls after layoffs based on political affiliation or support are an impermissible infringement on the First Amendment rights of public employees"); *Connick v. Myers,* 461 U.S. 138, 147, 146–47 (1983) (holding that the decision of a government employer to discharge an employee based on the employee's speech regarding a "personal interest" rather than a "public concern" is not subject to judicial review).

48. *See Metromedia, Inc. v. San Diego,* 453 U.S. 490, 493, 496, 521 (1981) (permitting some restrictions and noting that the restricted billboards have been used for political speech).

49. *See Members of the City Council of Los Angeles v. Taxpayers for Vincent,* 466 U.S. 789, 812 (1984) (approving municipal restrictions on the posting of signs and posters, including those with political content).

50. *See City of Ladue v. Gilleo,* 512 U.S. 43, 55 (1994) (noting that "residential signs play an important part in political campaigns").

51. *See Bethel Sch. Dist. No. 403 v. Fraser,* 478 U.S. 675, 682 (1986) (noting that children's rights of political expression in public school "are not automatically coextensive with the rights of adults in other settings").

52. *See Papish v. Board of Curators of Univ. of Mo.*, 410 U.S. 667, 670–71 (1973) (noting that "the mere dissemination of ideas . . . on a state university campus may not be shut off in the name alone of 'conventions of decency'").

53. *See Connick v. Myers,* 461 U.S. 138, 146–47 (1983) (juxtaposing the courts' role in protecting government employees' speech in matters of public concern and private concern).

54. *See Burson v. Freeman,* 504 U.S. 191, 211 (1992) (permitting restrictions on speech within one hundred feet of a polling place).

55. *See, e.g., FEC v. Mass. Citizens for Life, Inc.*, 479 U.S. 238 (1986) (striking down a federal law prohibiting a pro-life organization from identifying and supporting pro-life candidates in a newsletter).

56. *Buckley,* 424 U.S. at 15 (considering instead the larger question of whether campaign contributions and expenditures can best be characterized as conduct or political speech). The Court in *Buckley* moved freely, even on the same page of the opinion, between precedents involving the domain of general public discourse, such as *New York Times Co. v. Sullivan,* 376 U.S. 254 (1964) (cited in *Buckley,* 424 U.S. at 14) and precedents tied to the specific structural issues concerning elections, such as *Mills v. Alabama,* 384 U.S. 214 (1966) (cited in *Buckley,* 424 U.S. at 14). The Court did not undertake any discussion of whether principles and precedents applicable to public discourse should be modified in the context of elections. *See* Baker, *supra* note 4, at 29 ("*Buckley* did not even take up the possibility of viewing electoral speech as part of an institutionally bound governing process.").

57. 2 U.S.C.A. § 434(f)(3)(A)(i) (Supp. 203). The act also provided a backup definition of electioneering communication, in case this primary definition ran into constitutional problems.

58. For a comparison between BCRA and the concept of an "election period" in other democracies, *see* Samuel Issacharoff, *The Constitutional Logic of Campaign Finance Regulation,* 36 Pepp. L. Rev. 373 (2009) (discussing campaign finance regulations in other democracies).

59. Under preexisting federal law, however, corporations and unions were barred from engaging in express advocacy in support of federal candidates

without regard to the "election period" restrictions established by BCRA. 2 U.S.C. s 441(b).

60. 540 U.S. 93 (2003).

61. *Id.* at 205.

62. *Id.* at 206 n.88 (internal quotation marks omitted).

63. 130 S. Ct. 876 (2010).

64. 494 U.S. 652 (1990).

65. H.R. 5175, 111th Cong. (2010); S. 3295, 11th Cong. (2010).

66. Of course, there are disputes about whether Congress has drawn the boundaries on the "electoral sphere" in an appropriate way. For the ACLU's objections along these lines to the legislation, see http://www.aclu.org/files/assets/Ltr_to_Senate_re_ACLU_opposes_DISCLOSE_Act.pdf.

67. The specific language of Lessig's proposed amendment is: "Nothing in this Constitution shall be construed to restrict the power to limit, though not to ban, campaign expenditures of non-citizens of the United States during the last 60 days before an election." *See* Lawrence Lessig, Citizens Unite: *The Constitutional Amendment America Needs,* New Republic, March 16, 2010, http://www.tnr.com/article/politics/citizens-unite.

68. Ronald Dworkin, *The Decision That Threatens Democracy,* N.Y. Rev. Books, April 15, 2010, available at http://www.nybooks.com/articles/archives/2010/may/13/decision-threatens-democracy/.

69. Critics of campaign-finance reform sometimes recognize this point as well. *See, e.g.,* Sullivan, *supra* note 37, at 675 ("Campaign finance reform may not be predicated on equality of citizen participation in elections unless electoral speech can be conceptually severed from informal political discourse.").

4

1. *Citizens United v. Federal Elections Commission,* 558 U.S. 20 (2010).

2. *See* Frederick Schauer and Richard H. Pildes, *Electoral Exceptionalism and the First Amendment*, 77 Tex. L. Rev. 1803 (1999).

3. The Bipartisan Campaign Reform Act defined an "electioneering communication" as any "broadcast, cable, or satellite communication" that (I) "refers to a clearly identified candidate for Federal office; (II) is made within—(aa) 60 days before a general, special, or runoff election for the office sought

by the candidate; or (bb) 30 days before a primary or preference election, or a convention or caucus of a political party that has authority to nominate a candidate, for the office sought by the candidate; and (III) in the case of a communication which refers to a candidate other than President or Vice President, is targeted to the relevant electorate." 2 U.S.C. § 434(f)(3)(A)(i) (Supp. 2003).

4. *See* Geoffrey R. Stone, *Content-Neutral Restrictions*, 54 U. Chi. L. Rev. 46 (1987); John Ely, *Flag Desecration: A Case Study in the Roles of Categorization and Balancing in First Amendment Analysis*, 88 Harv. L. Rev. 1482 (1975); Elena Kagan, *Private Speech, Public Purpose: The Role of Government Motive in First Amendment Doctrine*, 63 U. Chi. L. Rev. 415, 446–463 (1996).

5. *See* Geoffrey R. Stone, *Content-Regulation and the First Amendment*, 25 Wm. & Mary L. Rev. 189 (1983); Paul Stephan, *The First Amendment and Content Discrimination*, 68 Va. L. Rev. 203 (1982); Kagan, *Private Speech, Public Purpose* , *supra* note 3, at 444–45.

6. *Hearings on the Nomination of John G. Roberts to Be Chief Justice of the Supreme Court of the United States before the Committee on the Judiciary*, 109th Cong., 1st Sess. 56 (2005) (testimony of John G. Roberts).

7. *Monitor Patriot Co. v. Roy,* 401 U.S. 265, 272 (1971).

8. Schauer and Pildes, *Electoral Exceptionalism, supra* note 2, at 1806.

9. *Tinker v. Des Moines School District,* 393 U.S. 503, 509 (1969).

10. *See* Geoffrey R. Stone, *The Rules of Evidence and the Rules of Public Debate*, 1993 U. Chi. Leg. F. 127.

11. *See Jones v. North Carolina Prisoners' Union,* 433 U.S. 119 (1977).

12. *Parker v. Levy,* 417 U.S. 733, 744 (1974).

13. *Id.*

14. *See Pickering v. Board of Education,* 391 U.S. 563 (1968).

15. *See* Geoffrey R. Stone, *Top Secret: When Our Government Keeps Us in the Dark*, 5–17 (2007).

16. *See, e.g., Arkansas Educational Television Commission v. Forbes,* 523 U.S. 666 (1998) (candidate debates); *Burdick v. Takushi,* 504 U.S. 428 (1992) (election ballots); *Burson v. Freeman,* 504 U.S. 191 (polling places).

17. For an example of an "unreasonable" restriction the Court invalidated, *see Anderson v. Celebrezze*, 460 U.S. 780 (1983) (invalidating an "unreasonable" time requirement for ballot access).

18. *See Clingman v. Beaver,* 544 U.S. 581 (2005) (uholding a state law prohibiting a political party from inviting registered members of other political parties to vote in its primary); *Burdick v. Takushi,* 504 U.S. 428 (1992) (upholding a statute prohibiting write-in voting); *California Democratic Party v. Jones,* 530 U.S. 567 (2000) (invalidating a state law permitting individuals who are not members of a political party to vote in that party's primary); *Anderson v. Celebrezze,* 460 U.S. 780 (1983) (invalidating a state statute requiring independent candidates to file their nominating petitions in mid-March in order to qualify for the ballot in the November election).

19. Pub. L. 107–155, 116 Stat. 81, enacted March 27, 2002.

20. *McConnell v. Federal Election Commission,* 540 U.S. 93 (2003).

21. *Federal Election Commission v. Wisconsin Right to Life,* 551 U.S. 449 (2007).

22. For an excellent analysis of these issues, *see* Richard Briffault, *Issue Advocacy: Redrawing the Elections/Politics Line,* 77 Tex. L. Rev. 1751 (1999).

23. Geoffrey R. Stone, *Free Speech in the Twenty-First Century: Ten Lessons from the Twentieth Century*, 36 Pepp. L. Rev. 273, 283–85 (2009); *Sex, Violence and the First Amendment*, 74 U. Chi. L. Rev. 1857, 1866–1867; *United States v. Stevens*, 130 S. Ct. 1577 (2010) (emphasizing the importance of history in defining "low value" speech).

24. *See Hague v. CIO*, 307 U.S. 496 (public forum); *Richmond Newspapers v. Virginia*, 448 U.S. 555 (1980) (criminal trials).

25. Schauer and Pildes, *Electoral Exceptionalism, supra* note 2, at 1806.

26. *Id.*

27. *Id.* at 1808.

28. *See Buckley v. Valeo*, 424 U.S. 1 (1976) (contributions, disclosure and subsidies); *Arkansas Educational Television Commission v. Forbes,* 523 U.S. 666 (1998) (candidate debates); *Burdick v. Takushi,* 504 U.S. 428 (1992) (election ballots); *Burson v. Freeman,* 504 U.S. 191 (polling places).

29. *See Arkansas Educational Television Commission v. Forbes*, 523 U.S. 666 (1998).

30. *See McConnell v. Federal Elections Commission,* 540 U.S. 93 (2003).

31. *Buckley v. Valeo*, 424 U.S. 1 (1976).

32. Consider the view stated by the Canadian Supreme Court in the landmark decision in *Libman v. Quebec,* [1997] 3 S.C.R. 569, 598-99 (Can.): "If the principle of fairness in the political sphere is to be preserved, . . . laws

limiting spending are needed to preserve the equality of democratic rights." *See* Samuel Issacharoff, *The Constitutional Logic of Campaign Finance Regulation*, 36 Pepp. L. Rev. 373 (2009).

33. *See* Stone, *supra* note 10.

5

1. *See* my article *Money Talks But It Isn't Speech,* 95 Minn. L. Rev. 953 (2011) for a discussion of how Supreme Court case doctrine links money to speech in these ways.

2. Mike Seidman has written an interesting and provocative article that does address this general question, but it is one of very few. *See* Louis Michael Seidman, *The Dale Problem: Property and Speech Under the Regulatory State*, 75 U. Chi. L. Rev. 1541 (2008).

3. 424 U.S. 1 (1976).

4. *Id.* at 19.

5. *Id.*

6. *Id.*

7. The idea of a penumbral right was introduced in *Griswold v. Connecticut*, 381 U.S. 479 (1965). In *Griswold* the court reasoned that the specific guarantees in the Bill of Rights depend on corollary, or "penumbral," rights which give the enumerated rights "life and substance." *Id.* at 484. *See also* Hellman, *supra* note 1 (discussing the relationship between money and constitutional rights).

8. Restrictions on spending money are subject to strict scrutiny while restrictions on giving money are subjected to heightened, but less exacting, review. *See Buckley*, 424 U.S. at 44–45.

9. *See Citizens United v. FEC,* 130 S. Ct. 876 (2010) (treating the connection between speech and money as obvious without citing to *Buckley*). *Citizens United* does cite *Buckley* at other points in the case, however. *Citizens United*, 130 S. Ct. *passim. See also* Hellman, *supra* note 1, at 954–55 (discussing the Court's treatment of the connection between money and speech in *Citizens United*).

10. 381 U.S. 479 (1965).

11. *Griswold* examined the constitutionality of two provisions of a Connecticut law. *Id.* at 480. The first punished any "person who uses any drug, medicinal article or instrument for the purpose of preventing

contraception" and the second punished anyone who helps another to do so. *Id.*

12. *Id.* at 485.

13. 405 U.S. 438 (1972).

14. In language cited often in later cases, the Court explains, "if the right of privacy means anything, it is the right of the *individual*, married or single, to be free from unwarranted governmental intrusion into matters so fundamentally affecting a person as the decision whether to bear or beget a child." *Id.* at 453.

15. *Id.* at 440.

16. 431 U.S. 678 (1977).

17. *Id.* at 681. The case also addressed whether provisions of the New York law forbidding sale of contraceptives to minors under 16 and forbidding the advertising of contraceptives were unconstitutional. *Id.* The Court struck down both provisions. *Id.*

18. *Id.* at 687 (explaining that "*Griswold* may no longer be read as holding only that a State may not prohibit a married couple's use of contraceptives. Read in light of its progeny, the teaching of *Griswold* is that the Constitution protects individual decisions in matters of childbearing from unjustified intrusion by the State").

19. *Id.* at 688.

20. *Id.* (reasoning that "an instructive analogy is found in decisions after *Roe v. Wade*, *supra*, that held unconstitutional statutes that did not prohibit abortions outright but limited in a variety of ways a woman's access to them").

21. *Id.* at 689.

22. *Id.* The Court goes on to consider whether a compelling governmental interest justifies the restriction on this right and finds that no such interest exists. *Id.* at 690.

23. 394 U.S. 557 (1969).

24. *Id.* at 567–68.

25. *Id.* at 559.

26. *Id.* at 568.

27. *Id. See also Roth v. U.S.*, 354 U.S. 476, 485 (1957) (in which Roth was convicted of mailing obscene materials); and its companion case, *Alberts v. California*, 354 U.S. 476, 481 (1957) (in which Alberts was convicted of "lewdly keeping for sale obscene and indecent books, and [of] writing, composing and publishing an obscene advertisement of them").

28. Justice Hugo Black pointed out the tension in the distinction in his dissent to the companion cases of *United States v. Thirty-Seven Photographs* and *United States v. Reidel*, when he noted that without the ability to purchase obscene material, a man could possess it "only when a man writes salacious books in his attic, prints them in his basement, and reads them in his living room." 402 U.S. 363, 382 (1971) (Black, J., dissenting).

29. *See, e.g., Smith v. United States,* 431 U.S. 291, 307 (1977) ("*Stanley* did not create a right to receive, transport, or distribute obscene material, even though it had established the right to possess the material in the privacy of the home."); *United States v. Orito,* 413 U.S. 139, 141 (1973) (holding that *Stanley*'s tolerance of obscenity within the privacy of the home created no "correlative right to receive it, transport it, or distribute it"); *United States v. Thirty-Seven (37) Photographs,* 402 U.S. 363, 376 (1971) ("That the private user under *Stanley* may not be prosecuted for possession of obscenity in his home does not mean that he is entitled to import it from abroad free from the power of Congress to exclude noxious articles from commerce"); *United States v. Reidel,* 402 U.S. 351, 354–55 (1971) (rejecting the argument that *Stanley* created a right to distribute or sell obscene material).

30. 402 U.S. at 356.

31. 473 U.S. 305 (1985).

32. *Id.* at 334.

33. *Id.* at 307.

34. *Id.* at 323.

35. *Id.* at 334–35.

36. *Id.* at 333–34.

37. *Id.* at 320.

38. *See Matthews v. Eldridge,* 424 U.S. 319, 335 (1976) (holding that evidentiary hearings are not required prior to the termination of disability benefits and setting forth the criteria to be applied in determining when more process is required).

39. *Walters*, 473 U.S. at 369–70 (Stevens, J., dissenting) (footnotes omitted).

40. Congress later amended the act at issue in this case and replaced with a system that allowed veterans to hire lawyers only after the decision of the Board of Veterans Affairs becomes final. This decision was challenged in *In re Fee Agreement of James W. Stanley*, 9 Vet. App. 203, 215 (1996) and upheld, following *Walters*.

41. *Walters*, 473 U.S. at 322–23.

42. *Id.* at 324–26.
43. *Id.* at 332–34.
44. *Id.* at 331.
45. *Id.* at 330–34.
46. This conclusion is also consistent with the Supreme Court's decision in *United States Department of Labor v. Triplett*, 494 U.S. 715 (1990) (upholding the discipline of a lawyer for improperly collecting fees in violation of the Black Lung Benefits Act and holding that the fee scheme in that act, which requires that attorney fees be reasonable, approved by the department, and collectible only at the close of a successful claim, does not violate the Due Process Clause of the Fifth Amendment because there was insufficient evidence to show that this scheme deprived claimants of adequate representation).
47. *In re Baby M*, 537 A.2d 1227 (N.J. 1988).
48. 487 N.W.2d 484 (Mich. Ct. App. 1992).
49. *Id.* at 484.
50. *Id.* at 485.
51. *Id.* at 486 (agreeing that "the Due Process Clauses of the state and federal constitutions, together with the penumbral rights emanating from the specific guarantees of the Bill of Rights, protect 'individual decisions in matters of childbearing from unjustified intrusions by the State'").
52. *Id.* at 489.
53. *Id.* at 485.
54. *Id.* at 486.
55. *Id.*
56. *Id.* at 487.
57. *Id.*
58. *Id.*
59. *Id.*
60. *Id.*
61. *Id.* at 486, 487.
62. *Id* at 487.
63. *Id.* at 486, 487.
64. *See, e.g.*, Elizabeth Anderson, *Value in Ethics and Economics* (1993).
65. 539 U.S. 558 (2003) (holding that a Texas law that prohibited sexual acts between same-sex partners was unconstitutional).
66. *See Williams v. Morgan*, 478 F.3d 1316 (11th Cir. 2007); *Williams v. Attorney General of Alabama*, 378 F.3d. 1232 (11th Cir. 2004); *Reliable Consultants, Inc. v. Earle*, 517 F.3d 738 (5th Cir. 2008).

67. The Eleventh Circuit found that *Lawrence* merely declared unconstitutional criminal prohibitions on consensual homosexual sodomy and refused to extrapolate from it a broader fundamental right to sexual privacy. *See Williams v. Attorney General*, 378 F.3d at 1236. In contrast, the Fifth Circuit characterized the right created in *Lawrence* broadly as the "right to be free from government intrusion regarding 'the most private human contact, sexual behavior.'" *Reliable Consultants*, 517 F.3d at 744 (quoting *Lawrence*, 539 U.S. at 567).

68. The Eleventh Circuit reasoned that because the *Lawrence* decision did not specifically invoke strict scrutiny or engage in a *Glucksberg* fundamental rights analysis, it was decided on rational basis grounds and therefore did not recognize a new fundamental right. *See Williams v. Attorney General*, 378 F.3d at 1238. On the other hand, the Fifth Circuit reasoned that although the *Lawrence* decision did not specifically categorize the right as fundamental, it did not need to do so because it gave specific instructions that interests in public morality cannot sustain a statute infringing on the right to sexual privacy. *See Reliable Consultants*, 517 F.3d at 745.

69. The Fifth Circuit found that Lawrence provided protection from governmental intrusion into sexual conduct. *Reliable Consultants*, 517 F.3d at 744. The Eleventh Circuit found that *Lawrence* offered protection for private sexual activity. *See Williams v. Morgan*, 478 F.3d at 1322.

70. *See Williams v. Morgan*, 478 F.3d at 1322 (explaining that "this statute targets *commerce* in sexual devices, an inherently public activity, whether it occurs on a street corner, in a shopping mall, or in a living room" (emphasis in original)).

71. *Id.*

72. *Id.*

73. It should be noted that the Eleventh Circuit declined to find that *Lawrence* held that such sexual privacy was a fundamental right. *Williams v. Attorney General*, 378 F.3d at 1236. As a result, the court in *Williams* applied only rational basis review. However, the court here treats the right to use sexual devices as analogous to the right to sexual privacy articulated in *Lawrence*. While *Lawrence* may decline to use the language of fundamental rights, clearly a right of some importance is protected. Thus, what the Eleventh Circuit has to say about use versus sale is relevant to the questions addressed in this chapter.

74. *Reliable Consultants*, 517 F.3d at 744.

75. *Id.*

76. *Id.*

77. *Walters v. National Association of Radiation Survivors,* 473 U.S. 305, 334 (1985).

78. *Id.*

79. *Id.* at 320.

80. *Carey v. Population Services,* 431 U.S. 678, 688 (1977).

81. *Buckley v. Valeo,* 424 U.S. 1, 19 (1976).

82. *Id.* at 21.

83. So far, this chapter has considered only the question whether restrictions on the right to spend one's own money on the exercise of a right violates that right. One obvious question that emerges from the theory is whether there is a positive right to adequate access to the means to effectuate constitutionally protected rights. Moreover, not all the cases fit as neatly within the adequacy analysis. Laws forbidding paid contract surrogacy illustrate the first point of this chapter—that not all constitutionally protected rights include a penumbral right to spend money—but may not fit the theory proposed to explain this delineation, that is, adequacy. While it is possible to tie this case to the adequacy analysis as well, the permissibility of laws forbidding paid surrogacy suggests that other factors may also be relevant.

84. *See supra, "The Blocked Strand and the First Amendment: The Stanley Approach."*

85. For example, in *Griswold v. Connecticut*, the Supreme Court emphasized the importance of privacy in the marital bedroom. 381 U.S. 479, 485–86 (1965). Several years later, in *Paris Adult Theater I v. Slaton*, the Court refused to apply *Stanley v. Georgia* because a theater did not warrant the same kind of privacy as a home. 413 U.S. 49, 65 (1973). In *Lawrence v. Texas*, the Court again emphasized the importance of the home, stating in the opening paragraph that "in our tradition the State is not omnipresent in the home." 539 U.S. 558, 562 (2003).

86. *See Osborne v. Ohio*, 495 U.S. 103, 108 (1990) (refusing to extend the right created in *Stanley* to at-home possession of child pornography).

87. Stanley has been so limited by subsequent Supreme Court decisions that it only applies to a very narrow right: the right to possess pornographic materials (not involving children) in one's own home for one's own personal use. This suggests that it may be truly limited to its facts.

88. 548 U.S. 230 (2006).

89. *Id.* at 236.

90. *Id.* at 248 (explaining that "at some point the constitutional risks to the democratic electoral process become too great").

91. *Id.*

92. *Id.* at 255.

93. *Id.* at 260.

6

1. *Citizens United v. FEC,* 130 S. Ct. 876 (2010).

2. *Id.* at 898. This case did not address the prohibition on the use of general treasury funds to finance contributions to candidates.

3. *Id.* at 913. The Court relies centrally on *First National Bank of Boston v. Bellotti,* 435 U.S. 765, which involved use of general treasury funds to finance ads relating to a state referendum on a state tax issue.

4. 130 S. Ct. at 913. The Court left for another case on another day the issue of whether foreign corporations were included in this broad assertion that all corporations are to be treated alike for purposes of First Amendment rights of political speech. *Id.* at 911.

5. *Id.* at 898–99.

6. *Id.* at 911.

7. *Id.* at 911 (citing *Bellotti,* 435 U.S. at 794).

8. *Austin,* 494 U.S. at 709–10. Citing *Bellotti,* 435 U.S. at 794, n. 34 as "noting 'crucial distinction' between union members and shareholders," Justice Kennedy rejected the relevance of such compelled speech cases as *Abood v. Detroit Board of Education,* 431 U.S. 209 (1977), noting crisply that "one need not become a member of the Michigan Chamber of Commerce in order to earn a living." *Austin,* 494 U.S. at 709–10.

9. *Austin,* 494 U.S. at 710.

10. *Id.* at 685–86.

11. *Id.* at 686–87.

12. *Id.* at 687.

13. *Id.* at 677.

14. *Id.* at 672 (emphasis in original).

15. *Id.* at 673.

16. For an analysis of voting decisions, *see* Samuel L. Popkin, *The Reasoning Voter: Communication and Persuasion in Political Campaigns* (1991).

17. Federal Election Campaign Act, 2 U.S.C. § 441b (FECA § 441b).

18. Both taxable business corporations and nonprofit advocacy organizations operate through managerial control, relatively weak boards, and shareholders or members with few rights to participate in organizational governance. While shareholders in business corporations vote for members of their boards and on certain issues specified in the corporations' organizing documents, most nonprofit advocacy organizations have no members with similar voting rights. The boards of nonprofit advocacy organizations are self-perpetuating boards that elect their own successors, or reelect themselves. For an analysis of managerial control that remains useful for understanding both business corporations and nonprofit advocacy organizations, *see* Adolf F. Berle and Gardiner C. Means, *The Modern Corporation and Private Property* (1932). *See also* Lucian A. Bebchuk and Robert J. Jackson, Jr., *Corporate Political Speech: Who Decides?* 124 Harv. L. Rev. 83 (2010).

19. U.S. Const. pmbl.

20. *Id.*

21. Declaration of Independence para 2. *See* Pauline Maier, *American Scripture: Making the Declaration of Independence* (1997).

22. *See generally* Pauline Maier, *Ratification: The People Debate the Constitution, 1787–1788* (2010); Akhil Reed Amar, *America's Constitution: A Biography* (2005).

23. Declaration of Independence para 2.

24. *See generally* Larry D. Kramer, *The People Themselves: Popular Constitutionalism and Judicial Review* 5 (2004).

25. *Id.* at 5–7. For a discussion of what he sees as disengagement from active participation at the very time that democratic institutions are spreading around the world, *see* Kramer, *Political Organization and the Future of Democracy,* in Jack M. Balkin and Reva B. Siegel, *The Constitution in 2020* at 166–78 (2009). Kramer expresses the concern that "leaders in the twenty-first century reach out to constituents primarily through the national media, apparently content to establish 'personal' contact through forms of address that are, in fact, one-sided and anything but personal." *Id.* at 176. Kramer concludes that "politics today has thus become a remote, passive activity for most of us." *Id.*

26. Kramer, *supra* note 24 at 7: "'The people' they knew could speak, and had done so. 'The people' they knew had fought a revolution, expressed dissatisfaction with the first fruits of independence, and debated

and adopted a new charter to govern themselves. Certainly the Founders were concerned about the dangers of popular Government, some of them obsessively so. But they were also captivated by its possibilities and in awe of its importance. Their Constitution remained, fundamentally, an act of popular will: the people's charter, made by the people. And, as we shall see, it was 'the people themselves'—working through and responding to their agents in the government—who were responsible for seeing that it was properly interpreted and implemented."

27. U.S. Const. Article VII. Amar, *supra* note 22 at 29 describes the Preamble and Article VII as "bookends."

28. U.S. Const. Article V.

29. U.S. Const. Article V.

30. Amar, *supra* note 22 at 471 describes the Preamble as "the Founder's foundation" and ratification as "the real constitutional drama." *Id.* at 468. For a detailed study of the drama of ratification in the state conventions, see Maier, *supra* note 22.

31. Amar, *supra* note 22 at 476.

32. William J. Brennan, Jr., *The Constitution of the United States: Contemporary Ratification,"* 27 S. Tx. L. Rev. 433 (1986) (originally delivered as a speech at Georgetown University on October 12, 1985).

33. Frances R. Hill, *Constitutive Voting and Participatory Association: Contested Constitutional Claims in Primary Elections,* 64 U. Miami L. Rev. 535, 538–53 (2010). *See also* Frances R. Hill, *Putting Voters First: An Essay on the Jurisprudence of Citizen Sovereignty in Federal Election Law,* 60 U. Miami L. Rev. 155 (2006).

34. *Ex parte* Yarbrough, 110 U.S. 651 (1884).

35. *Id.* at 666.

36. *Nixon v. Herndon,* 273 U.S. 536 (1927) (right to vote in primary); *Nixon v. Condon,* 286 U.S. 73 (1932) (striking down state statute authorizing state executive committee of political party to limit party membership to white voters); *Grovey v. Townsend,* 295 U.S. 45 (1935) (upholding state statute authorizing state convention of political party to limit party membership to white voters); *U.S. v. Classic,* 313 U.S. 299 (1941) (right to have vote counted in primary election); *Smith v. Allwright,* 321 U.S. 649 (1944) (overruling *Grovey v. Townsend*); *Terry v. Adams,* 345 U.S. 461 (1953) (striking down primary vote conducted by private association limited to white voters).

37. *See* Hill, *Constitutive Voting, supra* note 33 at 554–75.

38. *Baker v. Carr,* 369 U.S. 186 (1962)(state legislative districts). See also *Wesberry v. Sanders,* 376 U.S. 1 (1964)(congressional districts); *Reynolds v. Sims,* 377 U.S. 533 (1964)(state legislative districts).

39. Justice Brennan, *supra* note 38 at 442, said of these cases: "Recognition of the principle of 'one person, one vote' as a constitutional principle redeems the promise of self-governance by affirming the essential dignity of every citizen in the right to equal participation in the democratic process." In the same vein, Judge J. Skelly Wright, *Money and the Pollution of Politics: Is the First Amendment an Obstacle to Political Equality?* 82 Colum. L. Rev. 609 (1982), expressed concern that "the voices of individual citizens are being drowned out in elections campaigns." *Id.* at 609. Judge Wright said of political campaigns, "if the ideal of equality is trampled there, the principle of 'one person, one vote,' the cornerstone of our democracy, becomes a hollow mockery." *Id.*

40. Justice David H. Souter, Harvard University's 359th Commencement Address, 124 Harv. L. Rev. 429 (2010).

41. *Id.* at 435.

42. *Id.* at 434.

43. *Id.* at 433.

44. *Id.*

45. *Id.*

46. U.S. Const., Amend. I.

47. *NAACP v. Alabama ex rel. Patterson,* 357 U.S. 449 (1958); *Bates v. City of Little Rock,* 361 U.S. 516 (1960).

48. *Bates,* 361 U.S. at 522–23.

49. *Id.* at 528, citing *NAACP v. Alabama ex rel. Patterson.*

50. *Alabama ex. rel. Patterson*, 357 U.S. at 460.

51. *Id.*

52. *Roberts v. U.S. Jaycees,* 468 U.S. 609 (1984).

53. *Bd. of Dirs. of Rotary Int'l v. Rotary Club of Duarte,* 481 U.S. 537 (1981).

54. In *Roberts,* Justice Brennan, writing for the majority, described freedom of expressive association as "a right to associate for the purpose of engaging in those activities protected by the First Amendment—speech, assembly, petition for the redress of grievances, and the exercise of religion." *Roberts,* 468 U.S. at 612. He focused on the rights of individuals to associate, stating that "the Constitution guarantees freedom

of association of this kind as an indispensable means of preserving other individuals liberties." *Id.*

55. *Boy Scouts of America v. Dale,* 530 U.S. 640 (2000).

56. The Court extended its expressive association jurisprudence to political parties in a series of cases dealing with the rights of political parties in determining who can vote in primary elections. *See California Democratic Party v. Jones,* 530 U.S. 567 (2000) (decision announced two days after the decision in *Dale*).

57. *West Virginia Board of Education v. Barnette,* 319 U.S. 624 (1943) (compelled recitation of the Pledge of Allegiance in schools); *Wooley v. Maynard,* 430 U.S. 705 (1977)(compelled display of state motto on license plate).

58. An "agency shop" is a workplace in which all the workers are represented by a single union but not all the workers are required to become union members. Those who do not choose to become members are required to pay fees equivalent to union dues to support the collective bargaining activities from which they benefit.

59. *Abood v. Detroit Board of Education,* 431 U.S. 209 (1977).

60. *Id.* at 234.

61. *Id.* at 235.

62. *Id.* at 235–36.

63. *Davenport v. Washington Education Association,* 551 U.S. 177 (2007).

64. *Id.* at 185.

65. *Id.* 187 (emphasis in original).

66. *Id.* at 187.

67. *Id.* at 187, n. 2.

68. *Id.*

69. Justice Scalia applied a version of this argument in the context of commercial speech when he found that compelled speech is limited to situations in which funds are paid as a result of government compulsion and that compelled subsidization is distinguishable because it does not rest on government compulsion. *Johanns v. Livestock Mktg. Ass'n.,* 544 U.S. 550 (2005).

70. *Davenport,* 551 U.S. at 190–91.

71. *Id.* at 191, n. 4, citing *Beck* as an example of a content-based distinction by a private-sector union.

72. *Id.* at 191, n. 4.

73. *FEC v. Mass. Citizens for Life, Inc.*, 479 U.S. 238, 261–64 (1986).

74. The issue of donor intent was at the center of the six-year litigation between Princeton University and the Robertson family, which claimed that by operating the Woodrow Wilson School of Public and International Affairs as a center of scholarship the university failed to use the funds for training students for public service, particularly in foreign affairs. The parties settled the lawsuit at a cost to Princeton of some $90 million. For a summary of the litigation and the settlement, *see Princeton and Robertson Family Settle Titanic Donor-Intent Lawsuit,* The Chronicle of Higher Education, December 10, 2008. For a detailed chronology of the litigation, with links to relevant documents, including the Settlement Agreement, see http://www.princeton.edu/robertson/about.

75. *MCFL*, 479 U.S. at 261 ("[A]n individual desiring more direct control over the use of his or her money can simply earmark the contribution for a specific purpose, an option whose availability does not depend on the applicability of §441b").

7

1. For a history of the corporate free speech movement, *see generally* Robert L. Kerr, *The Corporate Free Speech Movement: Cognitive Feudalism and the Endangered Marketplace of Ideas* (2008); *see also* Linda L. Berger, *Of Metaphor, Metonymy, and Corporate Money: Rhetorical Choices in Supreme Court Decisions on Campaign Finance Regulation*, 58 Mercer L. Rev. 949 (2007).

2. *See, e.g.*, Dan Eggen and T. W. Farnam, *New "Super Pacs" Bringing Millions into Campaigns*, Wash. Post, September 28, 2010, at A01; Editorial, *The Secret Election*, N.Y. Times, September 19, 2010, at WK8; Michael Luo, *G.O.P. Allies Drive Ad Spending Disparity*, N.Y. Times, September 14, 2010, at A1.

3. 130 S. Ct. 876 (2010).

4. Geoffrey Stone has described low-value speech as speech that "might not sufficiently further the values and purposes of the First Amendment" to warrant strict-scrutiny protection against content-based regulation of speech. Geoffrey R. Stone, *Free Speech in the Twenty-First Century: Ten Lessons from the Twentieth Century*, 36 Pepp. L. Rev. 273, 283–285 (2009)

(providing overview of doctrine of low-value speech). Although Prof. Stone does not include campaign spending among his listed categories of low-value speech, the campaign finance case law has long treated contributions to candidates and parties as low-value speech. *See McConnell v. FEC,* 540 U.S. 93, 135 (2003) (noting that "the communicative value of large contributions inheres mainly in their ability to facilitate the speech of their recipients"); *Colo. Republican Fed. Campaign Comm. v. FEC,* 518 U.S. 604, 638 (1996) (Thomas, J., concurring in the judgment and dissenting in part) ("Contributions have less First Amendment value than expenditures because they do not involve speech by the donor.").

5. *See, e.g.*, Richard Briffault, *On Dejudicializing American Campaign Finance Law*, 34 N.Y.U. Rev. L. & Soc. Change (forthcoming April 2011) (discussing the incoherence of campaign finance decisions and asserting that such decisions are constitutionally and judicially unnecessary); Richard L. Hasen, Citizens United *and the Illusion of Coherence*, 109 Mich. L. Rev. 581 (2011); Samuel Issacharoff, *On Political Corruption*, 124 Harv. L. Rev. 118 (2010) (arguing for a reorientation of concept of corruption to focus on avoidance of "clientelist" relation between elected officials and interested parties); Zephyr Teachout, *A Wholesome Rule of Law: Corruption and Contract Law in the 19th Century*, 34 N.Y.U. Rev. L. & Soc. Change (forthcoming April 2011) (focusing on concerns about corruption). *But see* Kathleen M. Sullivan, *Two Concepts of Freedom of Speech*, 124 Harv. L. Rev 143 (2010) (analyzing *Citizens United* as interplay between two competing visions of First Amendment: freedom of speech as equality and freedom of speech as liberty).

6. Justice Thomas has usefully summarized the contributions/expenditures distinction as follows: "Contributions have less First Amendment value than expenditures because they do not involve speech by the donor." *Colo. Republican Fed. Campaign Comm.*, 518 U.S. at 638 (1996) (Thomas, J., concurring in the judgment and dissenting in part).

7. 424 U.S. 1 (1976).

8. *See id.* at 20–21 (stating that the size of political contributions provide only a rough measure of support, and therefore restrictions on contributions provide little restraint on political communication); *Cal. Med. Ass'n v. FEC,* 453 U.S. 182, 196 (1981) (stating contributions are not entitled to full First Amendment protection).

9. *See Citizens United*, 130 S. Ct. at 898 ("Premised on mistrust of governmental power, the First Amendment stands against attempts to

disfavor certain subjects or viewpoints. Prohibited, too, are restrictions distinguishing among different speakers, allowing speech by some but not others.") (citation omitted); *id.* at 884 ("It is irrelevant for First Amendment purposes that corporate funds may 'have little or no correlation to the public's support for the corporation's political ideas.'") (internal citation omitted).

10. 424 U.S. at 14. The best-known articulation of this theory of the deliberative aims of the First Amendment can be found in Alexander Meiklejohn, *Free Speech and Its Relation to Self-Government* (1948); *see also* Owen M. Fiss, *The Irony of Free Speech* (1996); Cass R. Sunstein, *Democracy and the Problem of Free Speech* (1993).

11. *Buckley*, 424 U.S. at 21.

12. *Id.*

13. *Va. State Bd. of Pharmacy v. Va. Citizens Consumer Council, Inc.*, 425 U.S. 748, 756 (1976).

14. *Buckley*, 424 U.S. at 21.

15. *Id.*

16. Separate First Amendment issues, of course, arise when part of a contributor's message is intended to be conveyed through the association through which she makes her contribution. Such associational issues are discussed *infra*, Section II.B.

17. *Buckley*, 424 U.S at 21–22.

18. *Id.* at 39–40.

19. *Id.* at 18 n.17.

20. *Id.* at 21.

21. *Id.* at 19.

22. *Id.* at 39.

23. *First Nat'l Bank of Bos. v. Bellotti,* 435 U.S. 765, 768 (1978).

24. *Id.* at 784.

25. *Id.* at 776.

26. *Id.* at 777.

27. *Id.*

28. 479 U.S. 238 (1986).

29. 494 U.S. 652 (1990).

30. 540 U.S. 93 (2003).

31. 479 U.S. at 260–61.

32. *Id.* at 263.

33. *Id.* at 252.
34. *Id.* at 258.
35. *Id.*
36. *Id.* at 259.
37. *Austin v. Mich. Chamber of Commerce,* 494 U.S. 652, 660 (1990).
38. *Citizens United v. FEC,* 130 S. Ct. 876, 907 (2010).
39. 494 U.S. at 654.
40. *Id.* at 654–55.
41. *Id.* at 660.
42. *Id.* at 660–61.
43. *McConnell,* 540 U.S. at 204 (quoting *FEC v. Beaumont,* 539 U.S. 146, 163 (2003)) (citations and internal quotation marks omitted). Notably, the Court in *Beaumont* upheld a corporate contribution ban as applied to nonprofit advocacy corporations, even while *MCFL* had struck down the expenditures restriction as applied to nonprofit advocacy corporations. *Beaumont,* 639 U.S. at 149. In rejecting the challenge to the contribution ban the Court emphasized the speech-by-proxy rationale, under which contributions are deemed to retain little of the volitional impulse of the original spender. *See id.* at 161 n.8. Thus, at the same time that the Court was importing a version of volitional analysis into the expenditures arena, it continued to employ volitional reasoning to accord political contributions only marginal First Amendment value.
44. *Citizens United,* 130 S. Ct. at 904 (quoting *First Nat'l Bank of Bos. v. Bellotti,* 435 U.S. 765, 777 (1978)).
45. *Id.* at 901–02.
46. *See id.* at 899 ("Quite apart from the purpose or effect of regulating content, moreover, the Government may commit a constitutional wrong when by law it identifies certain preferred speakers.").
47. *Id.* at 904 (noting that "*Buckley* rejected the premise that the Government has an interest 'in equalizing the relative ability of individuals and groups to influence the outcome of elections.'") (citation omitted).
48. *Id.* at 923 (Roberts, C. J., concurring) (quoting *Austin v. Mich. Chamber of Commerce,* 494 U.S. 652, 660 (1990)) (internal quotation marks omitted).
49. 494 U.S. at 660.
50. *Citizens United,* 130 S. Ct. at 905 (quoting *Austin,* 494 U.S. at 660) (internal quotation marks omitted).

51. *See supra, "Bellotti*: The Commodity Approach's Previous High-Water Mark."

52. *Buckley v. Valeo,* 424 U.S. 1, 97–98 (1976).

8

1. The term is from Richard Briffault.

2. Frank J. Sorauf, *Inside Campaign Finance* 238 (1992) (arguing for the interrelation between contribution and expenditure limits in the statutory FECA scheme).

3. *See* Samuel Issacharoff, Pamela S. Karlan, and Richard H. Pildes, *The Law of Democracy* 373 (3d ed. 2007) (providing the stable division on the Court over *Buckley*); J. Robert Abraham, *Note: Saving Buckley: Creating a Stable Campaign Finance Framework,* 110 Colum. L. Rev. 1078, 1091–92 (2010) (tallying half the justices that have served since 1976 as opposed to the *Buckley* framework).

4. Richard L. Hasen, *Buckley Is Dead, Long Live Buckley: The New Campaign Finance Incoherence of McConnell v. Federal Election Commission,* 153 U. Pa. L. Rev. 31, 37 (2004)

5. Samuel Issacharoff and Pamela S. Karlan, *The Hydraulics of Campaign Finance Reform,* 77 Tex. L. Rev. 1705, 1736 (1999) ("A generation has shown us that the expenditure/contribution distinction of Buckley not only is conceptually flawed, but has not worked").

6. I confess to being a participant in looking at the failures of Court doctrine, all the while conceding in articles and the classroom just how intractable the problem seemed. Indeed, writing with Pamela Karlan a decade ago, I concluded that not much could be done about the pull of finance in elections, such that the "hydraulic" of money finding its outlet led many campaign finance reform efforts to empower the unaccountable tertiary actors (the PACs, the 527s, and all the rest) at the expense of the candidates and parties who actually had to stand for election before We the People. *See id.*

7. 438 U.S. 265 (1978).

8. *See Buckley v. Valeo,* 424 U.S. 1, 26–28 (1976); *First Nat'l Bank v. Bellotti,* 435 US 765 (1978); *see also McConnell v. FEC,* 540 U.S. 93, 121 (2003).

9. *FEC v. National Conservative PAC*, 470 U.S. 480, 498 (1985).

10. 435 U.S. 765, 788, n. 26 (1978).

11. *Bellotti*, 435 U.S. at 790. *See also Meyer v. Grant,* 486 U.S. 414 (1998) (rejecting argument of undue influence of money in rejecting prohibition on paid signature gatherers for petition drives). The strongest exponent of this view—that the liberty protections of the First Amendment prohibit limitations on political expression—is Justice Thomas, whose opinions on campaign finance return consistently to the core prohibitory structure of the First Amendment. *See, e.g., Nixon v. Shrink Mo. Gov't PAC,* 528 U.S. 377, 410 (2000) (Thomas, J., dissenting) ("I begin with a proposition that ought to be unassailable: Political speech is the primary object of First Amendment protection").

12. *See Austin v. Michigan Chamber of Commerce,* 494 U.S. 652, 659–60 (1990) (expressing concern about the corrupting effect of "immense aggregations of wealth that are accumulated with the help of the corporate form"); *FEC v. Beaumont,* 539 U.S. 146, 155 (2003) (state has interest in prevent "war-chest corruption"); *McConnell v. FEC,* 540 U.S. 93, 143–45 (2003) (discussing the importance of prohibiting the appearance of "undue influence"); *FEC v. Wisconsin Right to Life, Inc.,* 551 U.S. 449, 479 (2007); *see also United States v. Int'l Union United Auto, Aircraft & Agric. Implement Workers of America,* 352 U.S. 567, 585 (1957) ("No less lively, although slower to evoke federal action, was popular feeling that aggregated capital unduly influenced politics, an influence not stopping short of corruption."); *First Nat'l Bank v. Bellotti,* 435 U.S. 765, 809 (White, J. dissenting).

13. *Austin*, 494 U.S. at 659.

14. David A. Strauss, *Corruption, Equality and Campaign Finance Reform*, 94 Colum. L. Rev. 1369, 1370 (1994).

15. *See Austin*, 494 U.S. at 660 ("the unique state-conferred corporate structure that facilitates the amassing of large treasuries warrants the limit on independent expenditures"); *see also Colorado Republican Fed'l Campaign Comm. v. FEC,* 533 U.S, 431, 441 (2001) (focusing on expenditures by political parties providing a path of circumvention of contribution limits).

16. *See* David Cole, *First Amendment Antitrust: The End of Laissez Faire in Campaign Finance,* 9 Yale L. & Pol'y Rev., 236, 237 (1991) (framing *Austin* as premised on the idea that "free market capitalism threatens the free marketplace of ideas by giving certain voices inordinate influence"); Owen M. Fiss, *The Irony of Free Speech* 4 (advocating state restriction of speech by

some and subsidies of others to equalize access to political discourse); Ronald Dworkin, *The Curse of American Politics*, N.Y. Rev. Books, October 17, 1996, at 19 ("When wealth is unfairly distributed and money dominates politics . . . [voters] are not equal in their own ability to command the attention of others for their own candidates, interests and convictions"). These arguments run into the teeth of *Buckley:* "the concept that government may restrict the speech of some elements of our society in order to enhance the relative voice of others is wholly foreign to the First Amendment," 424 U.S. at 48–49.

17. *See, e.g., Reynolds v. Sims,* 377 U.S. 522, 565 (1964) (all citizens should have an "equally effective voice" in the political process). The equality rationale appears in campaign finance cases through efforts to dampen money in general and the arms-race effects of needing to raise money. *See, e.g., Buckley v. Valeo,* 424 U.S. 1, 260 (1976) (White, J., concurring in part and dissenting in part) (justifying expenditure limitations as a legitimate means to "counter the corrosive effects of money in federal election campaigns"). *See also* Richard Hasen, *The Supreme Court and Election Law: Judging Equality from* Baker v. Carr *to* Bush v. Gore 114 (2003) ("*Austin* represents the first and only case in which a majority of the Court accepted, in deed if not in word, the equality rationale as a permissible state interest").

18. *Austin*, 494 U.S. at 659, *quoting FEC v. Mass. Citizens for Life, Inc.*, 479 U.S. 238, 257 (1986).

19. *See, e.g.*, Ronald Dworkin, *The Decision that Threatens Democracy,* N.Y. Rev. Books, May 13, 2010, at 63 (treating *Austin* as the controlling precedent on limitations on campaign expenditures).

20. *Shrink*, 528 U.S. at 390.

21. Bipartisan Campaign Reform Act of 2002, Pub. L. No. 107-155, 116 Stat. 81 (codified at 2 U.S.C. § 431-55).

22. *McConnell*, 540 U.S. at 143–44. Even this claim was short-lived as the Court soon held that corporations could not be barred from non-electoral speech, regardless of the advantages that might accrue to their corporate structure. *FEC v. Wis. Right to Life, Inc.,* 551 U.S. 449, 480 (2007).

23. *Citizens United v. FEC,* 130 S. Ct. 876, 913 (2010).

24. *FEC v. Colo. Republican Fed. Campaign Comm.,* 533 U.S. 431, 464 (2001) ("There is no significant functional difference between a party's coordinated expenditure and a direct party contribution to the candidate, and there is good reason to expect that a party's right of unlimited coordinated spending would attract increased contributions to parties to finance exactly that kind of spending").

25. *Randall v. Sorrell,* 548 U.S. 230 (2006) (striking down Vermont state contribution limits).

26. *Citizens United*, 130 S. Ct. at 904.

27. *Citizens United*, 130 S. Ct. at 962 (Stevens, J., dissenting).

28. *Citizens United v. FEC*, 130 S. Ct. 904, 909–10 (2010).

29. The Court started to grapple with this problem in *McConnell* in addressing "the danger that officeholders will decide issues not on the merits or the desires of their constituencies, but according to the wishes of those who have made large financial contributions valued by the officeholder . . . And unlike straight cash-for-votes transactions, such corruption is neither easily detected nor practical to criminalize. The best means of prevention is to identify and to remove the temptation." 540 U.S. at 153.

30. *See, e.g., Clientelism, Interests and Democratic Representation* (Simona Piattoni ed., 2001); Luis Roniger, *Political Clientelism, Democracy, and Market Economy*, 36 Comp. Pol. 353 (2004).

31. Alex Weingrod, *Patrons, Patronage and Political Parties*, 7 Comp. Stud. in Sci. & Hist. 377, 379 (1968).

32. Roniger, *supra* note 31, at 357 (describing clientelism as endemic in democracy).

33. *Id.* at 358.

34. Philip Keefer and Razvan Vlaicu, *Democracy, Credibility, and Clientelism*, 24 J. L. Econ. & Org. 371, 372–73 (2007).

35. *Id.* at 381–82, 387.

36. *See* Mancur Olson, *The Rise and Decline of Nations* 69–71 (1982).

37. *See* Rob Porter and Sam Walsh, *Earmarks in the Federal Budget Process* 8–9 (Harvard Law School Federal Budget Policy Seminar, Briefing Paper No. 16, 2006), http://www.law.harvard.edu/faculty/hjackson/Earmarks_16.pdf.

38. *The Federalist No. 10,* 56 (J. Madison) (P. Ford ed. 1898).

39. The most ambitious effort to read this definition of corruption cross-textually into the Constitution is found in Zephyr Teachout, *The Anti-Corruption Principle,* 94 Cornell L. Rev. 341, 374 (2009).

40. The leading effort was signaled in Cass R. Sunstein, *Public Values, Private Interests, and the Equal Protection Clause*, 1982 Sup. Ct. Rev. 127 (1982), which argued for applying different tiers of scrutiny to public and private regarding legislation.

41. Richard B. Stewart, *Regulation in a Liberal State: the Role of Non-Commodity Values*, 92 Yale L. J. 1537, 1542 (1983) (noting that "regulation

is viewed as a self-serving tool, manipulated either by well-organized economic interest groups to increase their wealth, or by ideological factions to impose their partisan values on society").

42. *See* Allica Adsera et al., *Are You Being Served? Political Accountability and Quality of Government* 37 (Inter-Am. Dev. Bank, Working Paper No. 438, 2000). Unfortunately, and paradoxically, the competitive uncertainty of elections may also increase pressures to deliver desired goods to any marginal constituency. *See* Jonathan Moran, *Democratic Transitions and Forms of Corruption,* 36 Crime, Law & Soc. Change 379, 381 (2001).

43. Roniger, *supra* note 30, at 367.

44. 130 S. Ct. at 911 (finding the prohibition on corporate independent expenditures both under- and overinclusive if the object is to protect shareholder interests).

45. 129 S. Ct. 2252 (2009).

46. *See* Robert A. Dahl, *A Preface to Democratic Theory* 145 (1956) (identifying the "'normal' American political process" in terms of "a high probability that an active and legitimate group in the population can make itself heard effectively at some crucial stage in the process of decision"); John Hart Ely, *Democracy and Distrust* 135 (1980) (similarly defining healthy democratic processes).

47. Harry H. Wellington and Ralph K. Winter, Jr., *The Limits of Collective Bargaining in Public Employment,* 78 Yale L. J. 1107, 1116, 1124-25 (1969) (developing this doubling of influence claims with regard to strikes by public sector unions). Professor Winter, now a judge on the Second Circuit, makes a significant reappearance in this area of law as counsel to Petitioner Buckley in *Buckley v. Valeo.*

48. *Id.* at 1121, 1123.

49. Hatch Act Amendments of 1940, Pub. L. No 76-252, § 5(a), 53 Stat. at 722.

50. Pub. L. No. 59–36, 34 Stat. 864; 2 U.S.C. § 441b(a). *See FEC v. Beaumont,* 539 U.S. 146, 149 (2003) (upholding constitutionality of Tillman Act, even as applied to not-for-profit corporations).

51. *Cf.* Peter Manikus, *Campaign Finance, Public Contracts and Equal Protection,* 59 Chi.-Kent L. Rev. 817, 817 (1983) (arguing that incentives for incumbents to use government powers to create loyalties among potential donors violated equal protection rights of challengers and campaign supporters).

52. *United Public Workers v. Mitchell,* 330 U.S. 75 (1947); *United States Civ. Serv. Comm'n v. Nat'l Ass'n of Letter Carriers,* 413 U.S. 548 (1973).

53. 2 U.S.C. § 441(c)(b) (1976), repealing Pub. L. No. 76-753, § 5(a), 54 Stat. 772 (1940).

54. *Id.* § 441c(a)(1).

55. *Id.* § 441c(a)(2).

56. *See Citizens United*, 130 S. Ct. at 909 ("[I]ndependent expenditures, including those made by corporations, do not give rise to corruption or the appearance of corruption").

57. *Id.* (emphasis added).

58. 129 S. Ct. 2252 (2009).

59. *Citizens United,* 130 S. Ct. at 910.

60. *Cf.* 17 C.F.R. §376.206(4)-5 (2010) (addressing pay-to-play issues in financial services).

61. For example, a recent Oregon referendum proposed using increased payroll taxes to finance public employment. Public employee unions raised almost 50 percent more than employer groups to push the measure through. *See* Brent Walth and Jeff Mapes, *Public Workers Flex Muscles in Tax Battle,* The Oregonian, January 21, 2010.

62. In Australia, corporate contributions to campaigns are legal yet prove to be limited, and generally corporate contributors have donated money to both major political parties. *See* I. Ramsey, G. Stapledon, and J. Vernon, *Political Donations by Australian Companies,* 29 Fed. L. Rev. 179, 203–4 (2001).

63. *Compare OpenSecrets*, http://www.opensecrets.org/bigpicture/index.php (documenting campaign expenditures) *with Opensecrets*, http://www.opensecrets.org/lobby/index.php (documenting lobbying expenditures of roughly the same total amount).

64. *See generally* Robert Reich, *Supercapitalism: The Transformation of Business, Democracy, and Everyday Life* 131–67 (2007) (chronicling the growth of lobbying to secure competitive advantage of firms vis-à-vis other firms).

65. *FEC v. Mass. Citizens for Life, Inc.,* 479 U.S. 238 (1986).

66. *FEC v. Wis. Right to Life, Inc.,* 551 U.S. 449 (2007).

67. *Citizens United,* 130 S. Ct. at 909 (no suggestion that "the Court should reconsider whether contribution limits should be subjected to rigorous First Amendment scrutiny").

68. In *Doe v. Reed,* No. 09-559, 201 U.S. LEXIS 5256 (June 24, 2010), the Court further rejected a First Amendment facial challenge to disclosure of names on a state petition drive.

69. Richard Briffault, *Reforming Campaign Finance Reform: A Review of* Voting With Dollars, 91 Cal. L. Rev. 643, 645 (2003).

70. *Id.* at 679 n.126. Translated to recent terms, John McCain received federal funds of $84 million for the general election cycle in 2008, compared to roughly $400 million raised independently and spent by the victorious Obama campaign. Michael Lou, *Obama Hauls in Record $750 Million for Campaign*, N.Y. Times, December 5, 2008, A29; Obama and McCain FEC Filings (Form 3Ps), http://query.nictusa.com/pres.

71. *See* Issacharoff and Karlan, *supra note* 6, at 1711 (drawing analogy to "giving a starving man unlimited trips to the buffet table but only a thimble-sized spoon with which to eat").

72. 128 S. Ct. 2759 (2008) (invalidating BCRA § 319(a) (codified at 2 U.S.C. § 441a-1(a))).

73. *Id.* at 2771.

74. *See* Emily C. Schuman, *Davis v. Federal Election Commission: Muddying the Clean Money Landscape*, 42 Loyola L.A. L. Rev. 737 (2009) (setting out basic framework of existing clean money schemes).

75. *McComish v. Bennett*, 130 S. Ct. 3408 (2010); *see also* A.R.S. § 16-940 to 16-961 (triggering extra public funds for participating candidates to match privately financed opponents).

76. *Davis*, 128 S. Ct. at 2772.

77. *Buckley*, 424 U.S. at 51 n.65 (upholding clean money program).

78. *See, e.g., Daggett v. Comm'n on Gov't Ethics and Election Practices*, 205 F.3d 445 (1st Cir. 2000) (holding that constraints on participating candidates in Maine outweighed effects of release from contribution limits in face of privately funded challengers); *Gable v. Patton*, 142 F.3d 940 (6th Cir. 1998) (upholding Kentucky statute that released participating candidates from expenditure and contribution limits in face of heavily financed challenger); *Vote Choice, Inc. v. DiStefano*, 4 F.3d 26 (1st Cir. 1993) (upholding similar Rhode Island law).

79. For example, under one current bill, the Fair Elections Now Act, H.R. 1826, 111th Cong. (2009); S. 752, 111th Cong. (2009), participating candidates in a federal clean money program would have to agree to accept no contribution greater than $100, even though the current federal limitation on contributions is $2,400.

80. The argument that excessive restrictions on candidate fund-raising promote politics dominated by single-issue special interests is central to Issacharoff and Karlan, *supra* note 5.

81. *See* 2 U.S.C. § 441a(a)(1), (c)(1)(A) (increasing limits on individual contributions to candidates and political parties, while indexing both sums to inflation).

82. President Obama's 2008 fund-raising and expenditure totals may be found at Center for Responsive Politics, Barack Obama Summary, at http://www.opensecrets.org/pres08/summary.php?cycle=2008&cid=N00009638.

83. Tahman Bradley, *Final Fundraising Figure: Obama's $750M*, ABC News, December 5, 2008, http://abcnews.go.com/Politics/Vote2008/story?id=6397572.

84. *See* Michael Malbin, *Revised and Updated 2008 Presidential Statistics*, Campaign Finance Institute, January 8, 2010, http://www.cfinst.org/Press/PReleases/10-01-08/Revised_and_Updated_2008_Presidential_Statistics.aspx (small donors gave $114 million to Obama).

85. *Id.* (noting Obama received more from small donors than McCain's whole public grant).

9

1. *Citizens United v. FEC,* 130 S. Ct. 876 (2010).

2. *Austin v. Michigan Chamber of Commerce*, 494 U.S. 652 (1990).

3. My argument was inspired in part by Professor Deborah Hellman's ideas, which are reflected in her chapter in this volume; Hellman examines the freedom of legislatures to limit the sale of items that they cannot outright ban; I examine the possibility of legislatures limiting the *enforcement* of contracts that they may not outright ban.

4. 130 S. Ct. 876 (2010).

5. *Id.* at 913.

6. *Id.* at 909–10.

7. *Id.*

8. *Id.* at 908–10.

9. *Id.* (referencing *Austin v. Michigan Chamber of Commerce,* 494 U.S. 652 (1990)). *Austin* had held that finance laws limiting corporate speech could be upheld if they served the purpose of protecting against a broader kind of corruption, including the corruption that comes from organizations with amassed wealth exercising undue influence over the political sphere.

10. *Citizens United*, 130 S. Ct. at 909–10.

11. *First Nat'l Bank of Bos. v. Belotti,* 435 U.S. 765 (1978).

12. *Buckley v. Valeo*, 424 U.S. 1 (1976).

13. For a nice discussion of this, see Richard L. Hasen, *Citizens United and the Illusion of Coherence*, 109 Mich. L. Rev. 581 (2011).

14. *Citizens United*, 130 S. Ct. at 910 (quoting *McConnell v. FEC*, 540 U.S. 93, 297 (2003)).

15. *Id.* at 961 (Stevens, J., dissenting).

16. *Id.* at 897.

17. *E.g.*, *id.* at 882, 895, 896.

18. *E.g.*, *id.* at 889, 891.

19. *Id.* at 904.

20. *Id.* at 908.

21. *See* 5 *Williston on Contracts* § 12 (4th ed. 2010).

22. Mark Pettit, Jr., *Freedom, Freedom of Contract, and the 'Rise and Fall,'* 79 B.U. L. Rev. 263, 291 (1999).

23. *Id.*

24. *Id.* at 325. As Professor Phillip H. Pettit argues, it is impossible to make absolute claims about diverse courts in a brief period of time, but some generalizations may be made about the willingness of courts to use public policy in ways that are currently out of practice.

25. *See id.* at 296–97 (discussing how modern courts examine unconscionability, and allow for a greater range of remedies depending on the equities between the parties).

26. These results came from non-comprehensive searches of Westlaw and Lexis.

27. *Elkhart Cnty. Lodge v. Crary,* 98 Ind. 238, 241–42 (1884).

28. *Bartle v. Nutt,* 29 U.S. 184, (1830).

29. Id. at 184, 185.

30. *Id.*

31. *Id.*

32. *Id.* at 188.

33. *Id.*

34. *Id.* at 189.

35. 88 U.S. 441 (1874).

36. *Id.* at 442

37. *Id.* at 445.

38. *Id.*

39. *Id.* at 451.

40. *Id.* at 450 & n.22 (citing Montesquieu, *The Spirit of Laws*).

41. *Id.* at 451.

42. *Buckley v. Valeo,* 424 U.S. 1, 27 (1976).

43. *Trist*, 88 U.S. at 451.
44. *Id.*
45. *Id.*
46. *See, e.g.*, Richard Briffault, *Lobbying and Campaign Finance: Separate and Together*, 19 Stan. L. & Pol'y Rev. 105, 107 (2008) ("Both lobbying and campaign finance are vital to representative democracy. Lobbying helps elected officials obtain the information they need to develop legislative or regulatory initiatives; to assess how proposals for government action will affect specific interests, industries, constituencies, or society at large; to determine how different groups view particular policy alternatives; and to decide how they will vote on the measures that come before them."); Vincent R. Johnson, *Regulating Lobbyists: Law, Ethics, and Public Policy*, 16 Cornell J. L. & Pub. Pol'y 1, 9 (2006) (footnotes omitted) ("Though widely vilified, lobbyists representing individuals or groups can make a valuable contribution to informed and effective government. Lobbyists can direct ideas and opinions to appropriate decision makers and clearly express the views of citizens who have too little time or skill to do so personally. Lobbyists also illuminate the practical consequences of proposed government conduct by ensuring that the insights and professional expertise of a particular business or industry become part of the deliberative process.").
47. *Elkhart Cnty. Lodge v. Crary*, 98 Ind. 238, 239 (1884).
48. *Id.*
49. *Id.*
50. *Id.* at 239–40.
51. *Id.* at 241.
52. *Id.* at 244.
53. 110 U.S. 651 (1884).
54. *Id.* at 666.
55. *Id.* at 657.
56. *Id.* at 667.
57. *Id.* at 658.
58. *See Citizens United v. FEC*, 130 S. Ct. 876, 896–914.
59. *See* Zephyr Teachout, *The Anti-Corruption Principle*, 94 Cornell L. Rev. 341, 373, 378 (2009).
60. *Id.* at 352–53.
61. *Marshall v. Balt. & Ohio R.R.*, 57 U.S. 314, 335 (1853).

62. *Bermudez Asphalt Paving Co. v. Critchfield,* 62 Ill. App. 221, 222, 228 (Ill. App. Ct. 1895) (holding that a road-paving contract calculated to influence legislative action to permit such paving was unenforceable as against public policy—no proof of illegality required).

63. *McGuffin v. Coyle & Guss,* 85 P. 954, 959 (Okla. 1906).

64. *Citizens United*, 130 S. Ct. at 910.

65. *King v. Randall,* 190 P. 979, 980–82 (Nev. 1920) (holding that a building contract based on the consideration of the location of a courthouse for a private benefit was unenforceable as it interfered with the public interest in the location of the courthouse).

66. *Davis v. Janeway,* 155 P. 241, 243 (Okla. 1916) (quoting 6 *Ruling Case Law* § 152 (William M. McKinney & Burdett A. Rich eds., 1915)).

67. For example, in an extensive discussion from a Delaware court (in the context of a criminal charge that an election officer refused to allow someone to vote for corrupt reasons), that court wrote: "It is difficult to define corruption, but we may say that it is the willfully and corruptly doing an act or omitting a duty which a person, acting in a public capacity, knows it to be his duty to do or omit, in disregard of his official duty, and the obligations of his oath." *State v. Colton,* 33 A. 259, 260 (Ct. Gen. Sess. of the Peace and Jail Delivery of Del. 1891).

68. *See* Hasen, *supra* note 13.

69. *See Crocker v. United States,* 240 U.S. 74, 78–79 (1916) (finding that there was "an obvious departure from recognized legal and moral standards" where a company employed an agent with "compensation contingent upon success, to secure the contract for furnishing . . . satchels" to the federal government. Because of their baneful tendency . . . [such] agreements . . . are deemed inconsistent with sound morals and public policy, and therefore invalid.").

70. *Restatement (Second) of Contracts* § 178(1) (2010).

71. *Rust v. Sullivan,* 500 U.S. 173, 197 (1991) (citing *Regan v. Taxation With Representation of Wash.*, 461 U.S. 545 (1983)).

72. *Regan*, 461 U.S. at 546.

73. *Id.* at 544.

74. *See Citizens United*, 130 S. Ct. at 910–17.

75. *Id.* at 898.

76. *Id.* at 908.

77. *Id.* at 904.

10

1. *See Buckley v. Valeo*, 424 U.S. 1 (1976).
2. *See Citizens United v. FEC*, 130 S. Ct. 876 (2010).
3. *See infra* Part III.A.
4. *See infra* Part III.B.
5. *See infra* Part III.C.
6. *See Citizens United.*
7. *See id.*
8. *Texas v. Johnson*, 491 U.S. 397, 414 (1989).
9. *N.Y. Times Co. v. Sullivan*, 376 U.S. 254, 270 (1964); *Cf.* Alexander Meiklejohn, *Free Speech and Its Relation to Self-Government* (1948).
10. *See Abrams v. United States*, 250 U.S. 616, 630 (1919) (Holmes, J., dissenting) ("The best test of truth is the power of the thought to get itself accepted in the competition of the market. . . ."). Of course, the marketplace of ideas is ideal in theory, but not always in practice, due to concentration of resources, media conglomerates, etc.
11. The Declaration of Independence para. 2 (U.S. 1776).
12. *Whitney v. California*, 274 U.S. 357, 375 (1927) (Brandeis, J., concurring).
13. *See* Thomas I. Emerson, *Toward a General Theory of the First Amendment*, 72 Yale L. J. 877, 885 (1963).
14. *See Butler v. Ala. Judicial Inquiry Comm'n*, 111 F. Supp. 2d 1224, 1231 (M.D. Ala. 2000) (quoting *United States v. Associated Press*, 52 F. Supp. 362, 372 (S.D.N.Y. 1943)) ("The First Amendment, said Judge Learned Hand, 'presupposes that right conclusions are more likely to be gathered out of a multitude of tongues, than through any kind of authoritative selection. To many this is, and always will be, folly; but we have staked upon it our all.'").
15. *Cohen v. California*, 403 U.S. 15, 24 (1971).
16. *See Eisner v. Stamford Bd. of Educ.*, 314 F. Supp. 832, 836 (D. Conn. 1970).
17. *United States v. N.Y. Times Co.*, 328 F. Supp. 324, 331 (S.D.N.Y. 1971).
18. *See Eisner*, 314 F. Supp. at 836 (internal quotation marks omitted).
19. Unregulated speech operates "as a catharsis throughout the body politic." Emerson, *supra* note 13, at 885.

20. *Landell v. Sorrell,* 406 F.3d 159, 168 (2d Cir. 2005) (Walker, C.J., dissenting).

21. *See Buckley*, 424 U.S. at 14; *see also N.C. Right to Life v. Leake,* 108 F. Supp. 2d 498, 511 (E.D.N.C. 2000) ("Implicit in the Court's ruling was the principle that core political speech, essential to the free flow of ideas in a democracy, occupies a highly protected place within First Amendment jurisprudence.").

22. *See Roth v. United States,* 354 U.S. 476, 484 (1957). *See also Stromberg v. California,* 283 U.S. 359, 369 (1931) ("The maintenance of the opportunity for free political discussion to the end that government may be responsive to the will of the people and that changes may be obtained by lawful means, an opportunity essential to the security of the Republic, is a fundamental principle of our constitutional system.").

23. *Monitor Patriot Co. v. Roy,* 401 U.S. 265, 272 (1971).

24. *See Buckley,* 424 U.S. at 7, 34 (The law imposed $1,000 limits on campaign contributions from individuals to candidates for federal office, and a $5,000 limit on contributions by political committees to candidates).

25. *Id.* at 7 (The law (1) limited the amount an individual could spend on a particular candidate to $1,000; and (2) curbed the amounts that candidates or their families could spend on their own election. The law also created disclosure requirements and public funding for presidential elections.).

26. *Id.* at 6.

27. *Id.* at 14 (quoting *Roth*, 354 U.S. at 484).

28. *See N.Y. Times Co. v. Sullivan,* 376 U.S. 254, 273 (1964) (Campaign contributions and expenditures, thus described as political speech, hit at "the central meaning of the First Amendment."). *See also Eu v. S.F. Cnty. Democratic Cent. Comm.*, 489 U.S. 214, 223 (quoting *Monitor Patriot Co.*, 401 U.S. at 272) ("The First Amendment 'has its fullest and most urgent application' to speech uttered during a campaign for political office.").

29. *See Buckley*, 424 U.S. at 16–17, 19.

30. *Id.* at 16.

31. *See id.* at 19 ("A restriction on the amount of money a person or group can spend on political communication during a campaign necessarily reduces the quantity of expression by restricting the number of issues discussed, the depth of their exploration, and the size of the audience reached. This is because virtually every means of communicating ideas in today's mass society requires the expenditure of money.").

32. *See FEC v. Nat'l Conservative Political Action Comm. (NCPAC)*, 470 U.S. 480, 497–98, 501 (1985) (The Court applied strict scrutiny to invalidate a federal statutory provision restricting gifts by political action committees in support of a presidential candidate. Since the expenditures were independent of and not coordinated with any candidate, the Court found that there was no danger of corruption and invalidated the restriction—it was not justified by a compelling governmental interest.). *See also Citizens Against Rent Control v. City of Berkeley*, 454 U.S. 290 (1981) (Where in analyzing a ballot referendum, as opposed to the election of a candidate, the Court focused on the *Buckley* corruption rationale, holding that absent an individual candidate, there was no risk of quid pro quo corruption, and therefore insufficient constitutional justification to restrict contributions to issue-related committees.).

33. *See Texas v. Johnson*, 491 U.S. 391, 414 (1989).

34. *See United States v. Drayton*, 536 U.S. 194 (2002) (Souter, J., dissenting) (As Justice Souter wrote in the criminal procedure context, there is "an air of unreality" in the Court's approach to campaign finance reform cases, and that unreality overlooks inequality in our politics.); *see also* Mark C. Alexander, *Money in Political Campaigns and Modern Vote Dilution*, 23 Law & Ineq. 239, 256–57 (2005).

35. Mark C. Alexander, *Let Them Do Their Jobs: The Compelling Government Interest in Protecting the Time of Candidates and Elected Officials*, 37 Loy. U. Chi. L. J. 669 (2006).

36. *See The Midterms: Surpassing $2 Billion in Campaign Spending*, NBC News (October 26, 2010), http://firstread.msnbc.msn.com/_news/2010/10/26/5352948-the-midterms-surpassing-2-billion-in-campaign-spending.

37. *See* Candice J. Nelson, *Spending in the 2000 Elections*, in *Financing the 2000 Election* 35–38 (David B. Magleby ed., 2002) ("Very few Americans contribute to political parties and candidates in the United States, and the percentage who do contribute has remained relatively stable during the past twenty years, even as the costs of elections have increased. Consequently, candidates need to spend more and more time trying to raise money from a very narrow donor base.").

38. *See* Center for Responsive Politics, *2010 Election Overview: Top Metro Areas*, http://www.opensecrets.org/overview/topmetro.asp (last visited February 4, 2011) (Combined, New York City, Washington, D.C.,

Los Angeles, San Francisco, Chicago, Boston, Philadelphia, and Houston account for over $500 million in individual campaign contributions. As a result, candidates spend much of their time flying back and forth across the country raising money.).

39. Martin Schram, *Speaking Freely: Former Members of Congress Talk about Money in Politics* (1995), pt. I, § 3, at 38 (quoting Rep. Leslie Byrne (D-VA)).

40. *See* Alexander, *Let Them Do Their Jobs*, *supra* note 35, at 696–701.

41. In a perhaps mundane sense, campaigns are simply job interviews, a mechanism by which we sort out those who will do the job of representing us in a legislative body, or perhaps as the chief executive of a branch of government.

42. *See* William J. Gore & Robert L. Peabody, *The Functions of the Political Campaign: A Case Study*, 11 W. Pol. Q. 55, 55 (1958). ("Campaigns are electioneering devices, means of getting candidates elected. But campaigns also embody traditional practices which manifest some of our answers to the most thorny aspects of the problem of representation.")

43 *Buckley v. Valeo*, 424 U.S. 1, 14–15 (1976).

44 *See* Ezra Klein, *For Lawmakers Like Evan Bayh, the Price of Fundraising Is Too Steep*, Wash. Post, October 31, 2010 (quoting Senator Evan Bayh) ("When candidates for public office are spending 90 percent of their time raising money . . . that's time they're not spending with constituents or with public policy experts").

45 *See* Alexander, *Let Them Do Their Jobs*, *supra* note 35, at 704–07.

46. *See id.* at 705–06.

47. Not only does time protection fit the *Buckley* framework, it promotes both equality speech interests, as candidates and officeholders can engage in broader and more meaningful conversations with a broad range of the citizenry. *But see* Vincent Blasi, *Free Speech and the Widening Gyre of Fund-Raising: Why Campaign Spending Limits May Not Violate the First Amendment*, 94 Colum. L. Rev. 1281, 1324 (1994) ("Campaign spending limits justified by the objective of candidate time protection should not be presumed to be unconstitutional.").

48. *See Randall v. Sorrell,* 548 U.S. 230, 278–79 (2006) (citations omitted).

49. *Id.* at 281–82 (Souter, J., dissenting).

50. *Id.* at 282 (Souter, J., dissenting).

51. *See id.* at 246.

52. Of course, there is no single silver bullet to be found. As the Court and scholars have warned, "money, like water, will always find an outlet. What problems will arise, and how Congress will respond, are concerns for another day." *McConnell v. FEC,* 540 U.S. 93, 224 (2003); *See also* Samuel Issacharoff and Pamela S. Karlan, *The Hydraulics of Campaign Finance Reform*, 77 Tex. L. Rev. 1705, 1708 (1999) (arguing that political money is like water in that it always has a place to go and is part of a broader "ecosystem"). Further, *Colorado Republican* made clear that reviewing courts can carefully examine the relationship between party money and individual candidates, and *McConnell* furthered that notion by lashing out against attempts to circumvent the letter and spirit of campaign finance laws. *See McConnell*, 540 U.S. at 137 (approvingly citing lower level of scrutiny for contributions, so as to "provide[] Congress with sufficient room to anticipate and respond to concerns about circumvention of regulations designed to protect the integrity of the political process"); *cf. FEC v. Colo. Republican Fed. Campaign Comm.*, 533 U.S. 431, 434 (2001) ("Parties thus perform functions more complex than simply electing their candidates: they act as agents for spending on behalf of those who seek to produce obligated officeholders."). Further injections of reality into jurisprudence can help stem the tide of evasive funding schemes.

53. *The Federalist No. 39,* at 182 (James Madison) (Terence Ball ed., 2003).

54. *Wesberry v. Sanders,* 376 U.S. 1, 7–8 (1964).

55. *See e.g.*, U.S. Const. amend. XIII; U.S. Const. amend. XIV; U.S. Const. amend. XV; U.S. Const. amend. XVII; U.S. Const. amend. XIX; U.S. Const. amend. XXIV, U.S. Const. amend. XXVI.

56. *See Wesberry*, 376 U.S. 1; *Reynolds v. Sims,* 377 U.S. 533 (1964); *WMCA, Inc. v. Lomenzo,* 377 U.S. 633 (1964); *Lucas v. Forty-Fourth Gen. Assembly of Colo.*, 377 U.S. 713 (1964); *Gray v. Sanders,* 372 U.S. 368 (1963).

57. *See supra* Part III.A.

58. *See* Alexander, *Money in Political Campaigns and Modern Vote Dilution*, *supra* note 34, at 241.

59. *See* Lisa Kass Boyle, *America, Inc.: How to Take the Country Back from Corporate Control*, Huffington Post (December 9, 2010), http://www.huffingtonpost.com/lisa-kaas-boyle/america-inc-how-to-take-t_b_794197.html.

60. As financial power increases so does access to elected officials. The correlation was noted in the U.S. District Court in the early stages of the *McConnell v. Federal Election Commission* litigation: "The record demonstrates that large donations . . . to the political parties provide donors with access to Members of Congress. The record is a treasure trove of testimony from Members of Congress, individual and corporate donors, and lobbyists, as well as documentary evidence, establishing that contributions . . . are given with the expectation they will provide the donor with access to influence federal officials, that this expectation is fostered by the national parties, and that this expectation is often realized." *McConnell v. FEC,* 251 F. Supp. 2d 176, 492 (D.D.C. 2003) (opinion of Kollar-Kotelly, J.).

61. *Gray v. Sanders,* 372 U.S. 368 (1963).

62. *See id.*; *Wesberry v. Sanders,* 376 U.S. 1 (1964); *Reynolds v. Sims,* 377 U.S. 533 (1964); Jamin Raskin and John Bonifaz, *The Constitutional Imperative and Practical Superiority of Democratically Financed Elections,* 94 Colum. L. Rev. 1160, 1164 (1994) (contending that "equal protection requires an inquiry into whether all citizens enjoy sufficient equality in the political field to participate meaningfully in public elections as voters, speakers, and candidates whenever they so desire.").

63. *Gray,* 372 U.S. at 379, 381 (1963) (In Equal Protection context, Court held that when one person is given multiple times the voting power of another person simply because of where that person lives that is discrimination similar to race- or gender-based discrimination.).

64. *Reynolds,* 377 U.S. at 555–65.

65. *Id.*

66. *See* Cass R. Sunstein, *Political Equality and Unintended Consequences,* 94 Colum. L. Rev. 1390, 1392 (1994) ("The 'one person-one vote' rule exemplifies the commitment to political equality.").

67. *See* Mark C. Alexander, *Campaign Finance Reform: Central Meaning and a New Approach,* 60 Wash. & Lee L. Rev. 767, 775 and nn.23–27 (2003).

68. Letter from Thomas Jefferson to Samuel Kercheval (July 12, 1816), *reprinted in* Thomas Jefferson, *Memoir, Correspondence, and Miscellanies: From the Papers of Thomas Jefferson* 285, 286 (F. Carr and Co. 1829). Thus, the republic was an apt form of government, for reasons of geography, or even practicality, as well.

69 *See* Alexander, *Campaign Finance Reform: Central Meaning and a New Approach*, *supra* note 67, at 780 & nn.51–55.

70. *See* U.S. Const. art. IV, § 4, cl. 1 ("The United States shall guarantee to every State in this Union a Republican Form of Government").

71. *See* Alexander, *Campaign Finance Reform: Central Meaning and a New Approach*, *supra* note 67, at 811–12 and nn.205–07.

72. There was a practical reason for the Guarantee Clause that was far clearer at the time of the Constitutional Convention than it is today. As originally created, the U.S. Senate was chosen by the legislatures of the respective states. U.S. Const. art. I, § 3, cl. 1. This was altered by a constitutional amendment that furthered the popular sovereignty notion by making senators subject to popular election. U.S. Const. amend. XVII. But the reality of state legislative involvement in the selection of the key chamber in the new national government gave the United States a vested interest in the forms of state government.

73. U.S. Const. art. IV, § 4, cl. 1.

74. *The Federalist No. 39,* at 182 (James Madison) (Terence Ball ed., 2003).

75. Plus, a supermajority of the people (no small feat to amass that many) has the power to amend the Constitution itself. *See* U.S. Const. art. V. *See also The Federalist No. 78,* at 381 (Alexander Hamilton) (Terence Ball ed., 2003) ("[I] trust the friends of the proposed constitution will never concur with its enemies in questioning that fundamental principle of republican government, which admits the right of the people to alter or abolish the established constitution whenever they find it inconsistent with their happiness").

76. Gerald Stourzh, *Alexander Hamilton and the Idea of Republican Government* 53 (1970) (Madison added: "The genius of Republican liberty, seems to demand on one side, not only that all power should be derived from the people; but, that those entrusted with it should be kept in dependence on the people by a short duration of their appointments; and, that, even during this short period, the trust should be placed not in a few, but a number of hands."); *See The Federalist No. 37,* at 170 (James Madison) (Terence Ball ed., 2003); *See also The Federalist No. 49,* at 245 (James Madison) (Terence Ball ed., 2003) ("As the people are the only legitimate fountain of power, and it is from them that the constitutional charter, under which the several branches of government hold their power, is derived; it seems strictly

consonant to the republican theory, to recur to the same original authority, not only whenever it may be necessary to enlarge, diminish or new-model the powers of government; but also whenever any one of the departments may commit encroachment on the chartered authorities of the others.").

77. *See* Alexander, *Campaign Finance Reform: Central Meaning and a New Approach*, *supra* note 67, at 815.

78. Bill Bradley, *The Journey from Here,* 85–86 (Laurie Orsec ed., 2000).

79. In addition, the money race in campaigns narrows the ultimate choices the people have in whom they elect. The need for large sums of money to mount a viable campaign reduces and eliminates competition. Uncertain of their ability to raise the necessary amount of money, many potential candidates forgo politics. Further, massive "war chests" that incumbents (and others) often amass have had the impact of scaring away would-be opponents. This equality concern also skews the republican form of government. *See* Spencer Overton, *But Some Are More Equal: Race, Exclusion, and Campaign Finance,* 80 Tex. L. Rev. 987 (2001) (arguing that the current political system has a disproportionately negative impact on the participation and representation of people of color); Jamin Raskin and John Bonifaz, *The Constitutional Imperative and Practical Superiority of Democratically Financed Elections*, 94 Colum. L. Rev. 1160 (1994) (arguing that the current system of elections and politics creates a wealth disparity and inequalities); Richard Briffault, *Dollars and Democracy* 3 (2000) ("The enormous burdens of fundraising on elected officials and candidates discourage many potentially serious candidates from participating in elections.").

80. *See* Alexander, *Campaign Finance Reform: Central Meaning and a New Approach*, *supra* note 67, at 782–83.

81. As a point of historical comparison, Thomas Paine complained as follows about the government of England: "Sir William Meredith calls it a republic; but in its present state it is unworthy of the name, because the corrupt influence of the crown, by having all the places in its disposal, hath so effectually swallowed up the power. . . ." Thomas Paine, *Common Sense* (January 10, 1776) *reprinted in* 2 *The Life and Works of Thomas Paine* 97–110, 114–20, 120–22 (William M. Van der Weyde ed., Patriots' Edition, Thomas Paine National Historical Association, 1925), http://press-pubs.uchicago.edu/founders/documents/v1ch4s4.html. Also, recall the discussion

earlier that initial English understandings of representative government eschewed special interest representation.

82. U.S. Const. art. IV, § 4.

11

1. 130 S. Ct. 876 (2010).
2. 424 U.S. 1 (1976).
3. Dan Eggen, *Poll: Large Majority Opposes Supreme Court's Decision on Campaign Financing*, Wash. Post, February 17, 2010.
4. *See, e.g., Harper v. Canada* (Attorney General) [2004] 1 S.C.R. 827, *Libman v. Quebec* (Attorney General) [1997] 3 S.C.R. 569.
5. *Bowman v. United Kingdom*, 26 Eur. Ct. Hum. Rt. 1 (1998).
6. 435 U.S. 765 (1978).
7. 459 U.S. 197 (1982).
8. 479 U.S. 238 (1986).
9. 494 U.S. 652 (1990).
10. 539 U.S. 146 (2003).
11. 540 U.S. 93 (2003).
12. 459 U.S. at 207.
13. 551 U.S. 449 (2007).
14. The complete ban on corporate contributions might be sustained under the secondary rationale put forward in *Beaumont*—that it is necessary to prevent circumvention of the limits on individual contributors that might result if an individual who has given the maximum permitted amount uses a corporation as a conduit for donating additional money. *See* 539 U.S. at 155. However, *Citizens United* criticized the anti-circumvention argument as a justification for regulation.
15. *Buckley*, 424 U.S. at 46–47 & n. 53; accord, *FEC v. Colo. Republican Fed. Campaign Comm.*, 533 U.S. 431, 442–43 (2001).
16. 518 U.S. 604 (1996).
17. 129 S. Ct. 2252 (2009).
18. *Id.* at 2263–64.
19. *Id.* at 2257, 2263–65.
20. 130 S. Ct. at 911.
21. 424 U.S. at 28.

22. *Nixon v. Shrink Missouri Gov't PAC*, 528 U.S. 377, 389 (2000).
23. *FEC v. Nat'l Cons. PAC*, 470 U.S. 480, 497 (1985).
24. *McConnell, supra* note 11, 540 U.S. at 147.
25. *Id.* at 142–54.
26. 130 S.Ct. at 910.
27. 548 U.S. 230 (2006).
28. *Id.* at 266–67. Justice Thomas had taken that position in several other cases. *See id.*
29. *Id.* at 265.
30. 548 U.S. at 273–81.
31. *Id.* at 281–84.
32. *Id.*
33. *Nixon*, supra note 22, 528 U.S. at 405.
34. 130 S.Ct. at 967.
35. *Reynolds v. Sims*, 377 U.S. 533 (1964).
36. *White v. Regester*, 412 U.S. 755 (1973).
37. *Harper v. Virginia Bd. of Elections*, 383 U.S. 663 (1966).
38. *Bullock v. Carter*, 405 U.S. 134 (1972).
39. *Hill v. Stone*, 421 U.S. 289 (1975).
40. *Buckley v. Valeo,* 424 U.S. 1, 48–49 (1976).
41. *Id.* at 50. The only cases the Court discussed to support its claim that the promotion of equality cannot justify spending limits were *Mills v. Alabama,* 384 U.S. 214 (1966), and *Miami Herald Publishing Co. v. Tornillo,* 418 U.S. 241 (1974). *Tornillo*, which struck down a Florida law that had sought to require a newspaper to make space available for a political candidate to reply to its criticism, seems completely inapposite. Campaign finance laws have never sought to require one candidate to make resources available to an opponent, which is, in effect, what the Florida law sought to do. *Mills*, which addressed a state law that barred a newspaper from publishing an editorial on election day urging the voters to vote a particular way on a ballot proposition, seems marginally closer to the campaign spending limits case, but even the relevance of *Mills* seems stretched. The Alabama law at issue in *Mills* reflected only a modest effort to prevent "confusive last-minute charges and countercharges . . . when as a practical matter, because of lack of time, such matters cannot be answered or their truth determined until after the election is over. 384 U.S. at 219–20 (quoting the opinion of the Alabama Supreme Court upholding the law). The Court quickly concluded that the law

was likely to be "wholly ineffective" in assuring adequate replies to campaign charges as people remained "free to hurl their campaign charges up to the last minute of the day before the election," *id.* at 220, and thus did not provide a reasonable basis for curtailing newspaper editorials. The broader question of whether voter equality can justify limitations on the use of private resources in campaigning was neither raised nor addressed in *Mills*, or in *Tornillo*.

42. 424 U.S. at 49.

43. *Nixon*, supra, 528 U.S. at 402.

44. *Id.*, citing *Storer v. Brown*, 415 U.S. 24, 736 (1974).

45. As early as 1910, federal law imposed limits on spending by candidates in federal elections; these limits were carried forward by the Federal Corrupt Practices Act of 1925, and were supplemented by limits imposed on spending by multistate political committees, labor unions, and corporations in the 1940s. Although typically evaded in practice, these limits remained on the books until the overhaul of federal campaign finance in the Federal Election Campaign Act of 1971. The states also sought to limit campaign expenditures starting in the late nineteenth century, and by 1932, thirty-nine states had laws limiting the size of campaign expenditures. *See* Louise Overacker, *Money in Elections* 302 (1932).

46. 554 U.S. 724 (2008).

47. 128 S. Ct. at 2773.

48. 424 U.S. at 48.

49. *See* Vincent Blasi, *Free Speech and the Widening Gyre of Fund-raising: Why Campaign Spending Limits May Not Violate the First Amendment After All*, 94 Colum L. Rev. 1281, 1282–83 (1994).

50. *See id.* at 1283.

51. *See, e.g., Homans v. City of Albuquerque*, 366 F.3d 900 (10th Cir. 2004); *Landell v. Sorrell*, 382 F.3d 91, 122 (2d Cir. 2004). *Cf. Kruse v. City of Cincinnati*, 142 F.3d 907, 919-20 (6th Cir. 1998) (Cohn, J., concurring).

52. 548 U.S. 230, 245–46 (2006).

53. *See Nixon v. Shrink Mo. Gov't PAC*, 528 U.S. 377, 397 (2000).

54. *Buckley v. Valeo*, 424 U.S. 1, 91 (1976).

55. *See, e.g., Baker v. Carr*, 369 U.S. 186, 191 (1962) (Tennessee legislature not reapportioned since 1901); *Wesberry v. Sanders*, 376 U.S. 1, 2 (1964) (Georgia congressional districts not redrawn since 1931); *Reynolds v. Sims*, 377 U.S. 533, 540 (1964) (Alabama legislature not reapportioned since 1900).

56. *See generally* Raymond J. LaRaja, *Small Change: Money, Political Parties and Campaign Finance Reform* (University of Michigan Press, 2008).

57. *Id.* at 45–56.

58. *Id.* at 56–65.

59. *Id.* at 106–18.

60. *Id.* at 72–75.

61. *Id.* at 104.

62. *See* Colin Feasby, *Constitutional Questions about Canada's New Political Finance Regime*, 45 Osgoode Hall L.J. 513 (2007).

63. *See, e.g.*, Frank J. Sorauf, *Inside Campaign Finance: Myths and Realities* (Yale University Press, 1992), 87–89, 254–55.

64. 393 U.S. 23 (1968).

65. *Id.* at 30–32.

66. *Jenness v. Fortson*, 403 U.S. 431 (1971).

67. *Storer v. Brown*, 415 U.S. 724 (1974). *See also American Party of Texas v. White*, 415 U.S. 767 (1974) (upholding law disqualifying voter who had voted in a primary from signing petition qualifying independent to run in the general election).

68. *Burdick v. Takushi*, 504 U.S. 428 (1992).

69. *Timmons v. Twin Cities Area New Party*, 520 U.S. 351 (1997).

70. *Id.* at 366.

71. *Id.*

72. 478 U.S. 109 (1986).

73. *See Vieth v. Jubelirer*, 541 U.S. 267, 279–80 and nn. 5–6.

12

1. 531 U.S. 98 (2000) (per curiam).

2. 130 S. Ct. 876 (2010).

3. *See* Mary Ann Case, *Are Plain Hamburgers Now Unconstitutional? The Equal Protection Component of* Bush v. Gore *as a Chapter in the History of Ideas About Law*, 70 U. Chi. L. Rev. 55, 56 (2003); Pamela S. Karlen, *Nothing Personal: The Evolution of the Newest Equal Protection from* Shaw v. Reno *to* Bush v. Gore, 79 N.C. L. Rev. 1346, 1364 (2001).

4. *See, e.g., A Badly Flawed Election: Debating Bush v. Gore, the Supreme Court and American Democracy* (Ronald Dworkin ed., 2002); *Bush v. Gore: The Question of Legitimacy* (Bruce Ackerman ed., 2002); *The Unfinished Election of 2000* (Jack Rakove ed. 2001); *The Vote:* Bush v. Gore *and the Supreme Court* (Cass R. Sunstein and Richard A. Epstein eds., 2001); Burt Neuborne, *Notes for the Unpublished Supplemental Separate Opinions in* Bush v. Gore, in *The Longest Night: Polemics and Perspective on the Election of 2000* (Arthur Jacobsen and Michael Rosenfeld eds., 2002).

5. 531 U.S. at 134 (Souter, J., dissenting); *id.* at 145–46 (Breyer, J., dissenting).

6. 531 U.S. at 110–11 (per curiam).

7. *See* Neuborne, *supra* note 4, at 216–18.

8. *See* Floyd Abrams, Citizens United *and Its Critics*, 120 Yale L. J. Online 77 (2010).

9. 369 U.S. 186 (1962).

10. For two well-known examples of the Court's willingness to wade into non-textual waters in defense of separation of powers and federalism, see *Youngstown Sheet & Tube Co. v. Sawyer*, 343 U.S. 579 (1952) (invalidating president's seizure of nation's steel mills to avert strike during the Korean War) and *Younger v. Harris*, 401 U.S. 37 (1971) (citing "Our Federalism" as the standard for determining scope of federal judicial authority over state courts).

11. It is possible that George Bush would have won the Florida recount. Even if the recount went beyond the safe-harbor period, no reason exists to believe that the democratic process for resolving contested presidential elections would have misfired. The only thing that can be said with certainty about *Bush v. Gore* is that the Supreme Court prevented democracy from working. For a summary of post-election investigation of the Florida ballots, *see* John Mintz and Peter Slavin, *Human Factor Was at Core of Vote Fiasco*, Wash. Post, June 1, 2001, at A1.

12. 369 U.S. 186, 289 (1962) (Frankfurter, J., dissenting) (courts are "not fit instruments of decision" when "standards meet for judicial judgment are lacking").

13. For one of the classic attacks on judicial review, see L. B. Boudin, *Government by Judiciary*, 26 Pol. Sci. Q. 238, 267 (1911). The leading modern critic of judicial review is Jeremy Waldron. *See* Jeremy Waldron, *The Core Case Against Judicial Review*, 115 Yale L. J. 1346 (2006).

14. *See generally* H. N. Hirsch, *The Enigma of Felix Frankfurter* (1981).

15. *Erie R.R. Co. v. Tompkins,* 304 U.S. 64, 78 (1938) (holding that federal courts did not have the power to create federal common law when ruling on state law claims in diversity jurisdiction).

16. *Ashwander v. Tenn. Valley Auth.,* 297 U.S. 288, 346 (1936) (Brandeis, J., concurring) (listing rules of judicial restraint).

17. For a comprehensive biography of Justice Brennan, *see* Seth Stern and Stephen Wermeil, *Justice Brennan: Liberal Champion* (2010). For the role played by race and fear of regional failure in the Warren Court's constitutional jurisprudence, *see* Burt Neuborne, *The Gravitational Pull of Race on the Warren Court,* 2010 Supreme Court Review (forthcoming).

18. U.S. Const. art. IV, § 4 ("The United States shall guarantee to every State in this union a Republican Form of Government"). The Court has refused, under the political question doctrine, to enforce this clause since *Luther v. Borden*, 7 How. 1 (1849).

19. I make a textual argument for a First Amendment right to vote *infra.*

20. *Baker v. Carr,* 369 U.S. 186, 237 (1962). The full-blown equality standard was not announced until the Chief Justice's opinion in *Reynolds v. Sims*, 377 U.S. 573 (1964).

21. *E.g., Harper v. Va. State Bd. of Elections,* 383 U.S. 663, 670 (1966).

22. *Reynolds v. Sims,* 377 U.S. 533 (1964) (one person, one vote for Alabama state legislature); *Gray v. Sanders,* 372 U.S. 368 (1963) (invalidating Georgia's county unit system for state primary elections).

23. 377 U.S. at 622–23 (Harlan, J., dissenting).

24. Forthcoming, *NYU Review of Law and Social Change.*

25. 18 U.S.C. § 608(c) (1970 & Supp. IV); *see also* Appendix, *Buckley v. Valeo,* 424 U.S. 1 (1976) (text of statute); 424 U.S. at 190–91 (statutory spending limits).

26. *See* 424 U.S. at 189, 193.

27. *See id.* at 200.

28. *See generally id.*

29. *Id.* at 93–108 (upholding discriminatory public subsidies), 23–28 (invalidating expenditure and spending limits), 12–23 (upholding $1,000 contribution limit), 60–84 (upholding disclosure rules).

30. *Id.* at 15–19.

31. *Buckley v. Valeo,* 519 F.2d 821, 840 (D.C. Cir. 1975).

32. 391 U.S. 367 (1968).

33. 424 U.S. at 17. Justice Stevens did not participate in *Buckley*. Over the years, he made it clear that he viewed campaign spending as mixed speech and conduct.

34. *Id.* at 48–51.

35. *Associated Press v. United States,* 326 U.S. 1, 20 (1945) ("The First Amendment, far from providing an argument against application of [antitrust law], . . . rests on the assumption that the widest possible dissemination of information from diverse and antagonistic sources is essential to the welfare of the public").

36. 424 U.S. at 12–23.

37. *Id.* at 23–38.

38. *Citizens United v. FEC,* 130 S. Ct. 876, 899–901 (2010).

39. *See Minneapolis Star & Tribune Co. v. Minn. Comm'r of Revenue,* 460 U.S. 575 (1983) (invalidating differential taxation of newspapers); *Ark. Writers Project v. Ragland,* 481 U.S. 227 (1987); *Rosenberger v. Rector,* 515 U.S. 819 (1995).

40. *Hale v. Henkel,* 201 U.S. 43, 69–70 (1906).

41. *Braswell v. United States,* 487 U.S. 99, 104–09 (1988).

42. 487 U.S. at 119 (Kennedy, J., dissenting) (emphasis added).

43. 130 S. Ct. at 900.

44. *See Santa Clara Cnty. v. S. Pac. R.R. Co.,* 118 U.S. 394, 394–95 ("Corporations are persons within the meaning of the Fourteenth Amendment" as regards protection of property).

45. *Va. Pharmacy Bd. v. Va. Citizens Consumer Council,* 425 U.S. 748, 770 (1976).

46. Burt Neuborne, *A Rationale for the Protection and Regulation of Commercial Speech*, 46 Brook. L. Rev. 437 (1980); Burt Neuborne, *The First Amendment and Government Regulation of Capital Markets*, 55 Brook. L. Rev. 5 (1989).

47. 130 S. Ct. at 898–99.

48. *Id.* at 904.

49. 494 U.S. 692 (1990).

50. 540 U.S. 93 (2004).

51. *Buckley v. Valeo,* 424 U.S. 1, 47 (1976).

52. 129 S. Ct. 2252 (2009).

53. Unfortunately, Justice Kennedy's arbitrary and inconsistent approach to precedent was made easier for him because the United States, in defense of the statute, failed to assert either the overbalancing or corruption

arguments, choosing to stand or fall on a far weaker claim about corporate governance that, as Justice Kennedy noted, might justify regulation of corporate electioneering, but not its prohibition. *See* 130 S. Ct. at 911.

54. *See Ashwander v. Tenn. Valley Auth.*, 297 U.S. 288, 346 (1936) (Brandeis, J., concurring).

55. *FEC v. Nat'l Rifle Ass'n*, 254 F.3d 173 (D.C. Cir. 2001).

56. *FEC v. Mass. Citizens for Life*, 479 U.S. 238, 263–64 (1986).

57. *McComish v. Bennett,* 130 S. Ct. 3408 (June 8, 2010) (staying enforcement of Arizona public financing law).

58. *Buckley v. Valeo,* 424 U.S. 1, 95 (1976).

59. *E.g.*, Ariz. Rev. Stat. Ann. § 16–952(A); N.C. Gen. Stat. Ann. § 163–278.67(a).

60. *McComish v. Bennett,* 611 F.3d 510 (9th Cir. 2010), *cert. granted,* 131 S. Ct. 644 (November 29, 2010). The Court started down this road in *Davis v. FEC*, 128 S. Ct. 2759 (2008), invalidating the so-called millionaire's amendment, which lifted the ceiling on campaign contributions to a candidate opposed by a wealthy, self-financed candidate. While the precise holding of *Davis* dealt with the unconstitutionality of imposing different fund-raising regimes on competing candidates on the basis of wealth, some have read the opinion as dooming efforts to link campaign subsidies to the success of an opponent's fund-raising.

61. 376 U.S. 254, 271 (1964).

62. *See* Burt Neuborne, *The House Was Quiet and the World Was Calm. The Reader Became the Book,* 57 Vand. L. Rev. 2007 (2004).

63. *See* Burt Neuborne, *Democracy and the Poor*, in *Law and Class in America* (Paul Carrington and Trina Jones eds., 2006).

Index

About the Contributors

Mark C. Alexander is a law professor at Seton Hall University, specializing in constitutional law and the intersection of law and politics. He was senior adviser to Barack Obama, worked on the Obama presidential campaign, and developed Senator Obama's signature policies. He clerked for Chief Judge Thelton Henderson of the United States District Court for the Northern District of California and was a litigator with Gibson, Dunn & Crutcher in San Francisco before joining the Seton Hall Law School faculty in 1996.

Richard Briffault is the Joseph P. Chamberlain Professor of Legislation at the Columbia School of Law. His primary areas of teaching, research and writing are state and local government law and the law of the political process. He is the coauthor of a casebook, *State and Local Government Law* (2004); author of *Balancing Acts: The Reality Behind State Balanced Budget Requirements* (1996); and author of *Dollars and Democracy: A Blueprint for Campaign Finance Reform* (2000), the report of the Commission on Campaign Finance Reform of the Association of the Bar of the City of New York.

Deborah Hellman is Professor of Law and Jacob France Research Professor at the University of Maryland School of Law, where she teaches constitutional law, professional responsibility, contracts, bioethics, and jurisprudence. Her main scholarly interests focus on equality, discrimination, political participation and professional role. She is the author of *When Is Discrimination Wrong?* (2008).

Frances R. Hill is professor of law at the University of Miami School of Law. Since joining the faculty, she has been a visiting professor of law at the University of Pennsylvania Law School and the University of Iowa. She has been actively involved in campaign finance reform, a topic on which she has testified before Congress and the Federal Election Commission.

SAMUEL ISSACHAROFF is Bonnie and Richard Reiss Professor of Constitutional Law at the NYU School of Law, where he focuses on voting rights and civil procedure. He is the author of *Civil Procedure* (2d. edition 2008), *Party Funding and Campaign Financing in International Perspective* (with K.D. Ewing) (2006) and *The State of Voting Rights Law* (1993), and coauthor of *When Elections Go Bad: The Law of Democracy and the Presidential Election of 2000* (2001) and of *The Law of Democracy: Legal Structure of the Political Process* (with Pamela Karlan and Richard Pildes) (3d. edition, 2007).

BURT NEUBORNE is Inez Milholland Professor of Civil Liberties at the NYU School of Law and was the founding legal director of the Brennan Center for Justice. He has been one of the nation's most active and successful civil liberties lawyers, has litigated a wide range of landmark cases in the U.S. Supreme Court and other federal and state courts, and has served as the national legal director of the American Civil Liberties Union. He is the author of *Building a Better Democracy: Reflections on Money, Politics and Free Speech* (2002) and coeditor of *Political and Civil Rights in the United States* (1976).

RICHARD H. PILDES is Sudler Family Professor of Constitutional Law and codirector of the Center on Law and Security at the NYU School of Law. His work focuses on democracy and the law, constitutional law and theory, comparative perspectives on democratic institutions, and national-security law. He is a member of the American Academy of Arts and Sciences, and has been a Guggenheim Fellow and a Carnegie Scholar. He was a law clerk to Justice Thurgood Marshall, U.S. Supreme Court. He is the coauthor of *The Law of Democracy* and coeditor of *The Future of the Voting Rights Act* (2006).

ROBERT POST is Dean and Sol & Lillian Goldman Professor of Law at Yale Law School. Before coming to Yale, he taught at the University of California, Berkeley, School of Law. His subject areas are constitutional law, the First Amendment, legal history, and equal protection. He has written and edited numerous books, including *For the Common Good: Principles of American Academic Freedom* (2009); *Prejudicial Appearances: The Logic of American Antidiscrimination Law* (2001);

and *Constitutional Domains: Democracy, Community, Management* (1995).

GEOFFREY R. STONE is the Edward H. Levi Distinguished Service Professor at the University of Chicago. He is the author or co-author of many books on constitutional law, including *Speaking Out: Reflections on Law, Liberty and Justice* (2010), *Top Secret: When Our Government Keeps Us in the Dark* (2007), *War and Liberty: An American Dilemma* (2007), and *Perilous Times: Free Speech in Wartime* (2004). He is also the co-author of two casebooks, one on *Constitutional Law* and the other on *The First Amendment*, and since 1991 he has been an editor of the *Supreme Court Review*.

ZEPHYR TEACHOUT is associate professor of law at the Fordham University School of Law. She has been visiting assistant professor of law at Duke University, national director of the Sunlight Foundation, and director of Internet organizing, Dean for America (Howard Dean's presidential campaign). She is author of *Corruption, the Constitution and the Courts: The Career of a Concept* (forthcoming) and coeditor of *Mousepads, Shoe Leather and Hope: Lessons from the Howard Dean Campaign for the Future of Internet Politics* (2007).

MONICA YOUN is senior counsel at the Brennan Center for Justice and will be the Brennan Center's inaugural Constitutional Fellow at NYU School of Law. Most recently, she led a team of attorneys in a high-stakes case defending Arizona's public campaign financing law before the U.S. Supreme Court. She has litigated campaign finance and election law issues in state and federal courts throughout the nation, and she has testified before Congress and published scholarly articles on campaign finance issues. Her work at the Brennan Center has been recognized by the New Leaders Council, which named her one of their "40 Under 40" nationwide leaders for 2010 and awarded her the Dipaola Foundation Democracy Rejuvenation Award. Her recent collection of poetry, *Ignatz*, was nominated for a 2010 National Book Award.